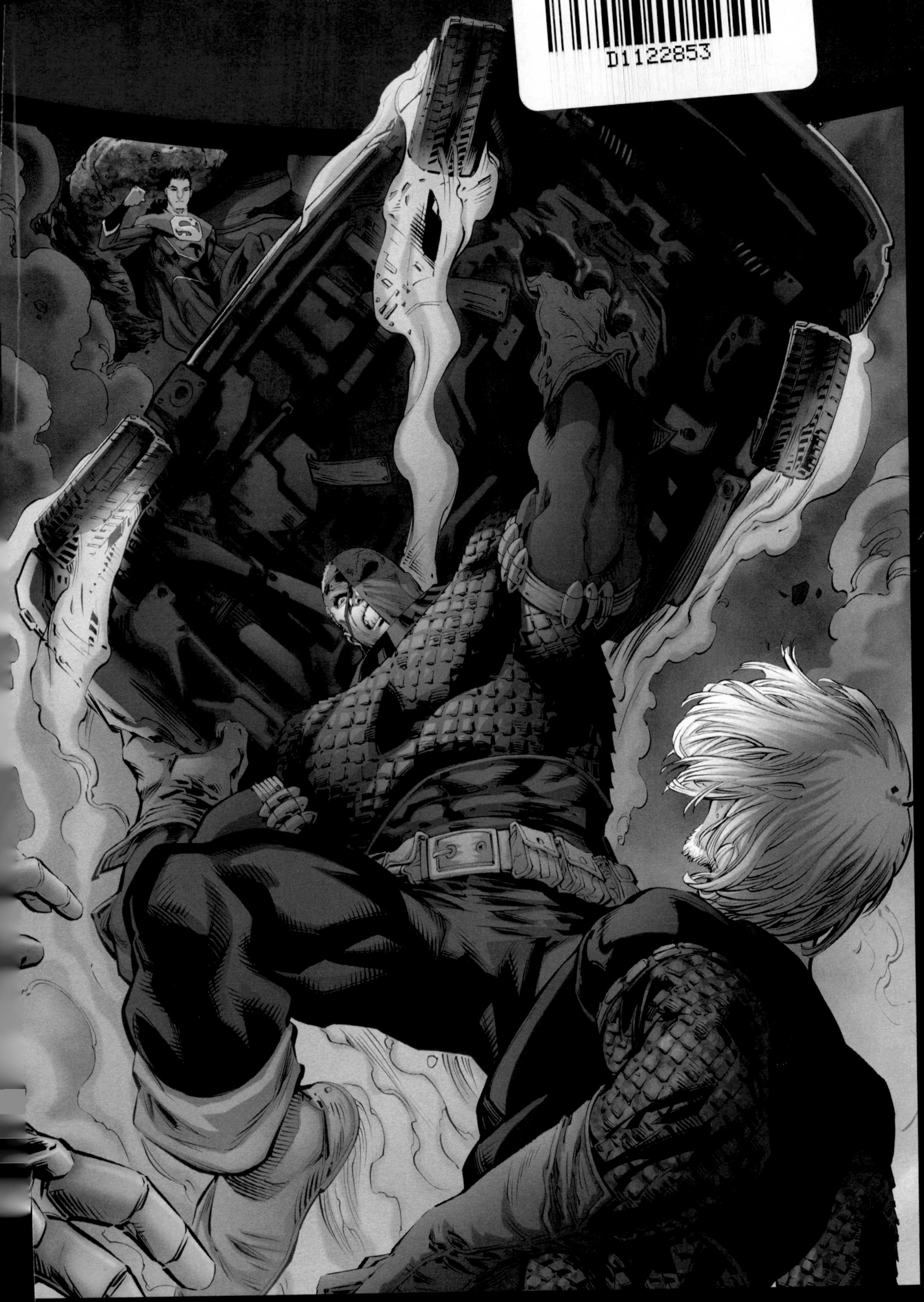

DEATHSTROKE

VOL.5 THE FALL OF SLADE

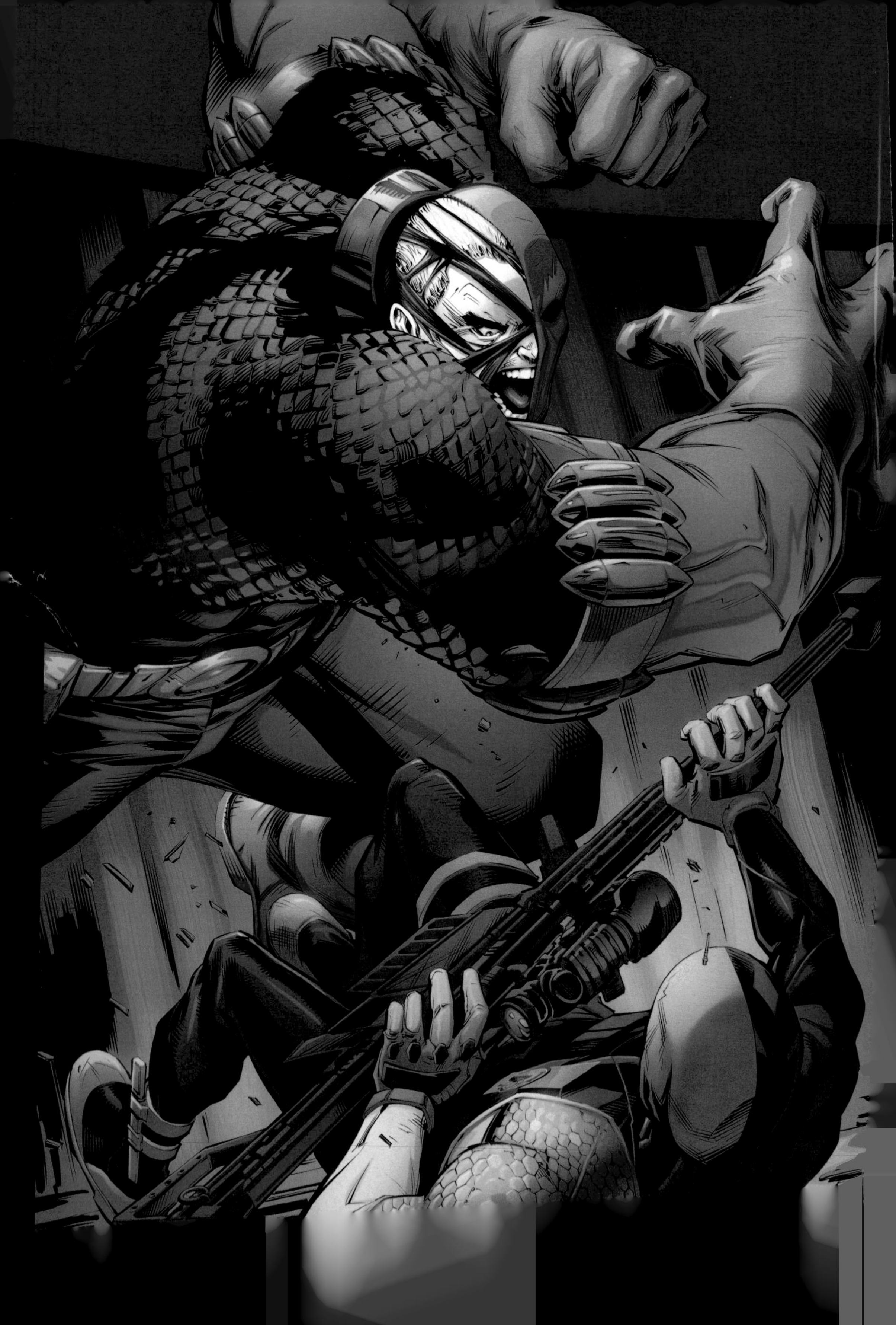

DEATHSTROKE

VOL.5 THE FALL OF SLADE

CHRISTOPHER PRIEST
writer

DIOGENES NEVES
DENYS COWAN
pencillers

TREVOR SCOTT * **SEAN PARSONS**
BILL SIENKIEWICZ
inkers

LARRY HAMA
breakdowns (ANNUAL #1)

JEROMY COX
colorist

WILLIE SCHUBERT * **DERON BENNETT**
letterers

RYAN SOOK
collection cover artist

DEATHSTROKE created by **MARV WOLFMAN** and **GEORGE PÉREZ**
SUPERMAN created by **JERRY SIEGEL** and **JOE SHUSTER**
By special arrangement with the Jerry Siegel family

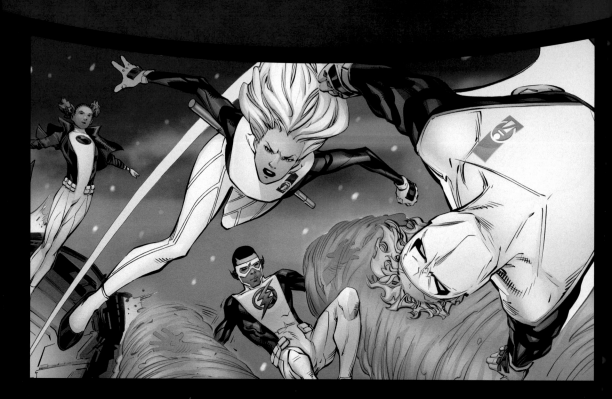

ALEX ANTONE Editor - Original Series * **DAVE WIELGOSZ** Assistant Editor - Original Series
JEB WOODARD Group Editor - Collected Editions * **ERIKA ROTHBERG** Editor - Collected Edition
STEVE COOK Design Director - Books * **MONIQUE NARBONETA** Publication Design

BOB HARRAS Senior VP - Editor-in-Chief, DC Comics
PAT McCALLUM Executive Editor, DC Comics

DAN DiDIO Publisher * **JIM LEE** Publisher & Chief Creative Officer
AMIT DESAI Executive VP - Business & Marketing Strategy, Direct to Consumer & Global Franchise Management
BOBBIE CHASE VP & Executive Editor, Young Reader & Talent Development * **MARK CHIARELLO** Senior VP - Art, Design & Collected Editions
JOHN CUNNINGHAM Senior VP - Sales & Trade Marketing * **BRIAR DARDEN** VP - Business Affairs
ANNE DePIES Senior VP - Business Strategy, Finance & Administration * **DON FALLETTI** VP - Manufacturing Operations
LAWRENCE GANEM VP - Editorial Administration & Talent Relations * **ALISON GILL** Senior VP - Manufacturing & Operations
JASON GREENBERG VP - Business Strategy & Finance * **HANK KANALZ** Senior VP - Editorial Strategy & Administration
JAY KOGAN Senior VP - Legal Affairs * **NICK J. NAPOLITANO** VP - Manufacturing Administration
LISETTE OSTERLOH VP - Digital Marketing & Events * **EDDIE SCANNELL** VP - Consumer Marketing
COURTNEY SIMMONS Senior VP - Publicity & Communications * **JIM (SKI) SOKOLOWSKI** VP - Comic Book Specialty Sales & Trade Marketing
NANCY SPEARS VP - Mass, Book, Digital Sales & Trade Marketing * **MICHELE R. WELLS** VP - Content Strategy

DEATHSTROKE VOL. 5: THE FALL OF SLADE

DC Comics, 2900 West Alameda Ave., Burbank, CA 91505
Printed by LSC Communications, Kendallville, IN, USA. 9/14/18. First Printing.
ISBN: 978-1-4012-7833-5

Library of Congress Cataloging-in-Publication Data is available.

PEFC Certified
Printed on paper from sustainably managed forests, controlled sources
PEFC
PEFC/29-31-337
www.pefc.org

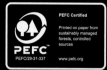

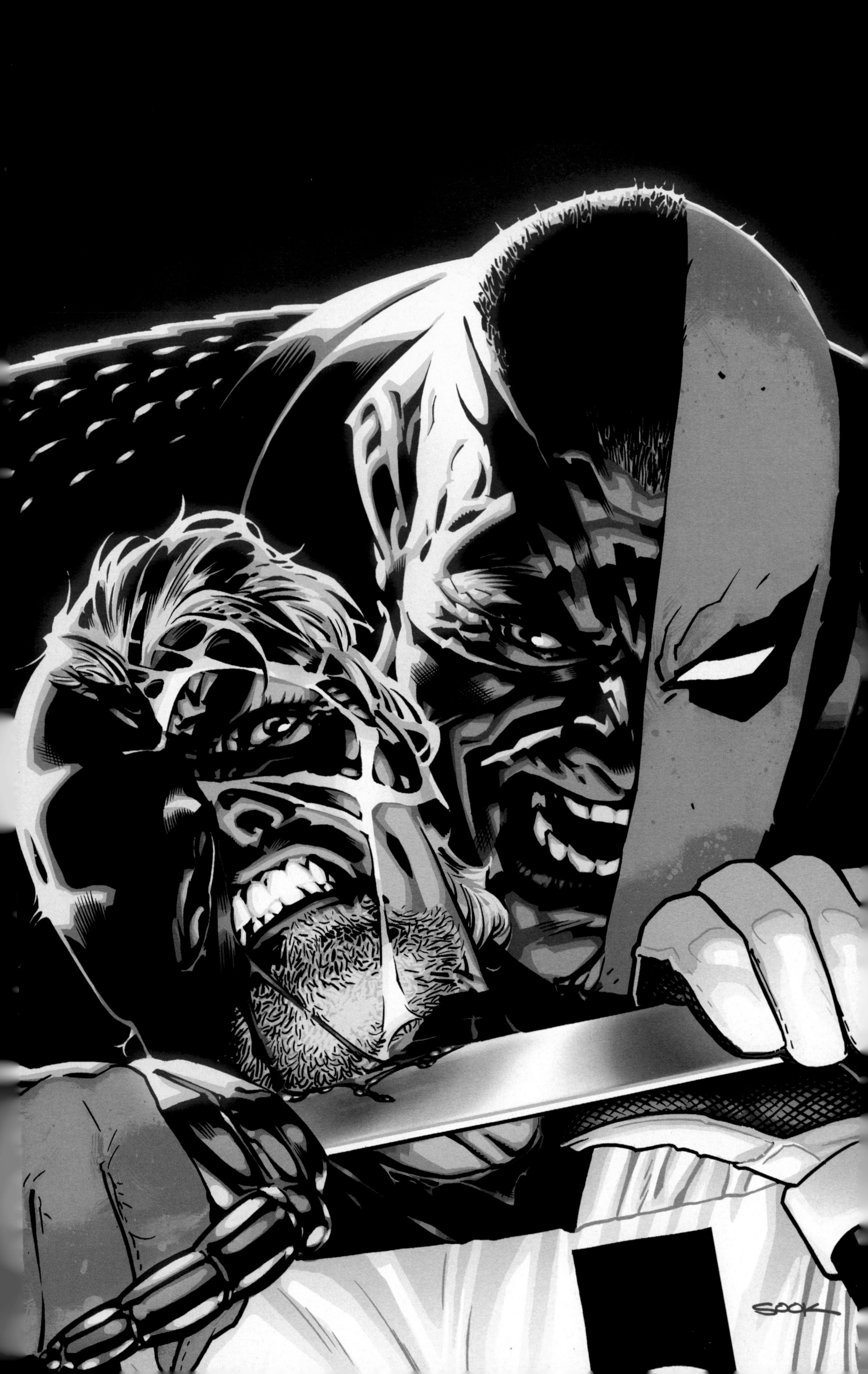

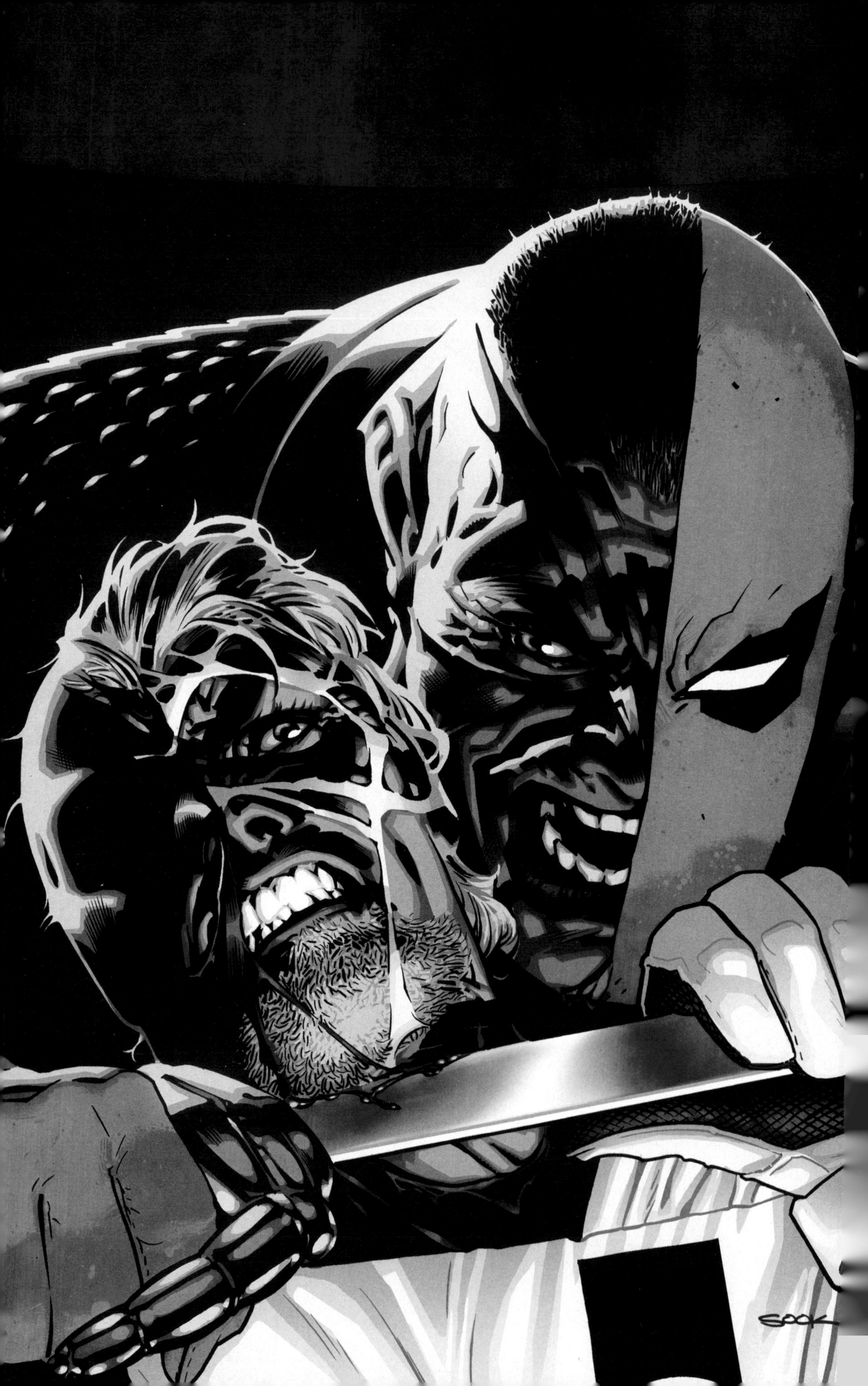
SOOK

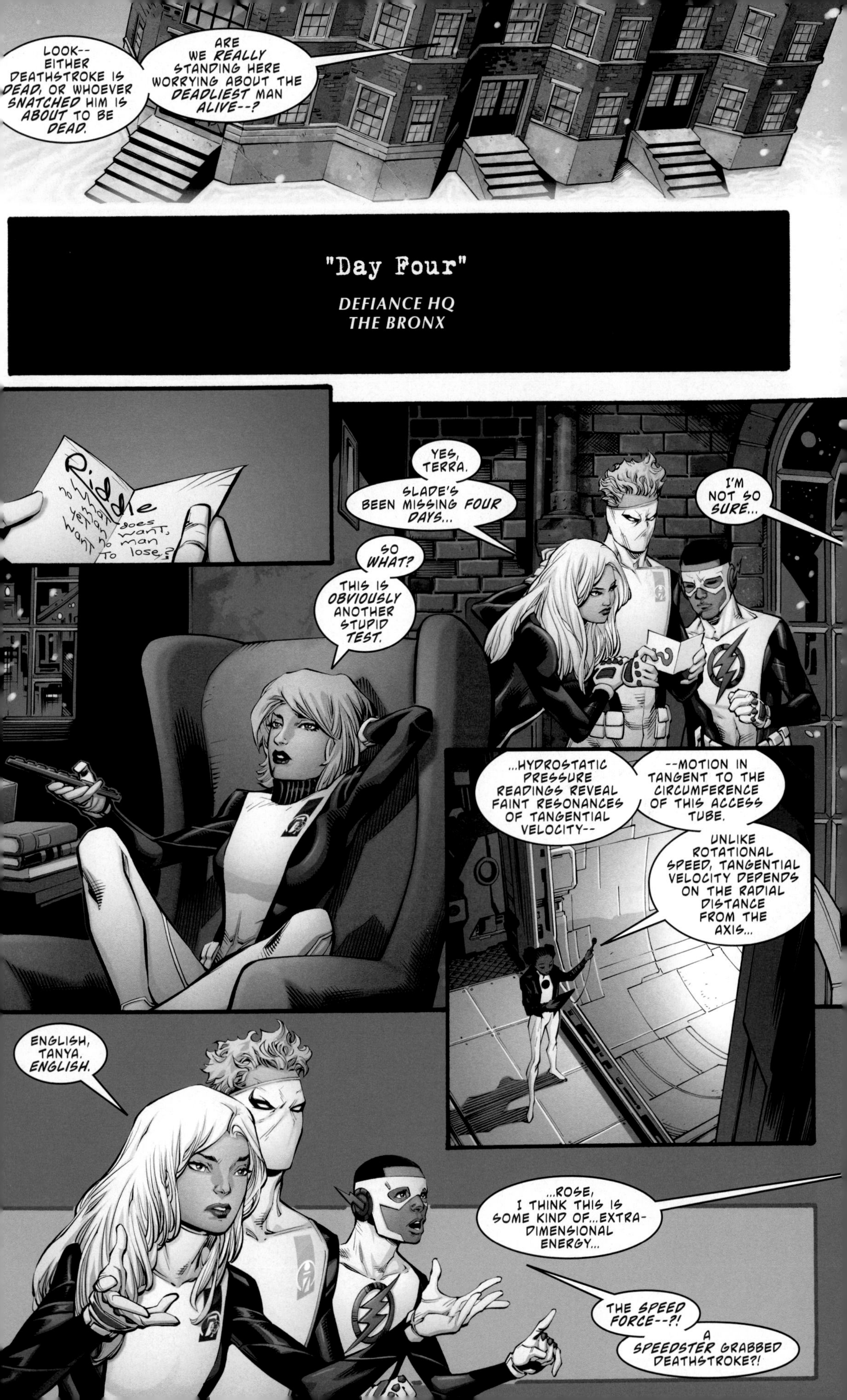

LOOK-- EITHER DEATHSTROKE IS DEAD, OR WHOEVER SNATCHED HIM IS ABOUT TO BE DEAD.
ARE WE REALLY STANDING HERE WORRYING ABOUT THE DEADLIEST MAN ALIVE--?
"Day Four"
DEFIANCE HQ
THE BRONX
Riddle
What goes
no man want,
yet no man
want to lose?
YES, TERRA.
SLADE'S BEEN MISSING FOUR DAYS...
SO WHAT?
THIS IS OBVIOUSLY ANOTHER STUPID TEST.
I'M NOT SO SURE...
...HYDROSTATIC PRESSURE READINGS REVEAL FAINT RESONANCES OF TANGENTIAL VELOCITY--
--MOTION IN TANGENT TO THE CIRCUMFERENCE OF THIS ACCESS TUBE.
UNLIKE ROTATIONAL SPEED, TANGENTIAL VELOCITY DEPENDS ON THE RADIAL DISTANCE FROM THE AXIS...
ENGLISH, TANYA. ENGLISH.
...ROSE, I THINK THIS IS SOME KIND OF...EXTRA-DIMENSIONAL ENERGY...
THE SPEED FORCE--?!
A SPEEDSTER GRABBED DEATHSTROKE?!

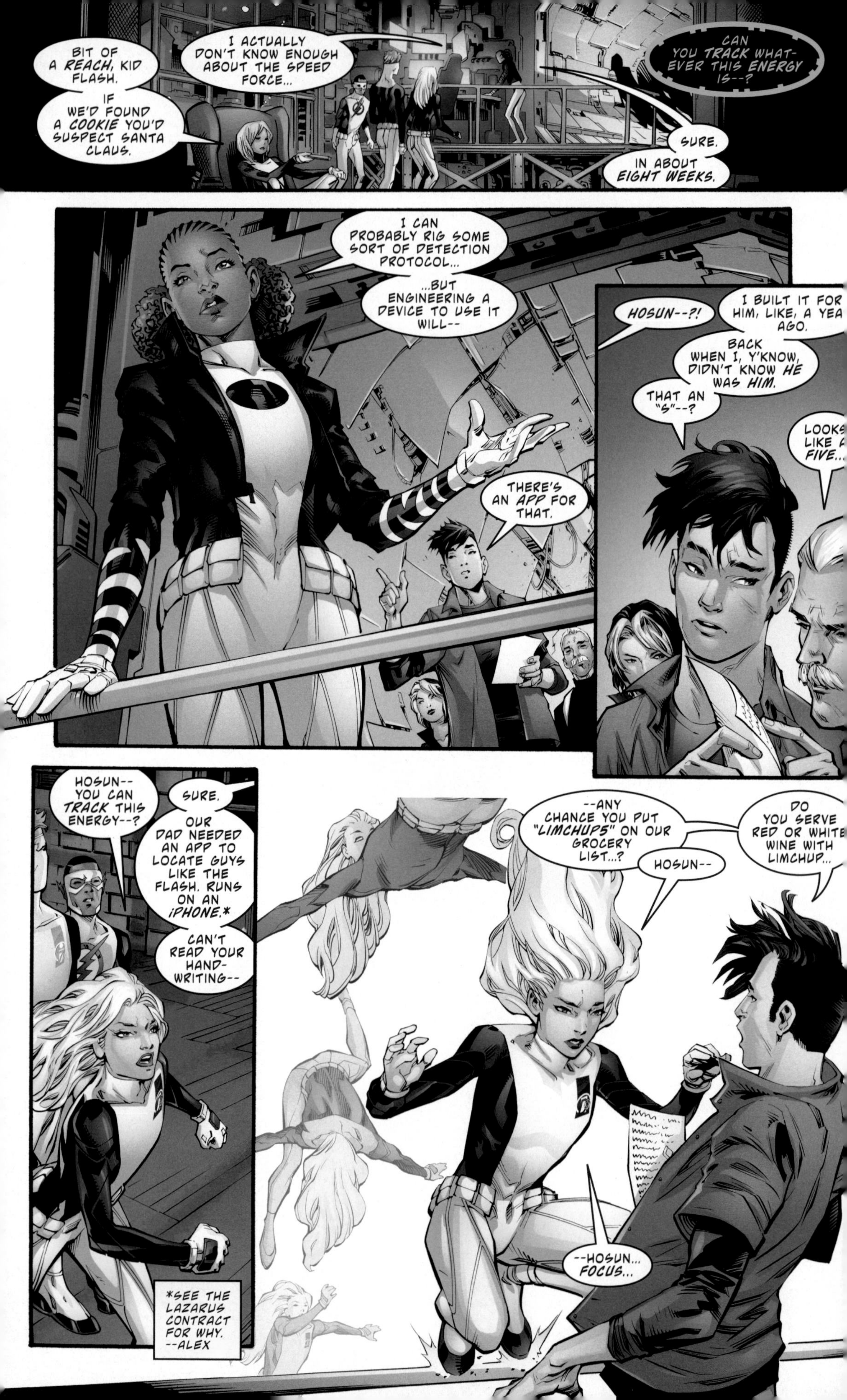
BIT OF A REACH, KID FLASH.
IF WE'D FOUND A COOKIE YOU'D SUSPECT SANTA CLAUS.
I ACTUALLY DON'T KNOW ENOUGH ABOUT THE SPEED FORCE...
CAN YOU TRACK WHATEVER THIS ENERGY IS--?
SURE.
IN ABOUT EIGHT WEEKS.
I CAN PROBABLY RIG SOME SORT OF DETECTION PROTOCOL...
...BUT ENGINEERING A DEVICE TO USE IT WILL--
THERE'S AN APP FOR THAT.
HOSUN--?!
I BUILT IT FOR HIM, LIKE, A YEA AGO.
BACK WHEN I, Y'KNOW, DIDN'T KNOW HE WAS HIM.
THAT AN "S"--?
LOOKS LIKE A FIVE...
HOSUN-- YOU CAN TRACK THIS ENERGY--?
SURE.
OUR DAD NEEDED AN APP TO LOCATE GUYS LIKE THE FLASH. RUNS ON AN iPHONE.*
CAN'T READ YOUR HAND-WRITING--
--ANY CHANCE YOU PUT "LIMCHUPS" ON OUR GROCERY LIST...?
HOSUN--
DO YOU SERVE RED OR WHITE WINE WITH LIMCHUP...
--HOSUN... FOCUS...
*SEE THE LAZARUS CONTRACT FOR WHY. --ALEX

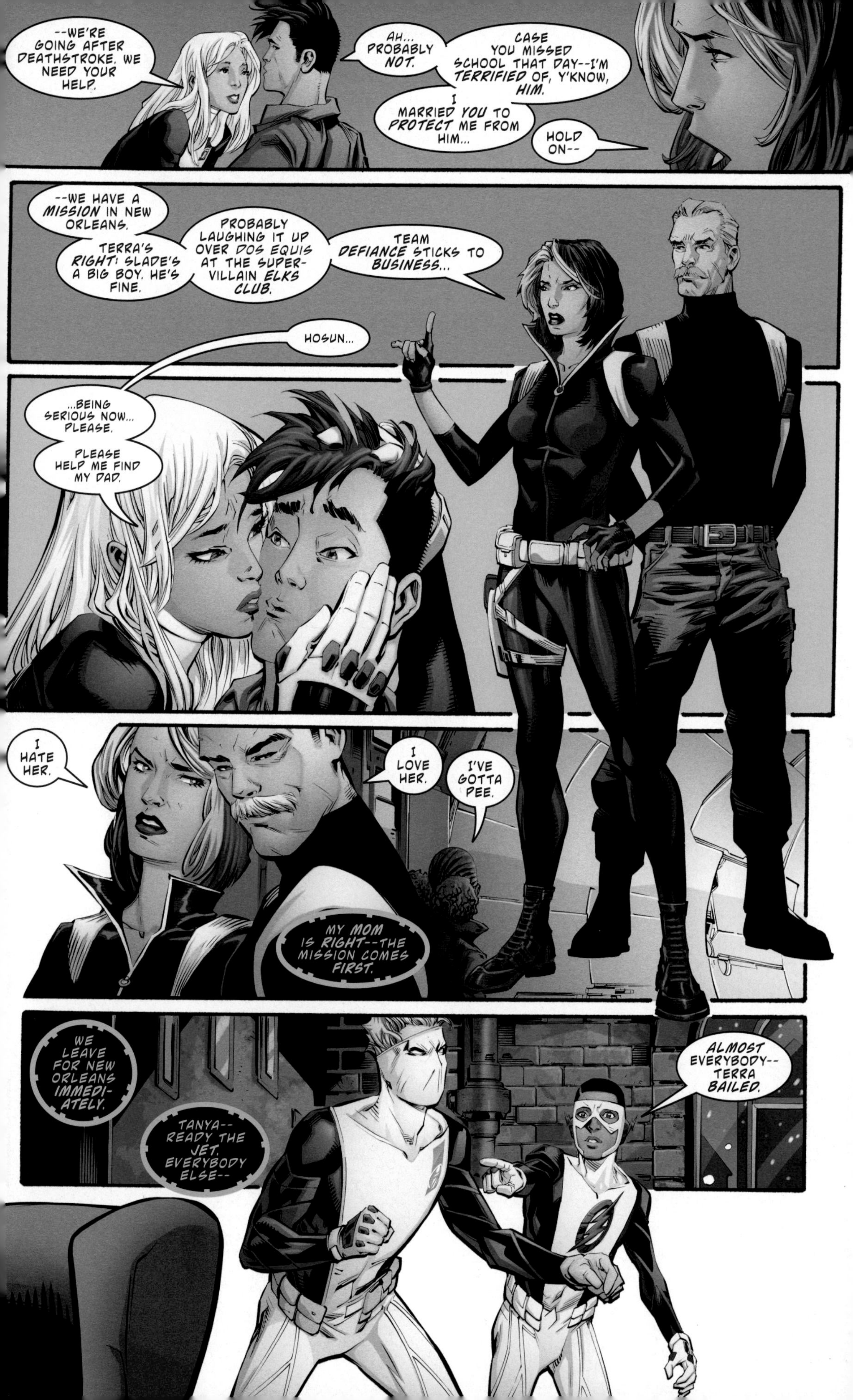
--WE'RE GOING AFTER DEATHSTROKE. WE NEED YOUR HELP.
AH... PROBABLY NOT.
CASE YOU MISSED SCHOOL THAT DAY--I'M TERRIFIED OF, Y'KNOW, HIM.
I MARRIED YOU TO PROTECT ME FROM HIM...
HOLD ON--
--WE HAVE A MISSION IN NEW ORLEANS.
TERRA'S RIGHT: SLADE'S A BIG BOY. HE'S FINE.
PROBABLY LAUGHING IT UP OVER DOS EQUIS AT THE SUPER-VILLAIN ELKS CLUB.
TEAM DEFIANCE STICKS TO BUSINESS...
HOSUN...
...BEING SERIOUS NOW... PLEASE.
PLEASE HELP ME FIND MY DAD.
I HATE HER.
I LOVE HER.
I'VE GOTTA PEE.
MY MOM IS RIGHT--THE MISSION COMES FIRST.
WE LEAVE FOR NEW ORLEANS IMMEDI-ATELY.
TANYA--READY THE JET. EVERYBODY ELSE--
ALMOST EVERYBODY--TERRA BAILED.

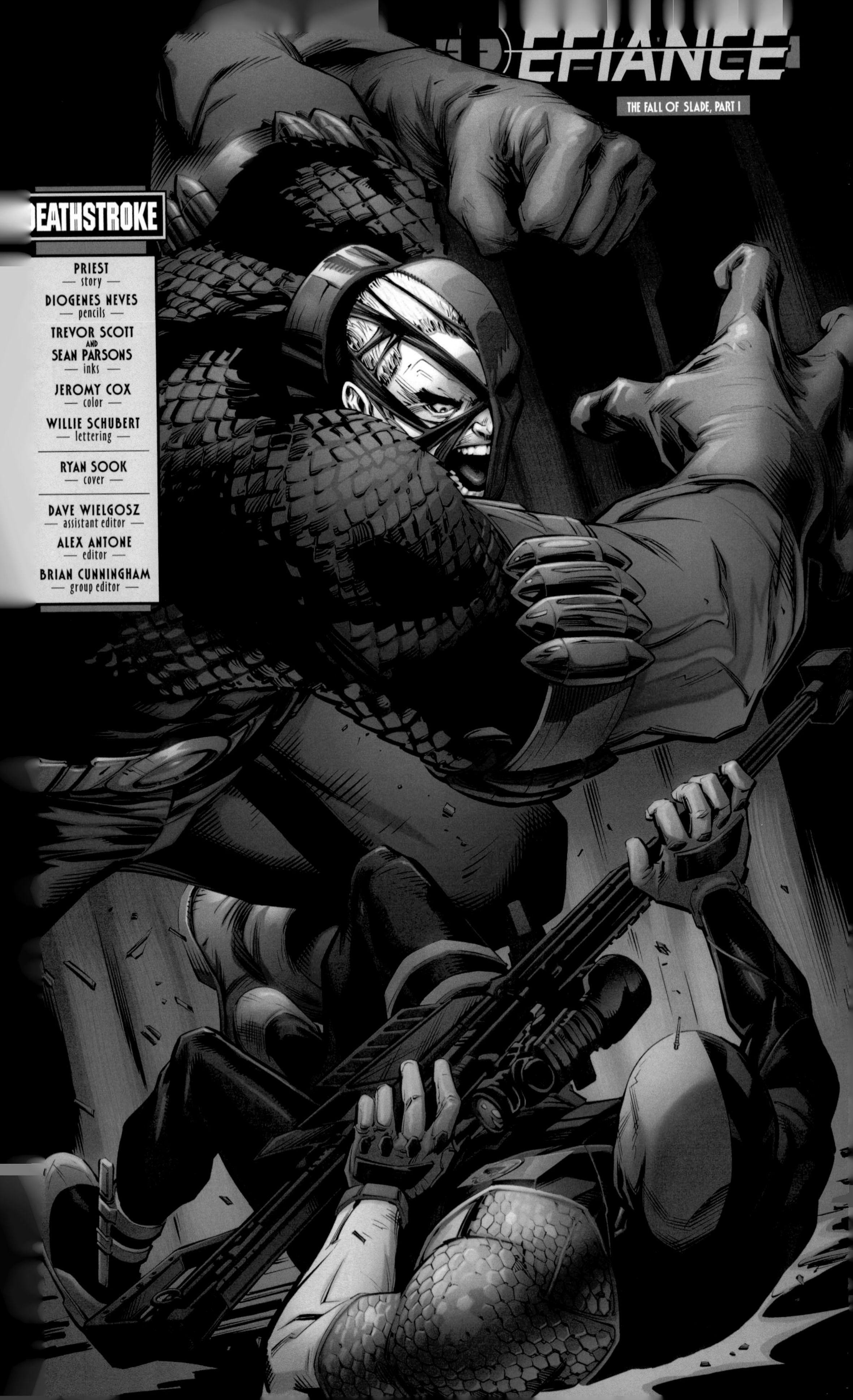
DEFIANCE
THE FALL OF SLADE, PART I
DEATHSTROKE
PRIEST — story —
DIOGENES NEVES — pencils —
TREVOR SCOTT AND SEAN PARSONS — inks —
JEROMY COX — color —
WILLIE SCHUBERT — lettering —
RYAN SOOK — cover —
DAVE WIELGOSZ — assistant editor —
ALEX ANTONE — editor —
BRIAN CUNNINGHAM — group editor —

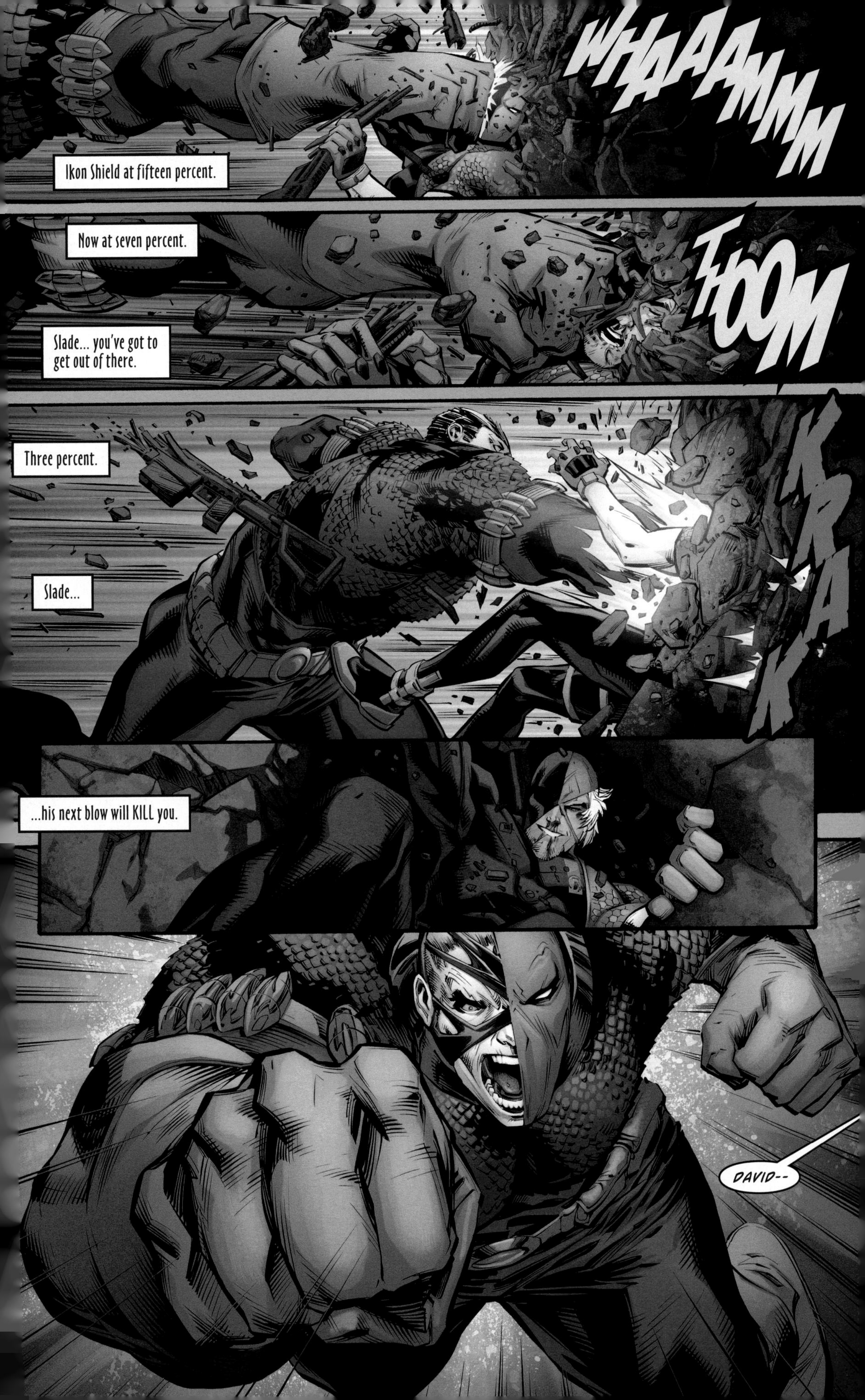
WHAAAMMM
Ikon Shield at fifteen percent.
Now at seven percent.
THOOM
Slade... you've got to get out of there.
Three percent.
KRAK
Slade...
...his next blow will KILL you.
DAVID--

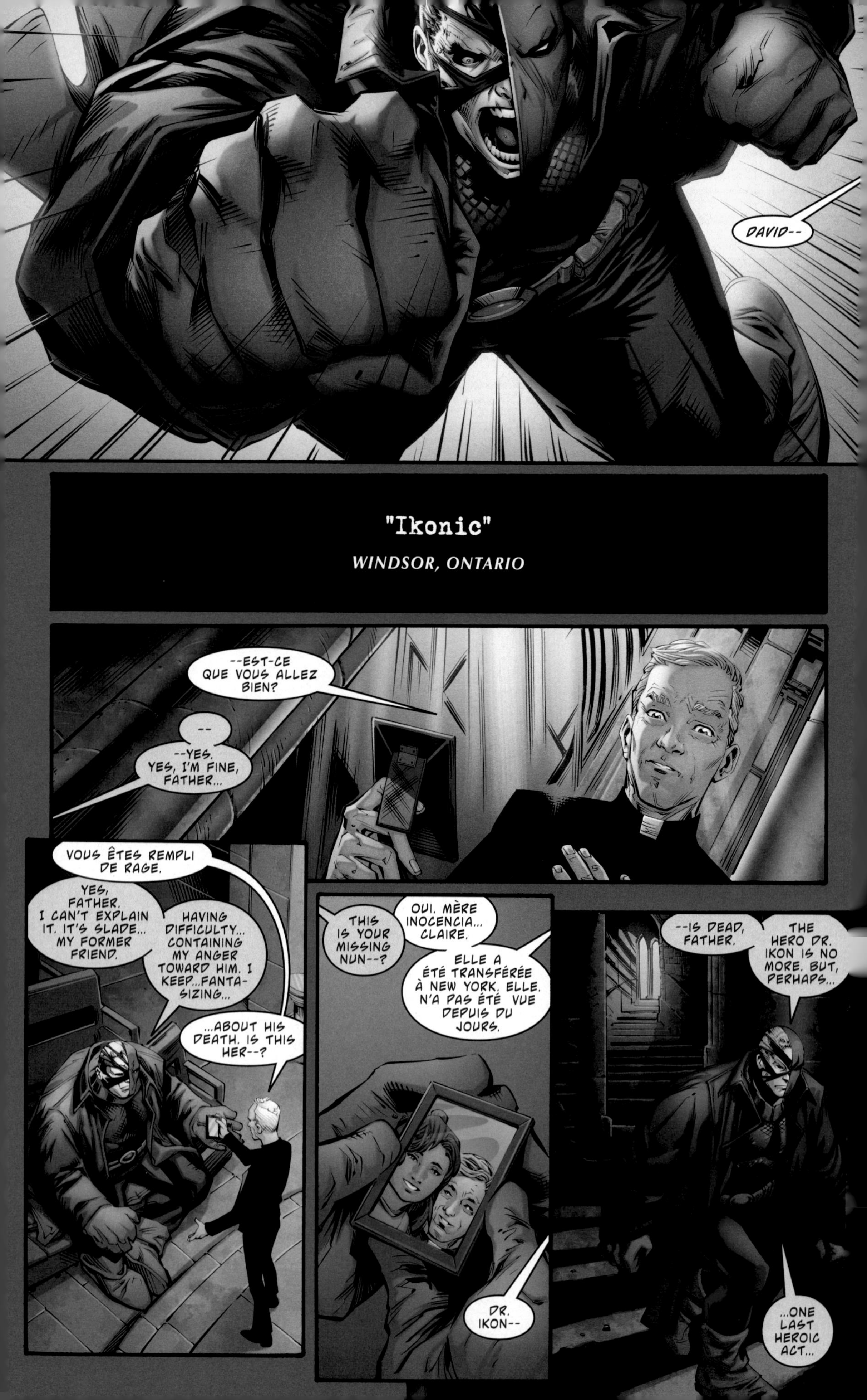
DAVID--
"Ikonic"
WINDSOR, ONTARIO
--EST-CE QUE VOUS ALLEZ BIEN?
--
--YES. YES, I'M FINE, FATHER...
VOUS ÊTES REMPLI DE RAGE.
YES, FATHER. I CAN'T EXPLAIN IT. IT'S SLADE... MY FORMER FRIEND.
HAVING DIFFICULTY... CONTAINING MY ANGER TOWARD HIM. I KEEP...FANTA-SIZING...
...ABOUT HIS DEATH. IS THIS HER--?
THIS IS YOUR MISSING NUN--?
OUI. MÈRE INOCENCIA... CLAIRE.
ELLE A ÉTÉ TRANSFÉRÉE À NEW YORK. ELLE N'A PAS ÉTÉ VUE DEPUIS DU JOURS.
DR. IKON--
--IS DEAD, FATHER.
THE HERO DR. IKON IS NO MORE. BUT, PERHAPS...
...ONE LAST HEROIC ACT...

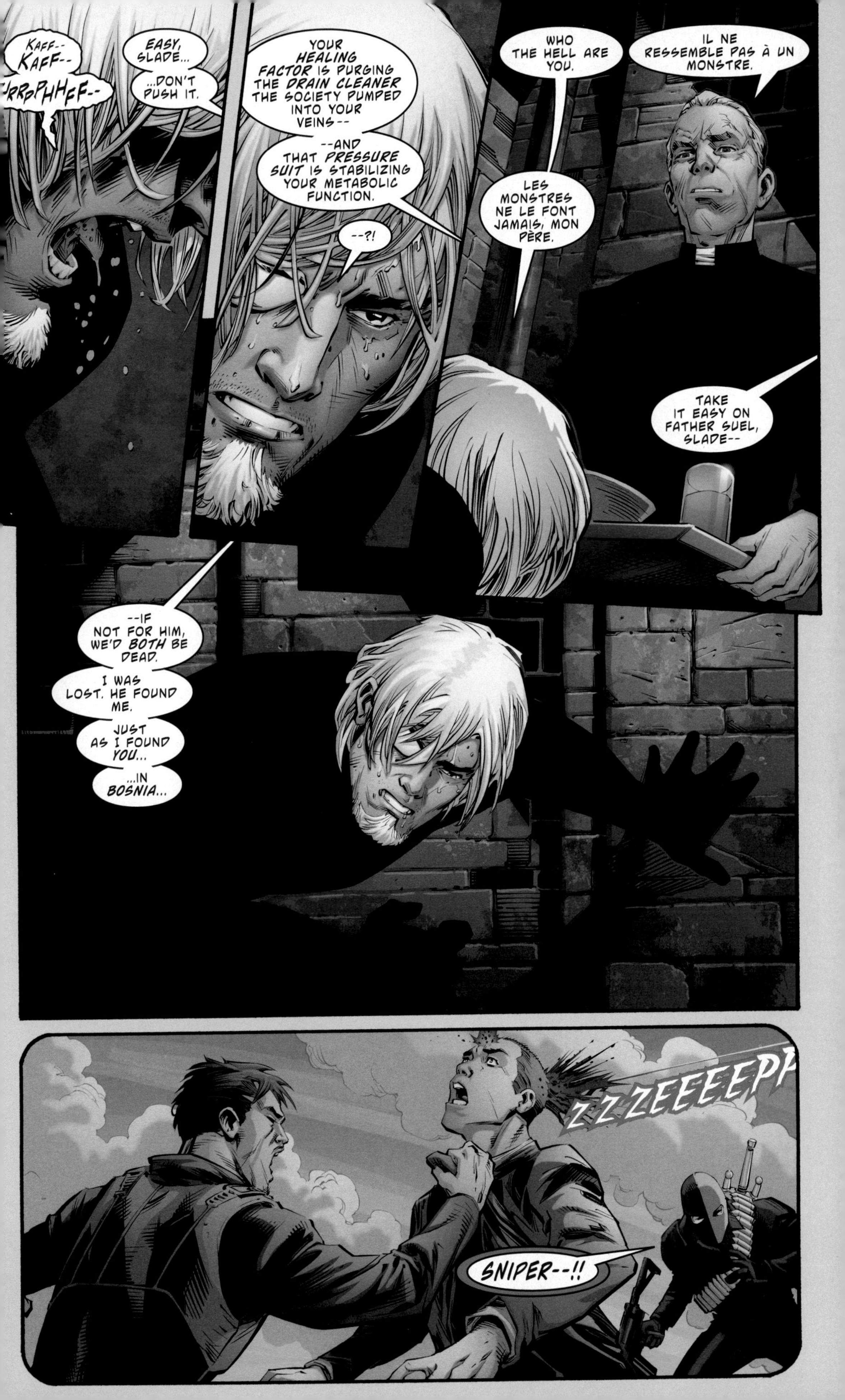
KAFF--
KAFF--
RRRPHHFF--
EASY, SLADE...
...DON'T PUSH IT.
YOUR HEALING FACTOR IS PURGING THE DRAIN CLEANER THE SOCIETY PUMPED INTO YOUR VEINS--
--AND THAT PRESSURE SUIT IS STABILIZING YOUR METABOLIC FUNCTION.
--?!
WHO THE HELL ARE YOU.
IL NE RESSEMBLE PAS À UN MONSTRE.
LES MONSTRES NE LE FONT JAMAIS, MON PÈRE.
TAKE IT EASY ON FATHER SUEL, SLADE--
--IF NOT FOR HIM, WE'D BOTH BE DEAD.
I WAS LOST. HE FOUND ME.
JUST AS I FOUND YOU...
...IN BOSNIA...
ZZZEEEEEPP
SNIPER--!!

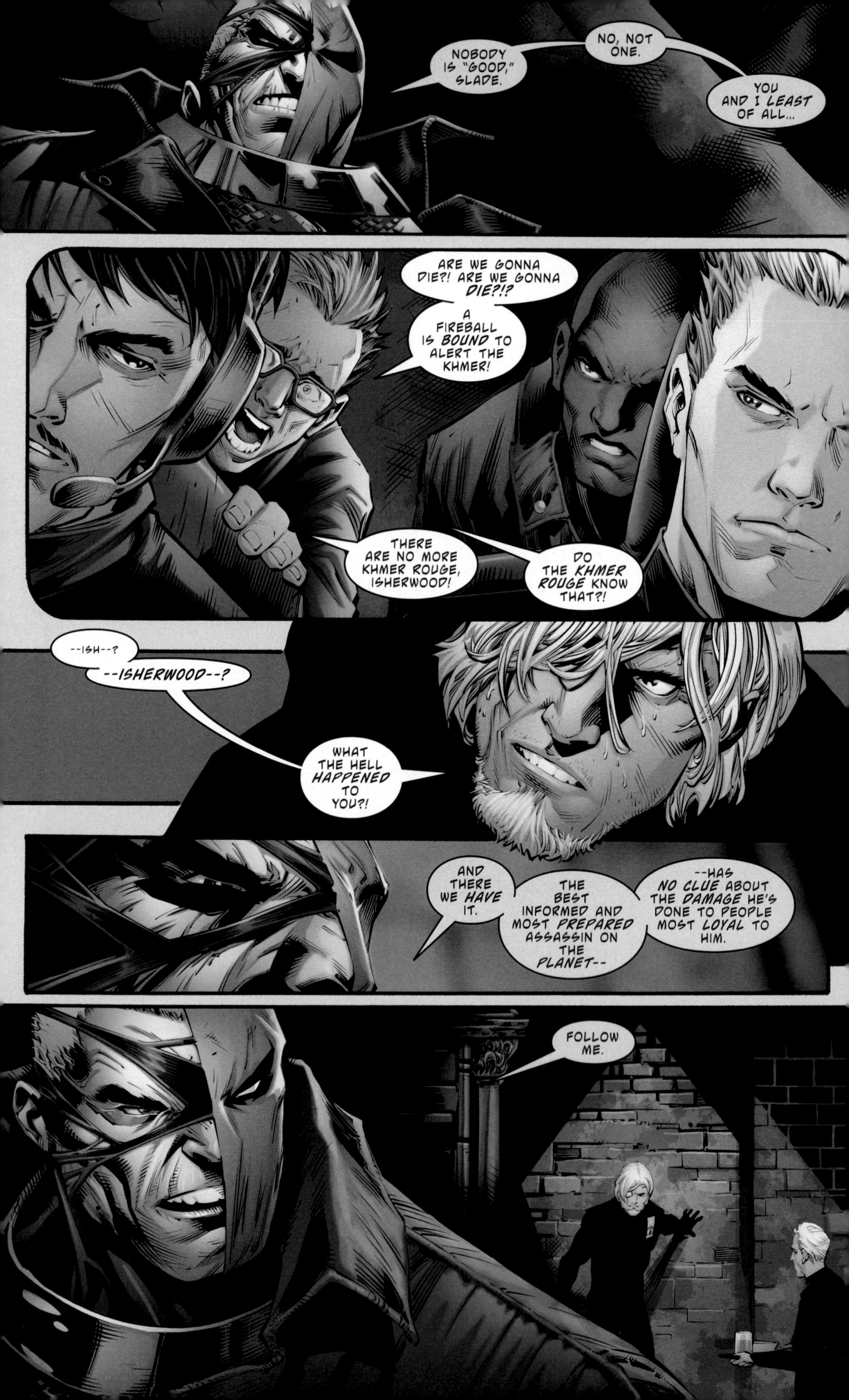
NOBODY IS "GOOD," SLADE.
NO, NOT ONE.
YOU AND I *LEAST* OF ALL...
ARE WE GONNA DIE?! ARE WE GONNA *DIE?!?*
A FIREBALL IS *BOUND* TO ALERT THE KHMER!
THERE ARE NO MORE KHMER ROUGE, ISHERWOOD!
DO THE *KHMER ROUGE* KNOW THAT?!
--ISH--?
--*ISHERWOOD*--?
WHAT THE HELL *HAPPENED* TO YOU?!
AND THERE WE *HAVE* IT.
THE BEST INFORMED AND MOST *PREPARED* ASSASSIN ON THE *PLANET*--
--HAS *NO CLUE* ABOUT THE *DAMAGE* HE'S DONE TO PEOPLE MOST *LOYAL* TO HIM.
FOLLOW ME.

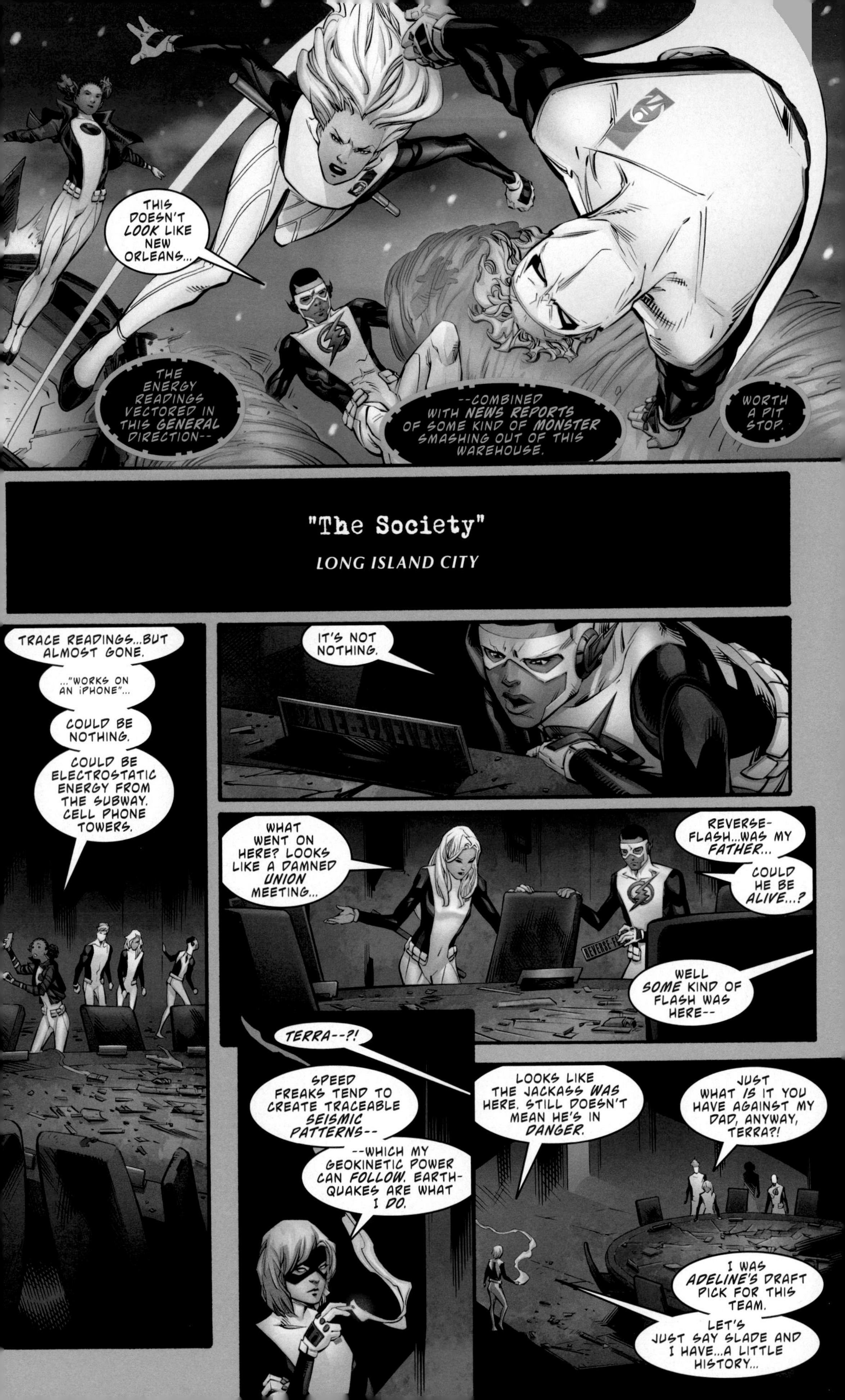

THIS DOESN'T LOOK LIKE NEW ORLEANS...
THE ENERGY READINGS VECTORED IN THIS GENERAL DIRECTION--
--COMBINED WITH NEWS REPORTS OF SOME KIND OF MONSTER SMASHING OUT OF THIS WAREHOUSE.
WORTH A PIT STOP.
"The Society"
LONG ISLAND CITY
TRACE READINGS...BUT ALMOST GONE.
..."WORKS ON AN iPHONE"...
COULD BE NOTHING.
COULD BE ELECTROSTATIC ENERGY FROM THE SUBWAY. CELL PHONE TOWERS.
IT'S NOT NOTHING.
WHAT WENT ON HERE? LOOKS LIKE A DAMNED UNION MEETING...
REVERSE-FLASH...WAS MY FATHER...
COULD HE BE ALIVE...?
WELL SOME KIND OF FLASH WAS HERE--
TERRA--?!
SPEED FREAKS TEND TO CREATE TRACEABLE SEISMIC PATTERNS--
--WHICH MY GEOKINETIC POWER CAN FOLLOW. EARTHQUAKES ARE WHAT I DO.
LOOKS LIKE THE JACKASS WAS HERE. STILL DOESN'T MEAN HE'S IN DANGER.
JUST WHAT IS IT YOU HAVE AGAINST MY DAD, ANYWAY, TERRA?!
I WAS ADELINE'S DRAFT PICK FOR THIS TEAM.
LET'S JUST SAY SLADE AND I HAVE...A LITTLE HISTORY...

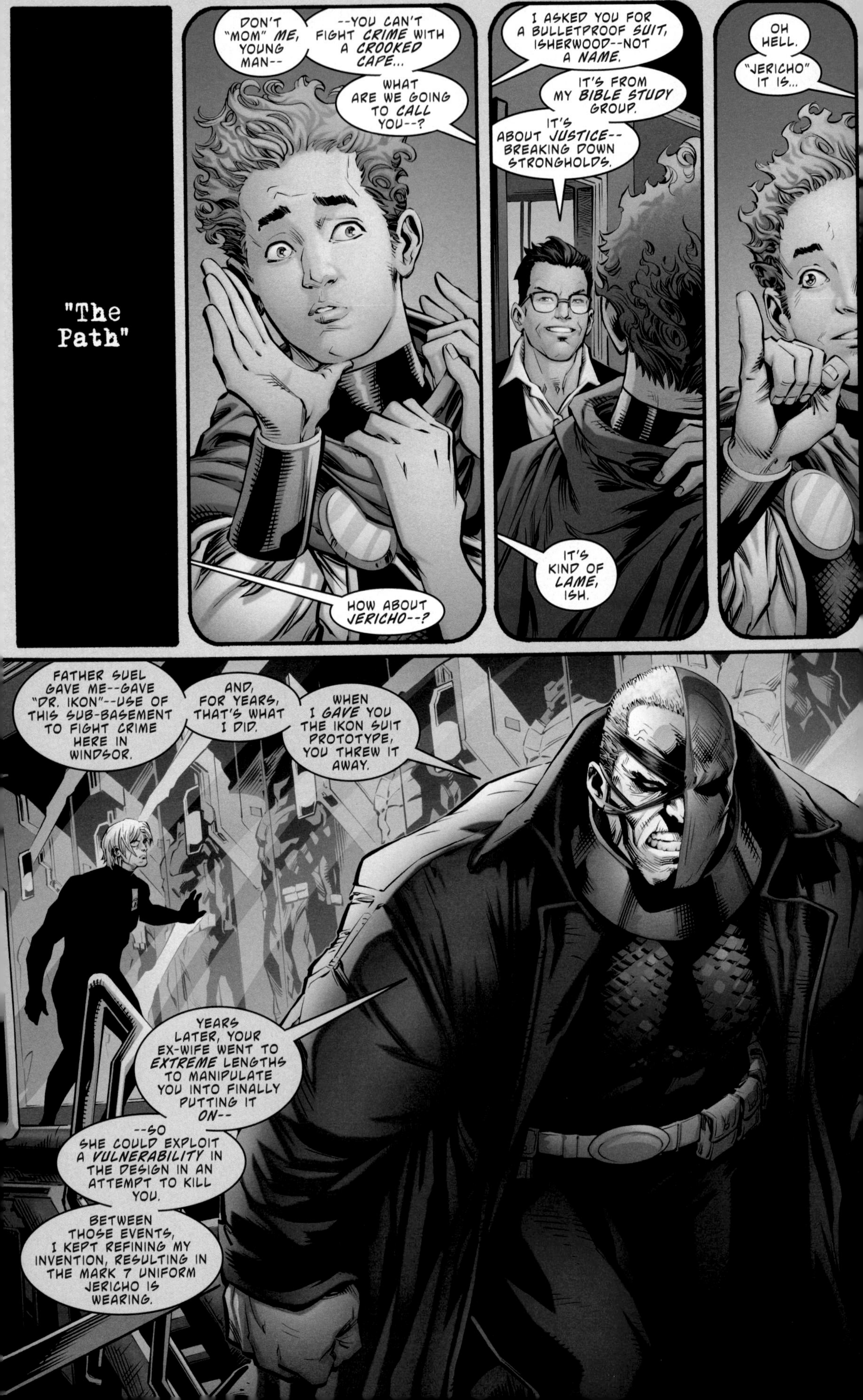
"The Path"
DON'T "MOM" ME, YOUNG MAN--
--YOU CAN'T FIGHT CRIME WITH A CROOKED CAPE...
WHAT ARE WE GOING TO CALL YOU--?
HOW ABOUT JERICHO--?
I ASKED YOU FOR A BULLETPROOF SUIT, ISHERWOOD--NOT A NAME.
IT'S FROM MY BIBLE STUDY GROUP.
IT'S ABOUT JUSTICE--BREAKING DOWN STRONGHOLDS.
IT'S KIND OF LAME, ISH.
OH HELL. "JERICHO" IT IS...
FATHER SUEL GAVE ME--GAVE "DR. IKON"--USE OF THIS SUB-BASEMENT TO FIGHT CRIME HERE IN WINDSOR.
AND, FOR YEARS, THAT'S WHAT I DID.
WHEN I GAVE YOU THE IKON SUIT PROTOTYPE, YOU THREW IT AWAY.
YEARS LATER, YOUR EX-WIFE WENT TO EXTREME LENGTHS TO MANIPULATE YOU INTO FINALLY PUTTING IT ON--
--SO SHE COULD EXPLOIT A VULNERABILITY IN THE DESIGN IN AN ATTEMPT TO KILL YOU.
BETWEEN THOSE EVENTS, I KEPT REFINING MY INVENTION, RESULTING IN THE MARK 7 UNIFORM JERICHO IS WEARING.

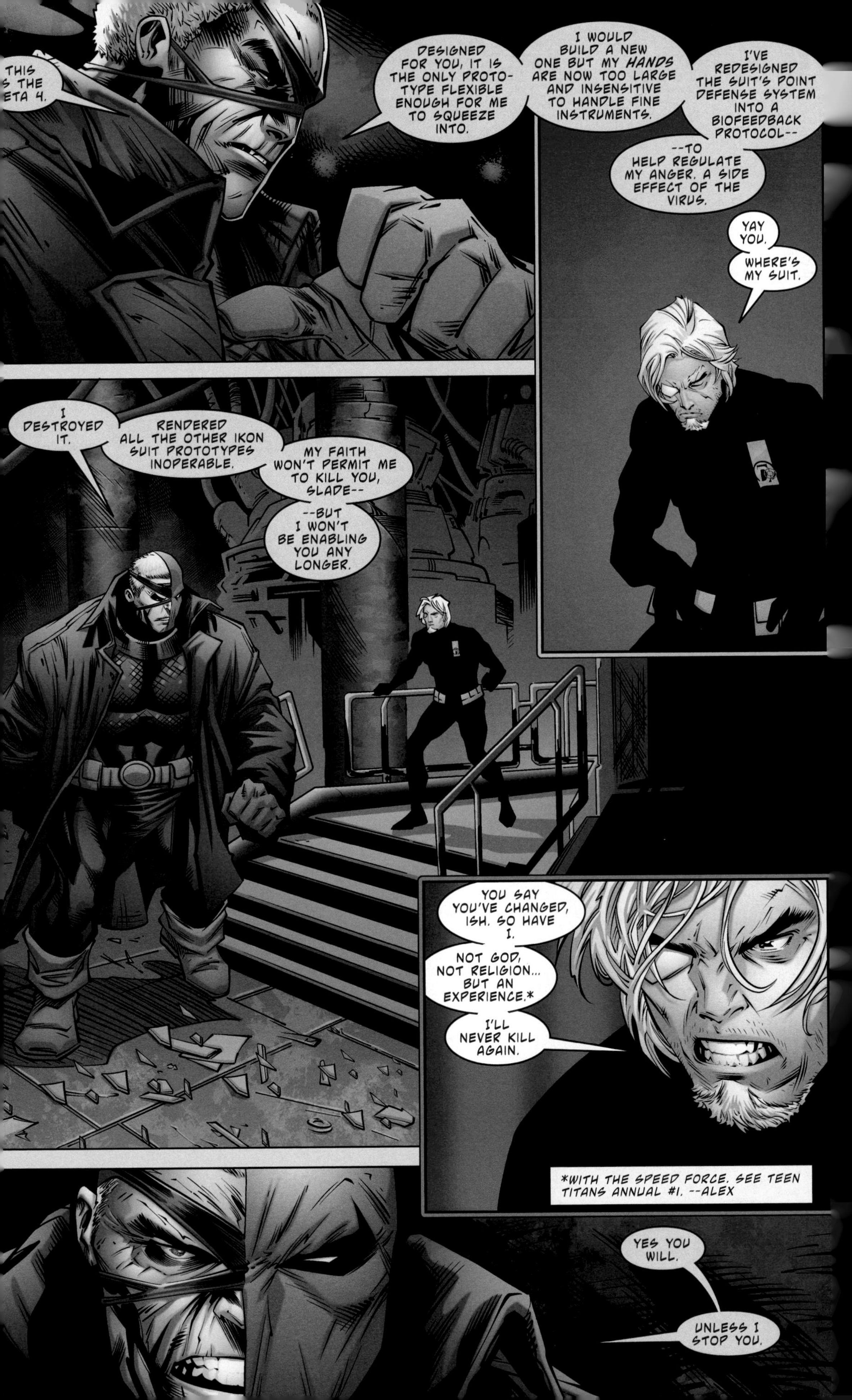
THIS ...S THE ...ETA 4.
DESIGNED FOR YOU, IT IS THE ONLY PROTOTYPE FLEXIBLE ENOUGH FOR ME TO SQUEEZE INTO.
I WOULD BUILD A NEW ONE BUT MY HANDS ARE NOW TOO LARGE AND INSENSITIVE TO HANDLE FINE INSTRUMENTS.
I'VE REDESIGNED THE SUIT'S POINT DEFENSE SYSTEM INTO A BIOFEEDBACK PROTOCOL--
--TO HELP REGULATE MY ANGER. A SIDE EFFECT OF THE VIRUS.
YAY YOU.
WHERE'S MY SUIT.
I DESTROYED IT.
RENDERED ALL THE OTHER IKON SUIT PROTOTYPES INOPERABLE.
MY FAITH WON'T PERMIT ME TO KILL YOU, SLADE--
--BUT I WON'T BE ENABLING YOU ANY LONGER.
YOU SAY YOU'VE CHANGED, ISH. SO HAVE I.
NOT GOD, NOT RELIGION... BUT AN EXPERIENCE.*
I'LL NEVER KILL AGAIN.
*WITH THE SPEED FORCE. SEE TEEN TITANS ANNUAL #1. --ALEX
YES YOU WILL.
UNLESS I STOP YOU.

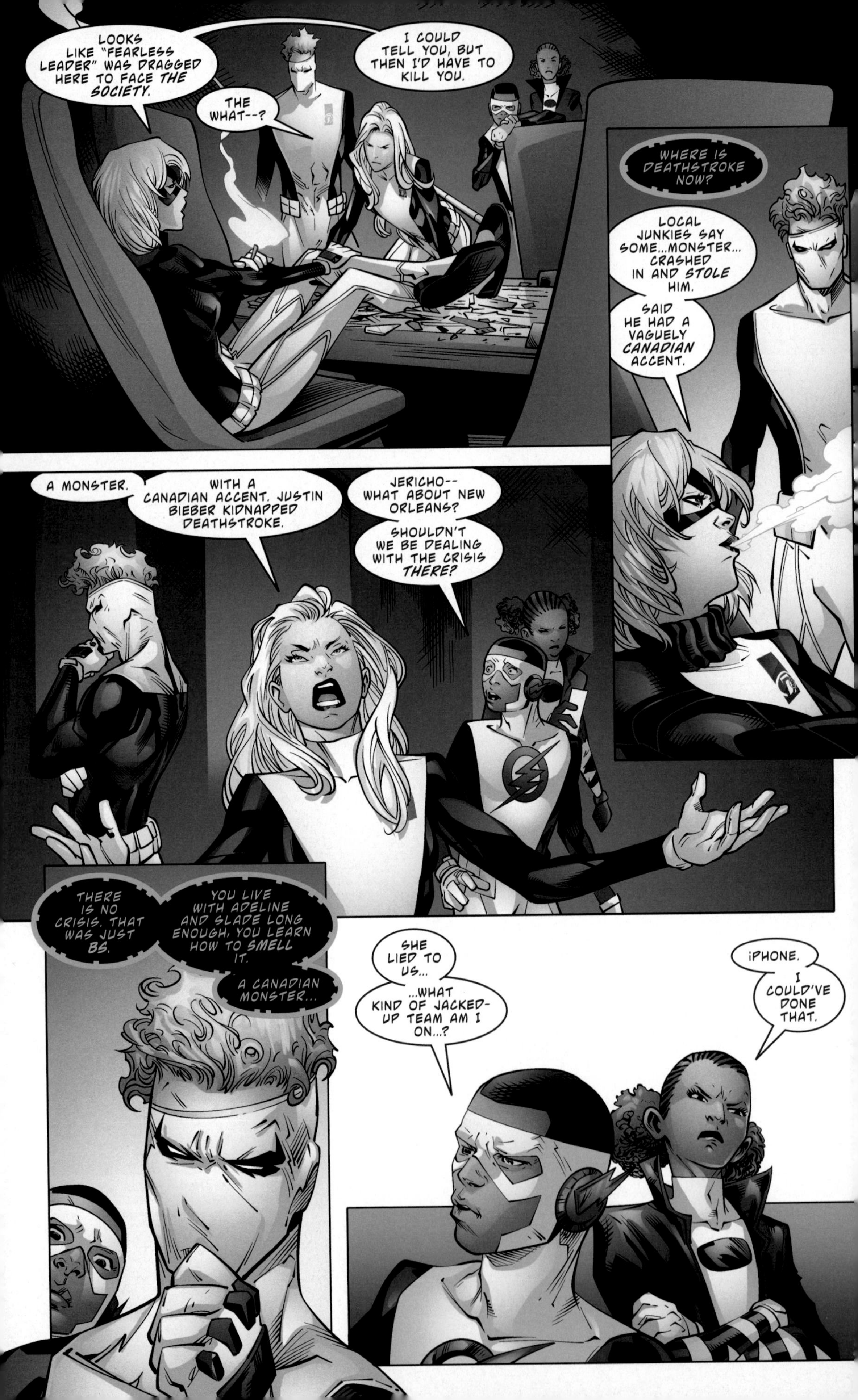
LOOKS LIKE "FEARLESS LEADER" WAS DRAGGED HERE TO FACE THE SOCIETY.
THE WHAT--?
I COULD TELL YOU, BUT THEN I'D HAVE TO KILL YOU.
WHERE IS DEATHSTROKE NOW?
LOCAL JUNKIES SAY SOME...MONSTER... CRASHED IN AND STOLE HIM.
SAID HE HAD A VAGUELY CANADIAN ACCENT.
A MONSTER.
WITH A CANADIAN ACCENT. JUSTIN BIEBER KIDNAPPED DEATHSTROKE.
JERICHO-- WHAT ABOUT NEW ORLEANS?
SHOULDN'T WE BE DEALING WITH THE CRISIS THERE?
THERE IS NO CRISIS. THAT WAS JUST BS.
YOU LIVE WITH ADELINE AND SLADE LONG ENOUGH, YOU LEARN HOW TO SMELL IT.
A CANADIAN MONSTER...
SHE LIED TO US...
...WHAT KIND OF JACKED-UP TEAM AM I ON...?
iPHONE.
I COULD'VE DONE THAT.

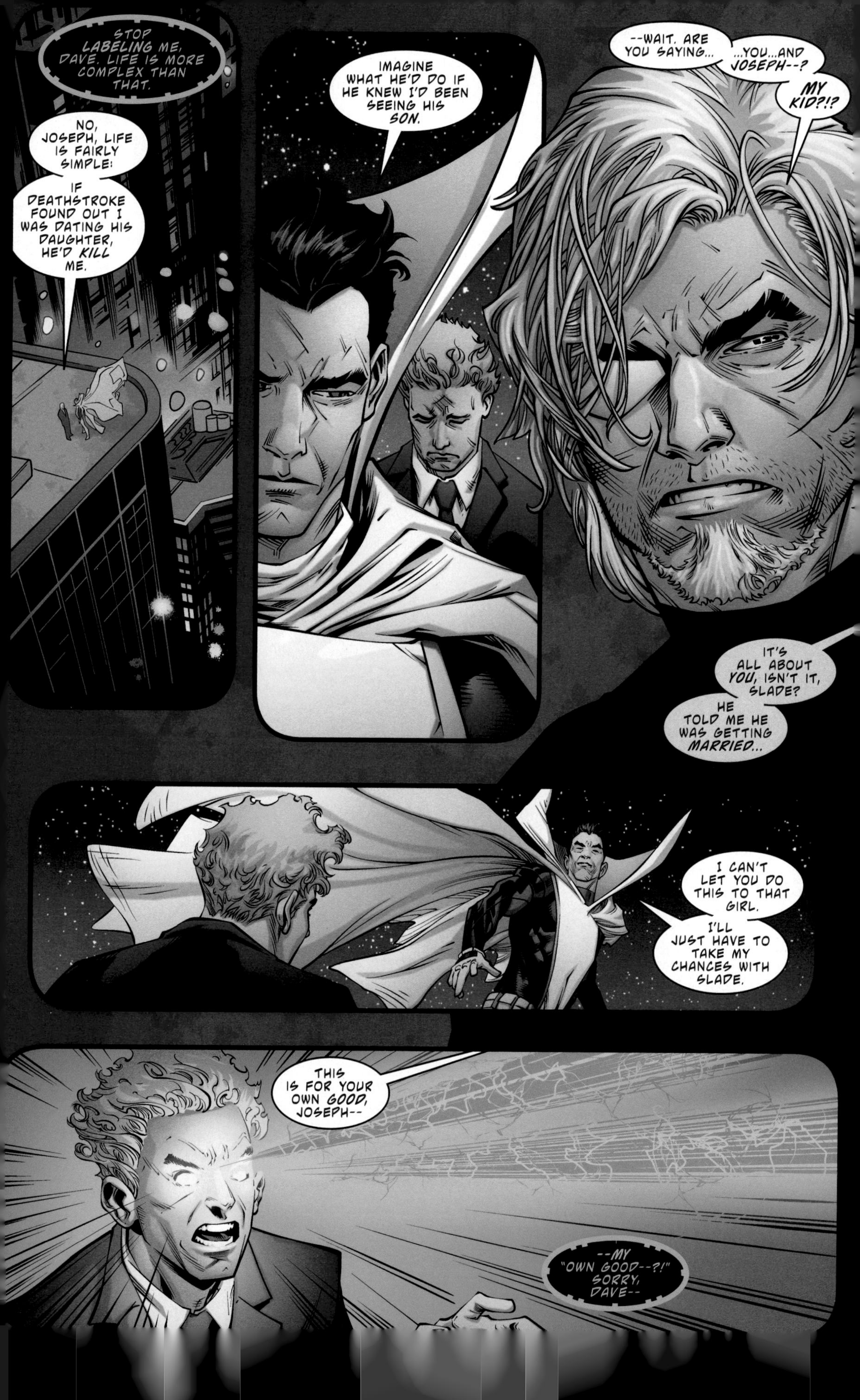
STOP LABELING ME, DAVE. LIFE IS MORE COMPLEX THAN THAT.
NO, JOSEPH, LIFE IS FAIRLY SIMPLE:
IF DEATHSTROKE FOUND OUT I WAS DATING HIS DAUGHTER, HE'D KILL ME.
IMAGINE WHAT HE'D DO IF HE KNEW I'D BEEN SEEING HIS SON.
--WAIT. ARE YOU SAYING...
...YOU...AND JOSEPH--?
MY KID?!?
IT'S ALL ABOUT YOU, ISN'T IT, SLADE?
HE TOLD ME HE WAS GETTING MARRIED...
I CAN'T LET YOU DO THIS TO THAT GIRL.
I'LL JUST HAVE TO TAKE MY CHANCES WITH SLADE.
THIS IS FOR YOUR OWN GOOD, JOSEPH--
--MY "OWN GOOD--?!" SORRY, DAVE--

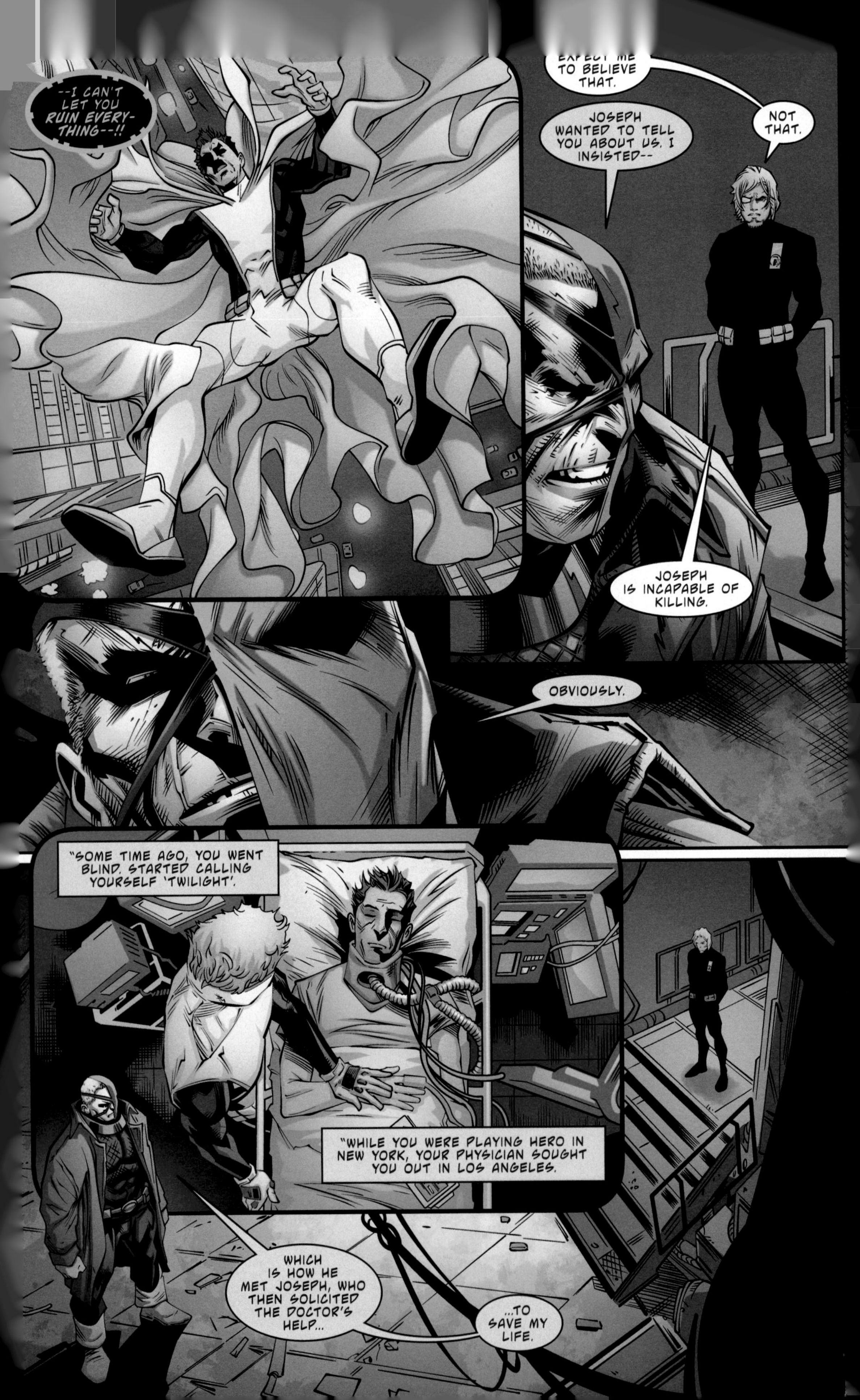
--I CAN'T LET YOU RUIN EVERY-THING--!!
TO BELIEVE THAT.
NOT THAT.
JOSEPH WANTED TO TELL YOU ABOUT US. I INSISTED--
JOSEPH IS INCAPABLE OF KILLING.
OBVIOUSLY.
"SOME TIME AGO, YOU WENT BLIND. STARTED CALLING YOURSELF 'TWILIGHT'.
"WHILE YOU WERE PLAYING HERO IN NEW YORK, YOUR PHYSICIAN SOUGHT YOU OUT IN LOS ANGELES.
WHICH IS HOW HE MET JOSEPH, WHO THEN SOLICITED THE DOCTOR'S HELP...
...TO SAVE MY LIFE.

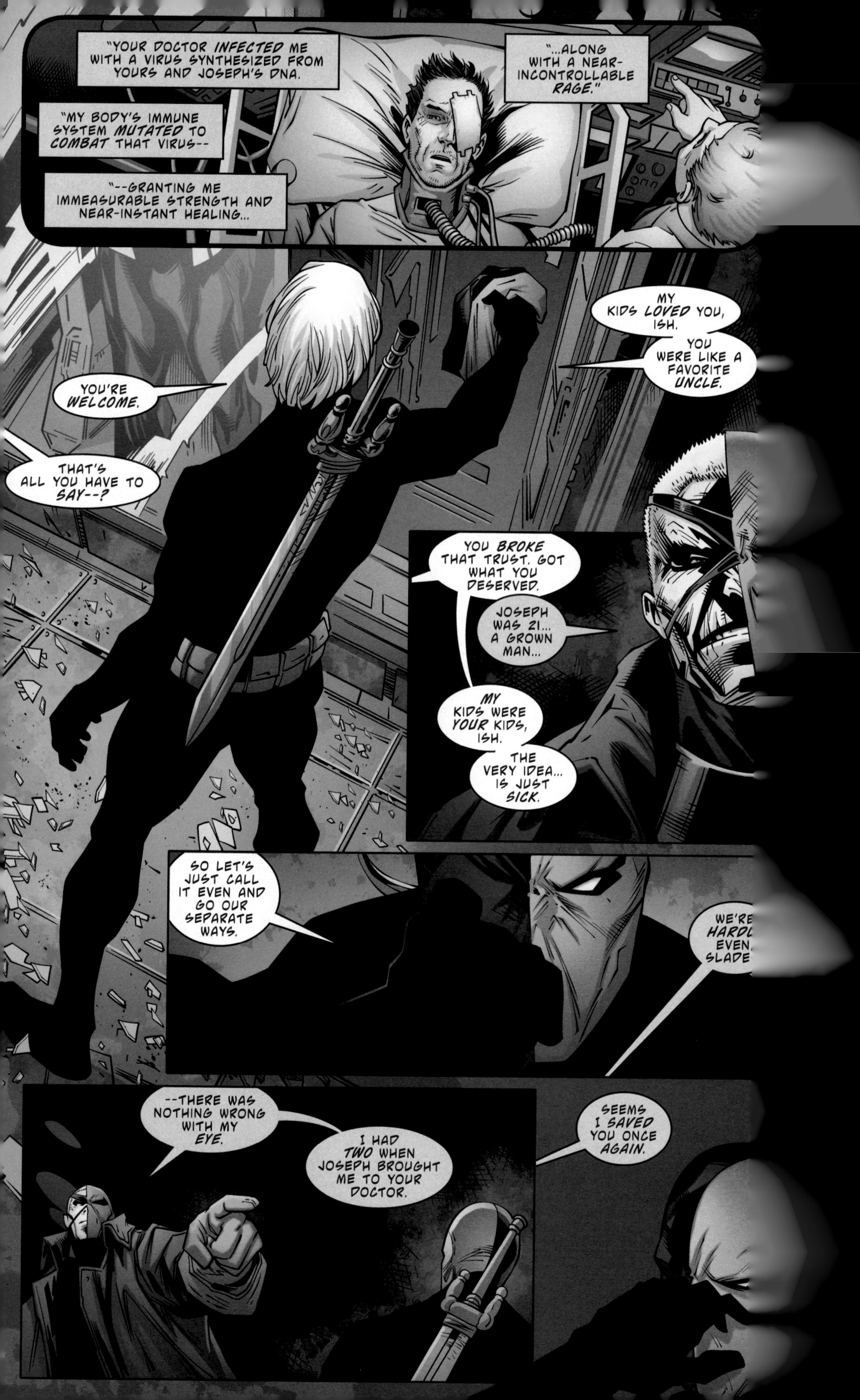
"YOUR DOCTOR INFECTED ME WITH A VIRUS SYNTHESIZED FROM YOURS AND JOSEPH'S DNA.
"MY BODY'S IMMUNE SYSTEM MUTATED TO COMBAT THAT VIRUS--
"--GRANTING ME IMMEASURABLE STRENGTH AND NEAR-INSTANT HEALING...
"...ALONG WITH A NEAR-INCONTROLLABLE RAGE."
YOU'RE WELCOME.
THAT'S ALL YOU HAVE TO SAY--?
MY KIDS LOVED YOU, ISH.
YOU WERE LIKE A FAVORITE UNCLE.
YOU BROKE THAT TRUST. GOT WHAT YOU DESERVED.
JOSEPH WAS 21... A GROWN MAN...
MY KIDS WERE YOUR KIDS, ISH.
THE VERY IDEA... IS JUST SICK.
SO LET'S JUST CALL IT EVEN AND GO OUR SEPARATE WAYS.
--THERE WAS NOTHING WRONG WITH MY EYE.
I HAD TWO WHEN JOSEPH BROUGHT ME TO YOUR DOCTOR.
SEEMS I SAVED YOU ONCE AGAIN.

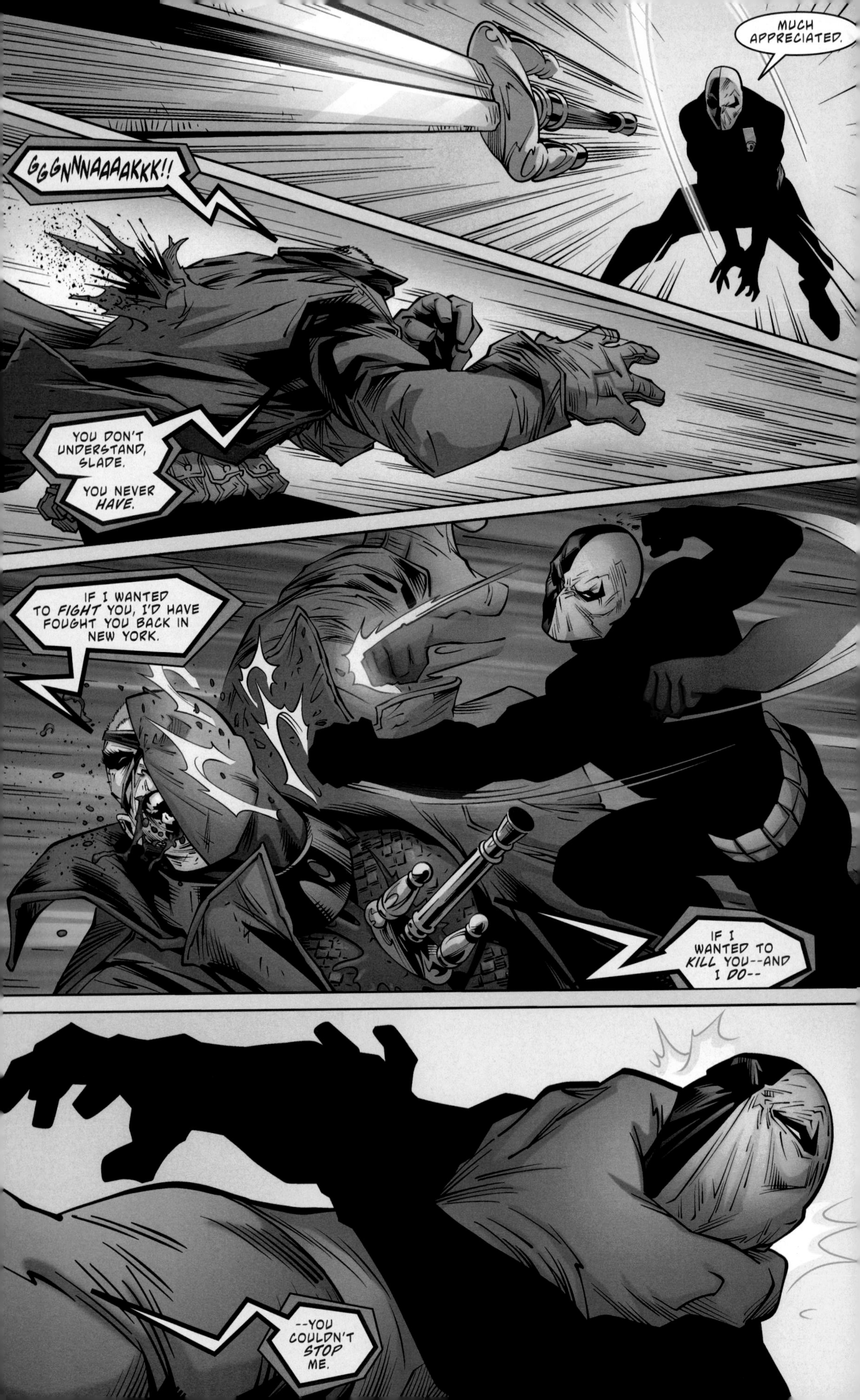
MUCH APPRECIATED.
GGGNNNAAAAKKK!!
YOU DON'T UNDERSTAND, SLADE.
YOU NEVER HAVE.
IF I WANTED TO FIGHT YOU, I'D HAVE FOUGHT YOU BACK IN NEW YORK.
IF I WANTED TO KILL YOU--AND I DO--
--YOU COULDN'T STOP ME.

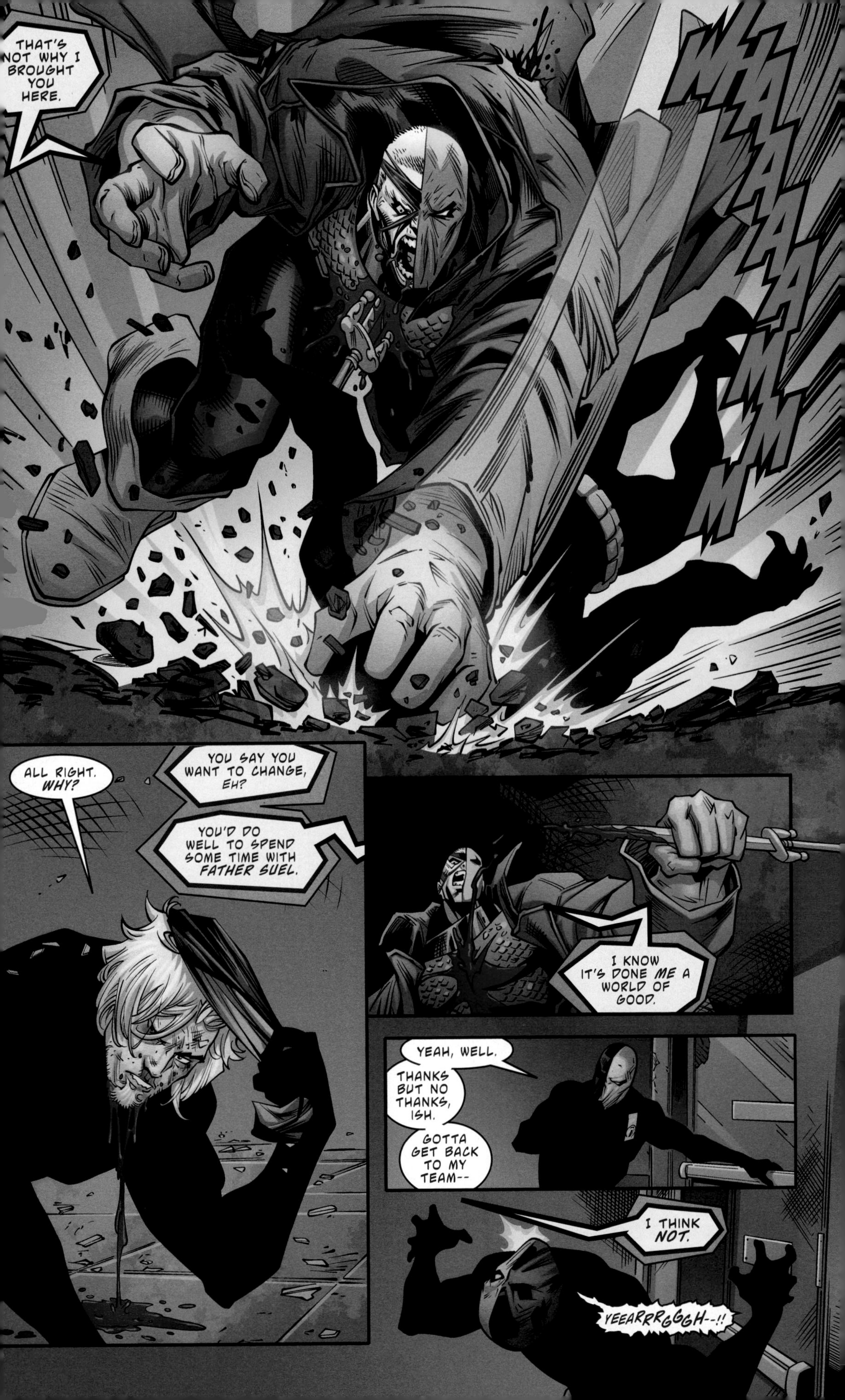
THAT'S NOT WHY I BROUGHT YOU HERE.
WHAAAAMMMM
ALL RIGHT. *WHY?*
YOU SAY YOU WANT TO CHANGE, EH?
YOU'D DO WELL TO SPEND SOME TIME WITH *FATHER SUEL.*
I KNOW IT'S DONE *ME* A WORLD OF GOOD.
YEAH, WELL.
THANKS BUT NO THANKS, ISH.
GOTTA GET BACK TO MY TEAM--
I THINK *NOT.*
YEEARRRGGGH--!!

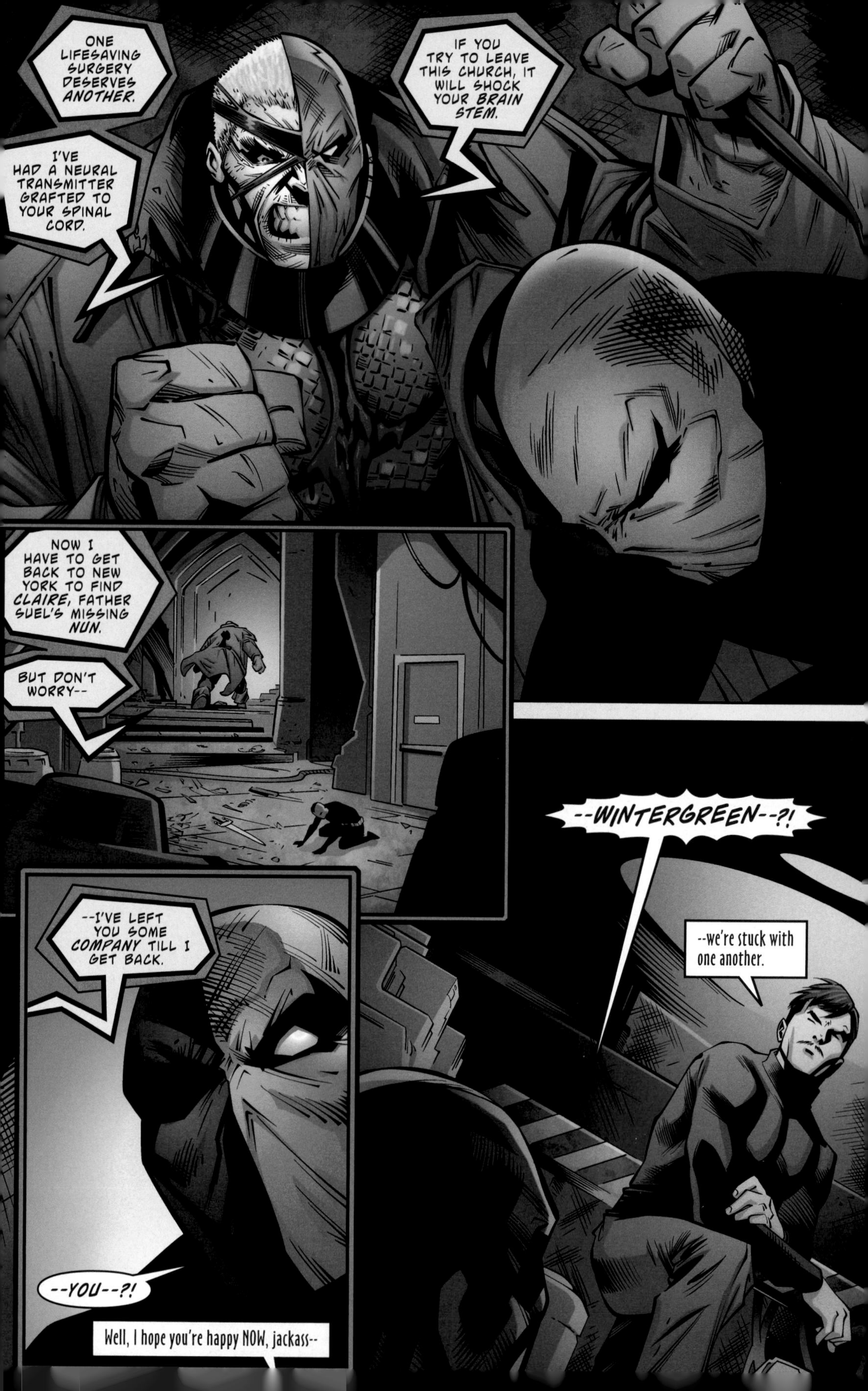
ONE LIFESAVING SURGERY DESERVES ANOTHER.
I'VE HAD A NEURAL TRANSMITTER GRAFTED TO YOUR SPINAL CORD.
IF YOU TRY TO LEAVE THIS CHURCH, IT WILL SHOCK YOUR BRAIN STEM.
NOW I HAVE TO GET BACK TO NEW YORK TO FIND CLAIRE, FATHER SUEL'S MISSING NUN.
BUT DON'T WORRY--
--I'VE LEFT YOU SOME COMPANY TILL I GET BACK.
--YOU--?!
Well, I hope you're happy NOW, jackass--
--WINTERGREEN--?!
--we're stuck with one another.

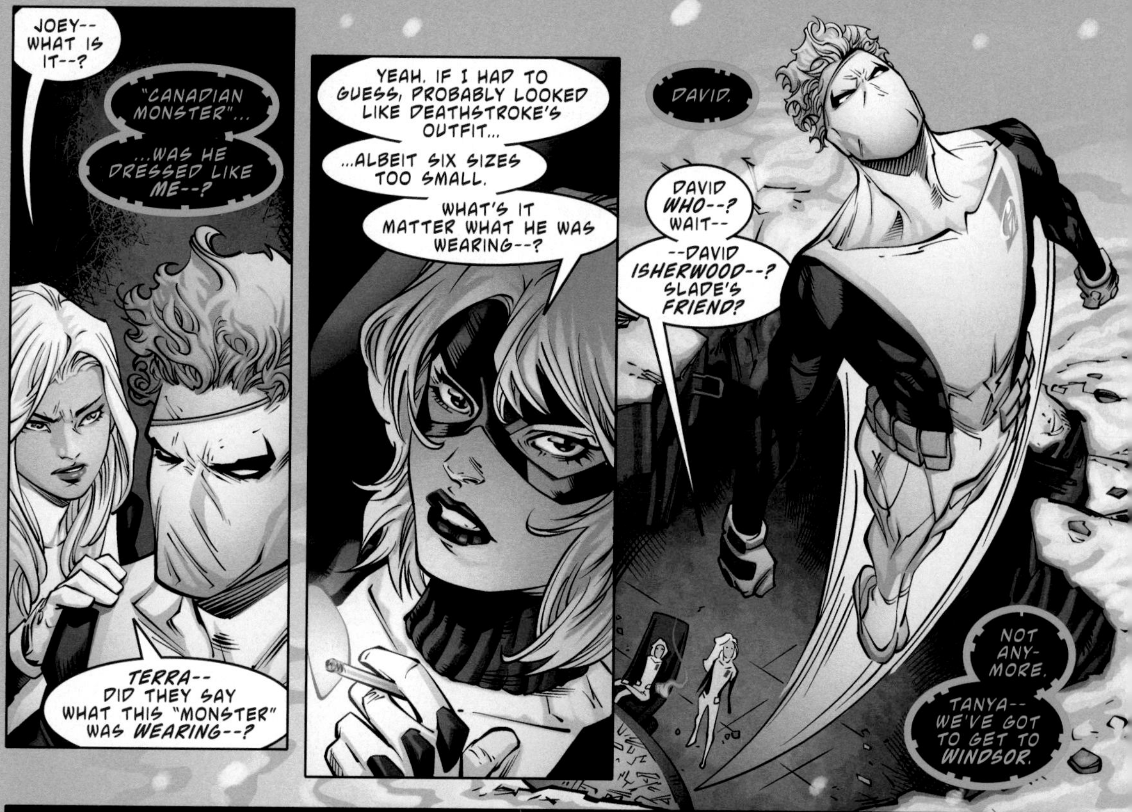
JOEY--
WHAT IS IT--?
"CANADIAN MONSTER"...
...WAS HE DRESSED LIKE ME--?
TERRA--
DID THEY SAY WHAT THIS "MONSTER" WAS WEARING--?
YEAH. IF I HAD TO GUESS, PROBABLY LOOKED LIKE DEATHSTROKE'S OUTFIT...
...ALBEIT SIX SIZES TOO SMALL.
WHAT'S IT MATTER WHAT HE WAS WEARING--?
DAVID.
DAVID WHO--? WAIT--
--DAVID ISHERWOOD--? SLADE'S FRIEND?
NOT ANY-MORE.
TANYA--
WE'VE GOT TO GET TO WINDSOR.

"Made in China"

DEFIANCE HQ
THE BRONX

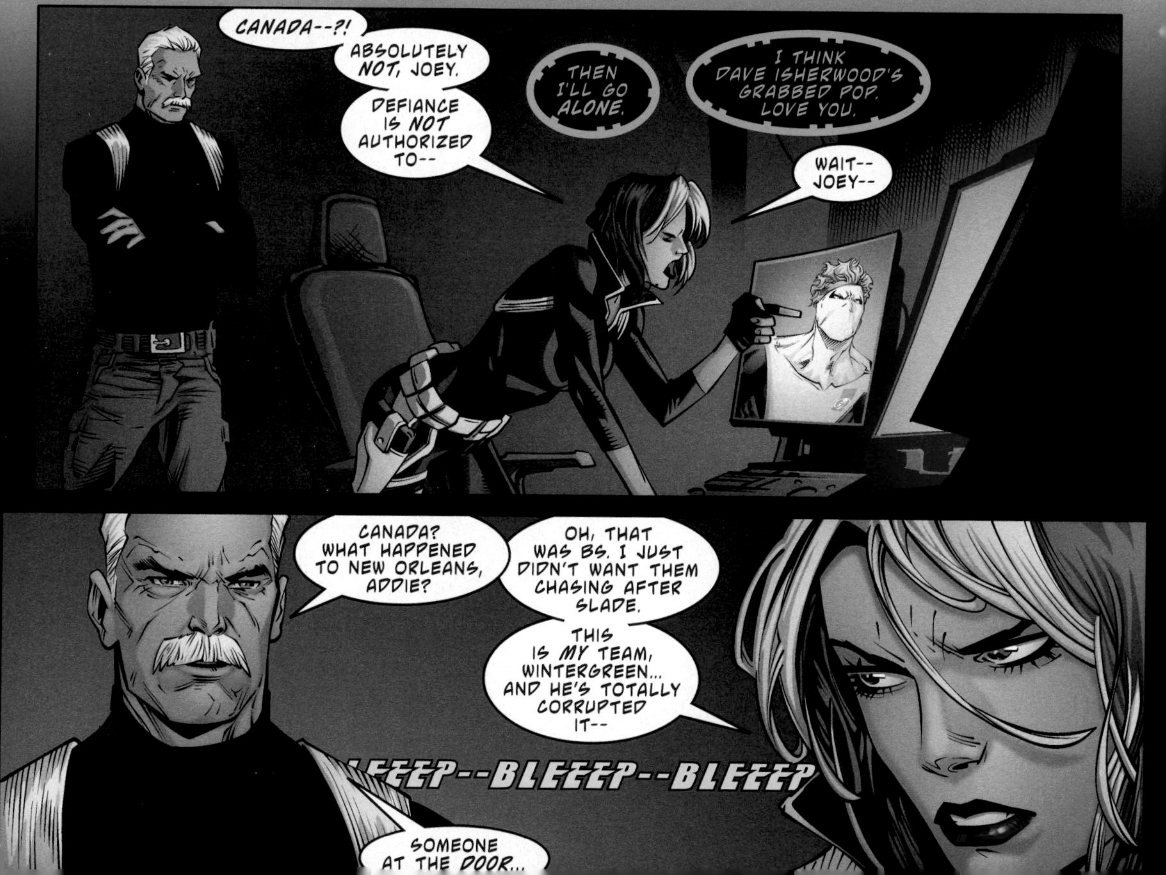
CANADA--?!
ABSOLUTELY NOT, JOEY.
DEFIANCE IS NOT AUTHORIZED TO--
THEN I'LL GO ALONE.
I THINK DAVE ISHERWOOD'S GRABBED POP. LOVE YOU.
WAIT--
JOEY--
CANADA? WHAT HAPPENED TO NEW ORLEANS, ADDIE?
OH, THAT WAS BS. I JUST DIDN'T WANT THEM CHASING AFTER SLADE.
THIS IS MY TEAM, WINTERGREEN... AND HE'S TOTALLY CORRUPTED IT--
LEEEP--BLEEEP--BLEEEP
SOMEONE AT THE DOOR...

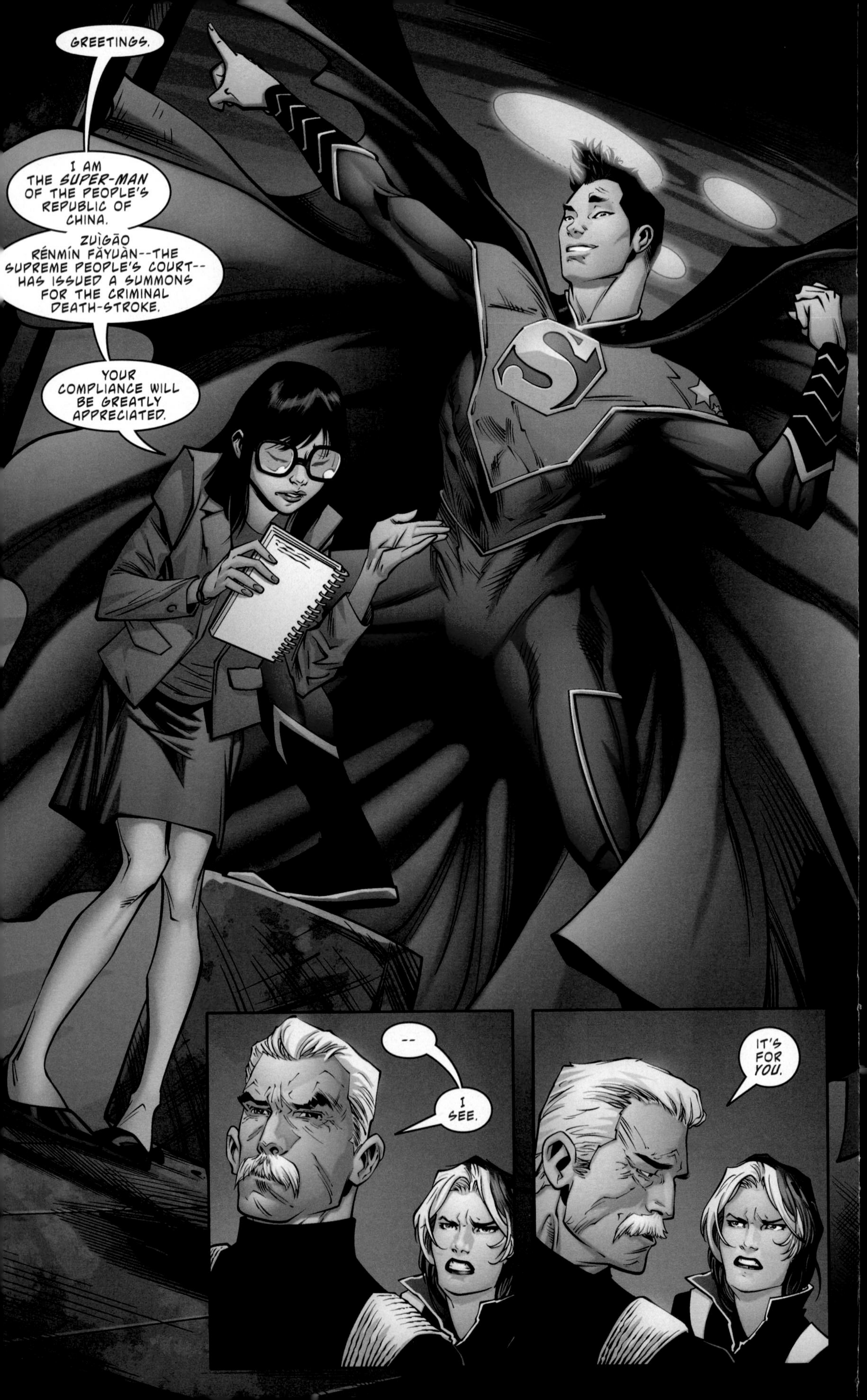
GREETINGS.
I AM THE *SUPER-MAN* OF THE PEOPLE'S REPUBLIC OF CHINA.
ZUÌGĀO RÉNMÍN FǍYUÀN--THE SUPREME PEOPLE'S COURT--HAS ISSUED A SUMMONS FOR THE CRIMINAL DEATH-STROKE.
YOUR COMPLIANCE WILL BE GREATLY APPRECIATED.
--
I SEE.
IT'S FOR *YOU*.

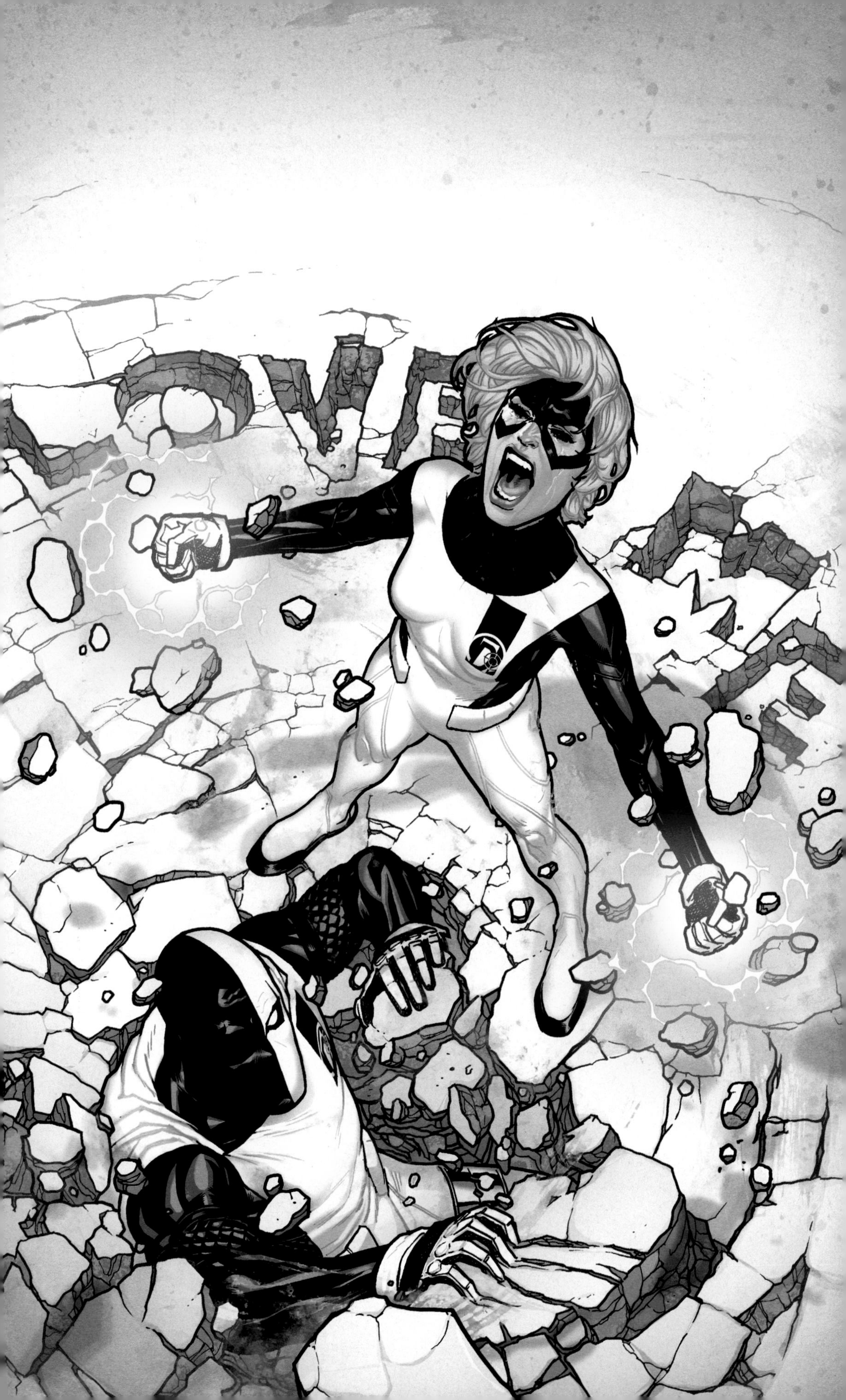

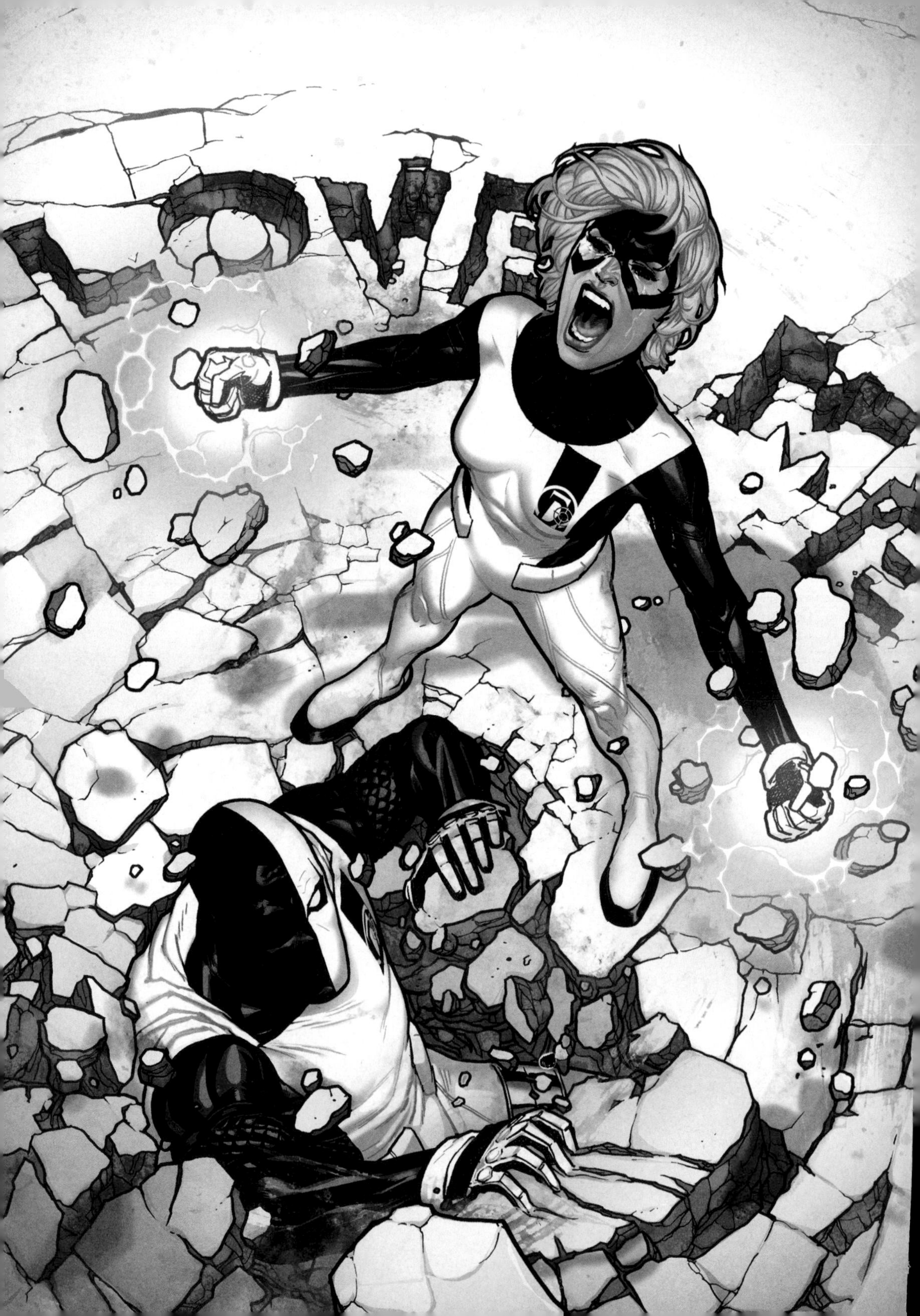

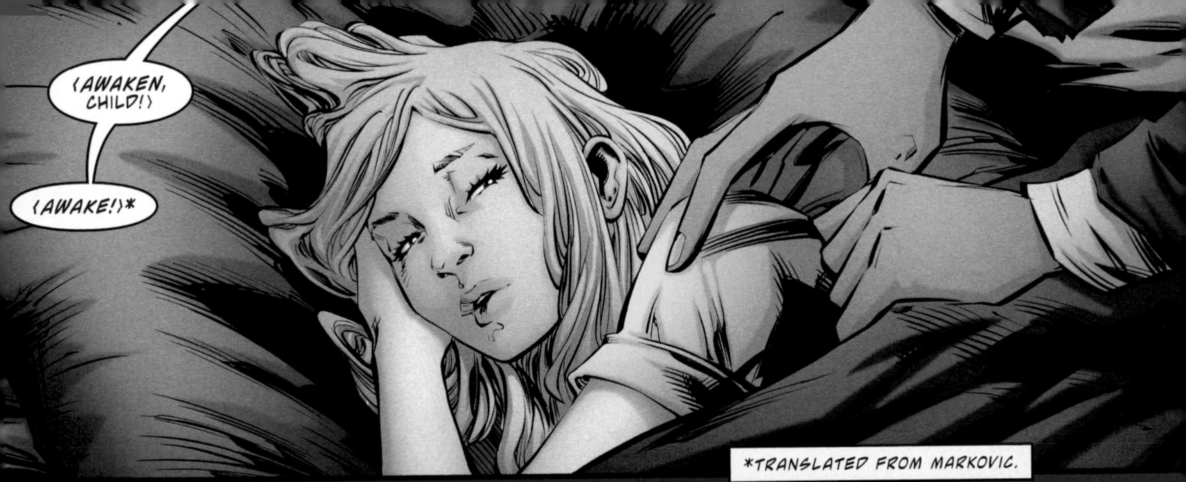

⟨AWAKEN, CHILD!⟩
⟨AWAKE!⟩*
*TRANSLATED FROM MARKOVIC.

"The Princess"

MARKOVIA

YEARS AGO

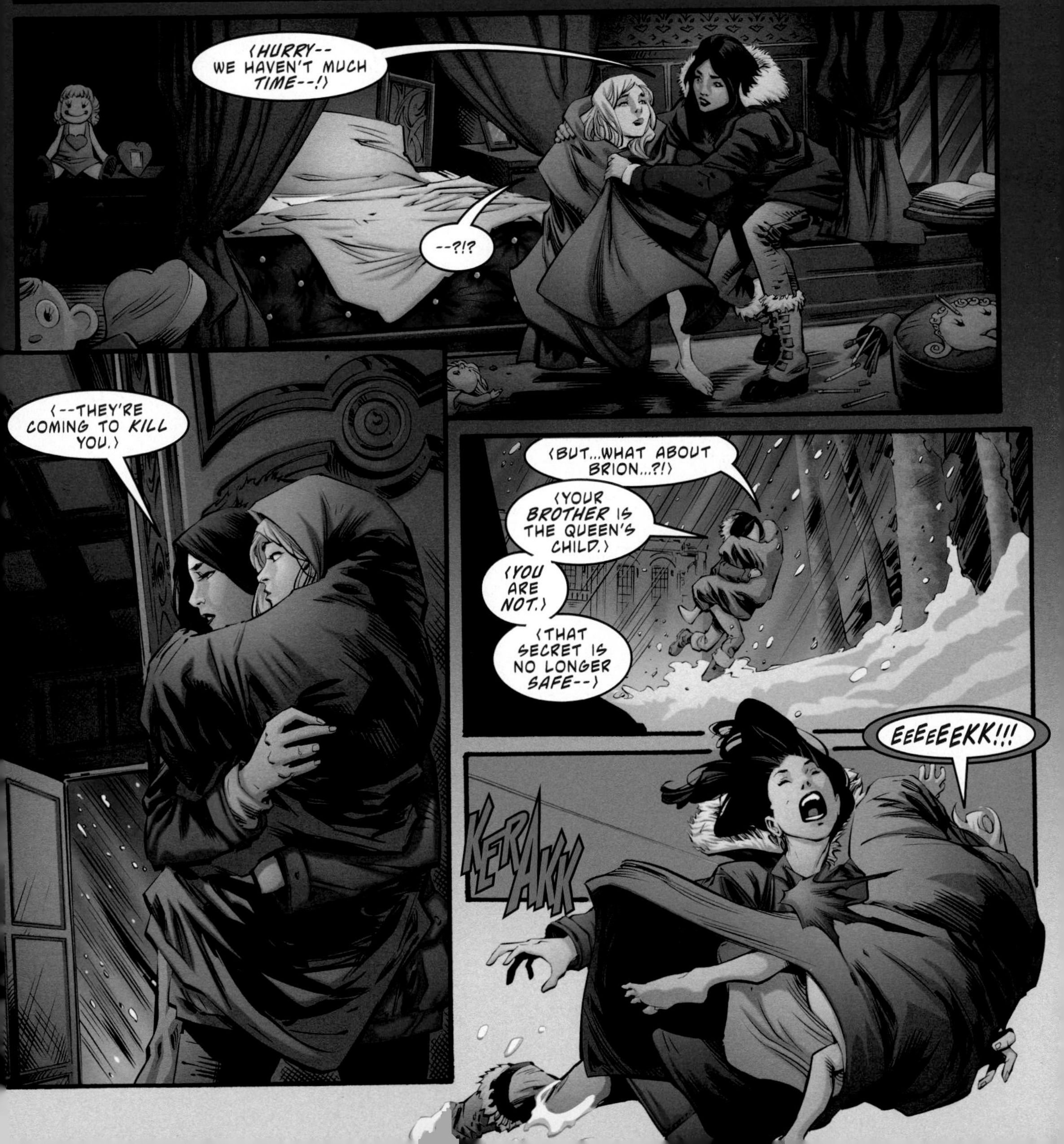

⟨HURRY-- WE HAVEN'T MUCH TIME--!⟩
--?!?
⟨--THEY'RE COMING TO KILL YOU.⟩
⟨BUT...WHAT ABOUT BRION...?!⟩
⟨YOUR BROTHER IS THE QUEEN'S CHILD.⟩
⟨YOU ARE NOT.⟩
⟨THAT SECRET IS NO LONGER SAFE--⟩
KERAKK
EEEEEEKK!!!

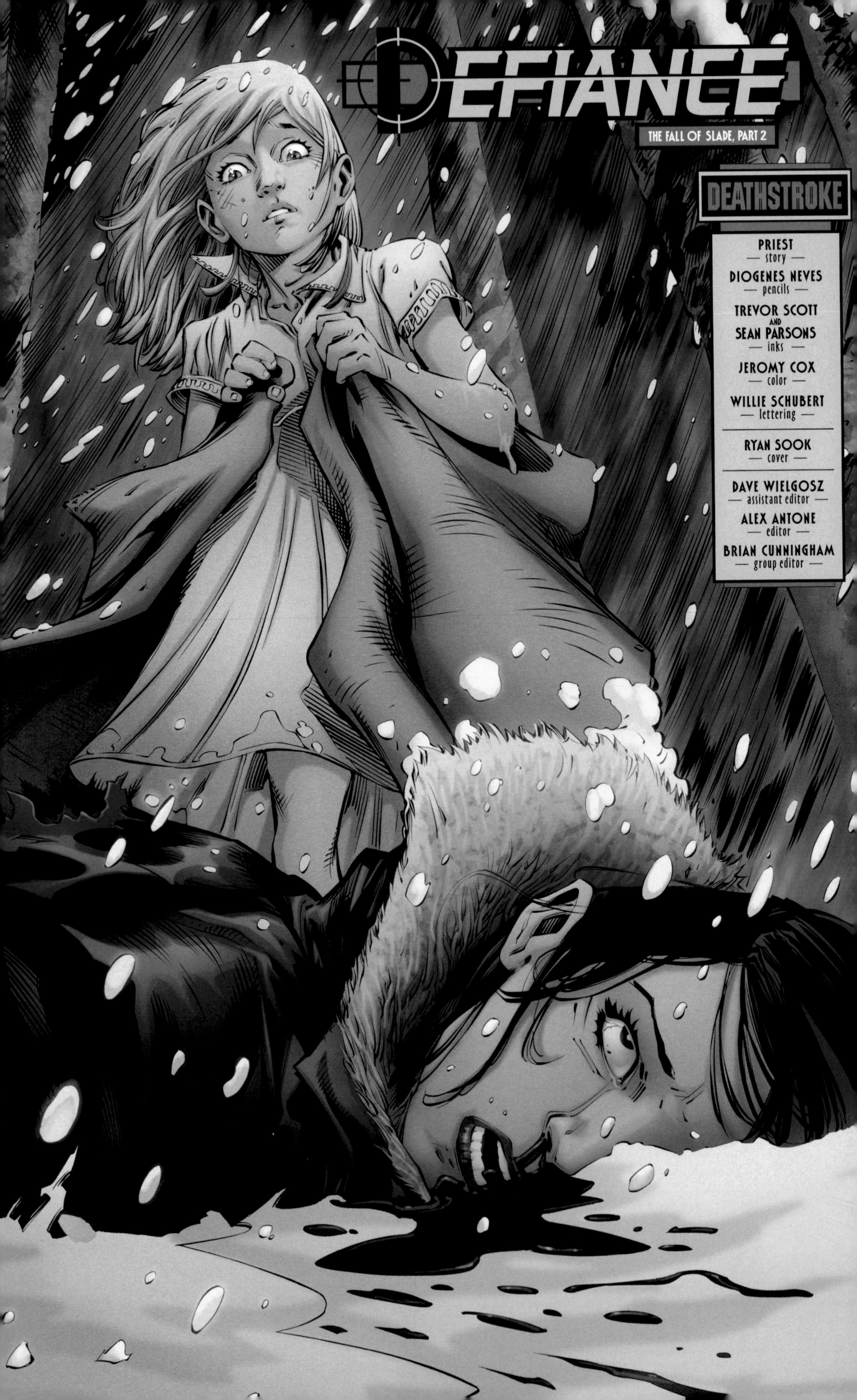
DEFIANCE
THE FALL OF SLADE, PART 2
DEATHSTROKE
PRIEST
— story —
DIOGENES NEVES
— pencils —
TREVOR SCOTT
AND
SEAN PARSONS
— inks —
JEROMY COX
— color —
WILLIE SCHUBERT
— lettering —
RYAN SOOK
— cover —
DAVE WIELGOSZ
— assistant editor —
ALEX ANTONE
— editor —
BRIAN CUNNINGHAM
— group editor —

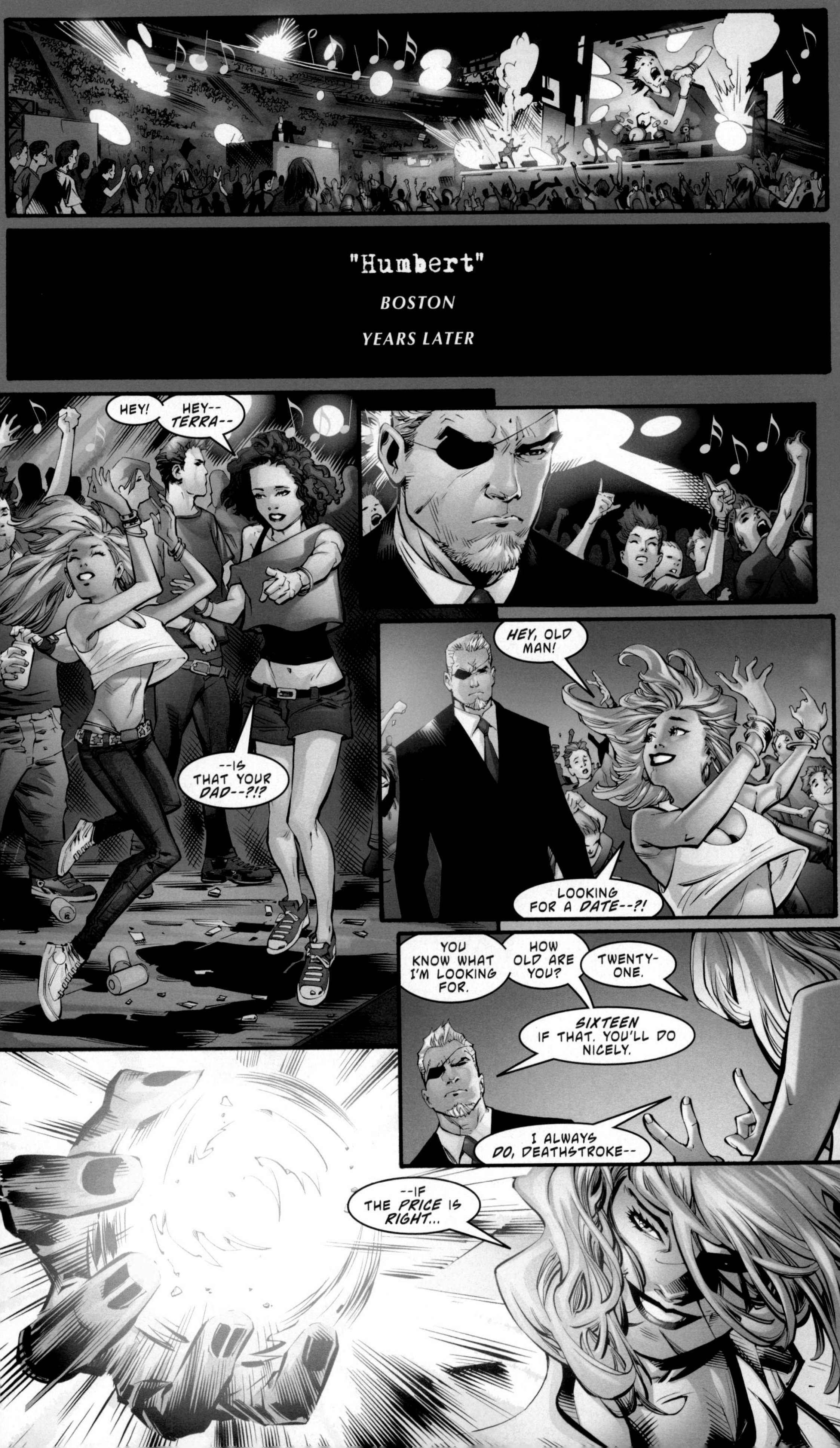
"Humbert"
BOSTON
YEARS LATER
HEY!
HEY--TERRA--
--IS THAT YOUR DAD--?!?
HEY, OLD MAN!
LOOKING FOR A DATE--?!
YOU KNOW WHAT I'M LOOKING FOR.
HOW OLD ARE YOU?
TWENTY-ONE.
SIXTEEN IF THAT. YOU'LL DO NICELY.
I ALWAYS DO, DEATHSTROKE--
--IF THE PRICE IS RIGHT...

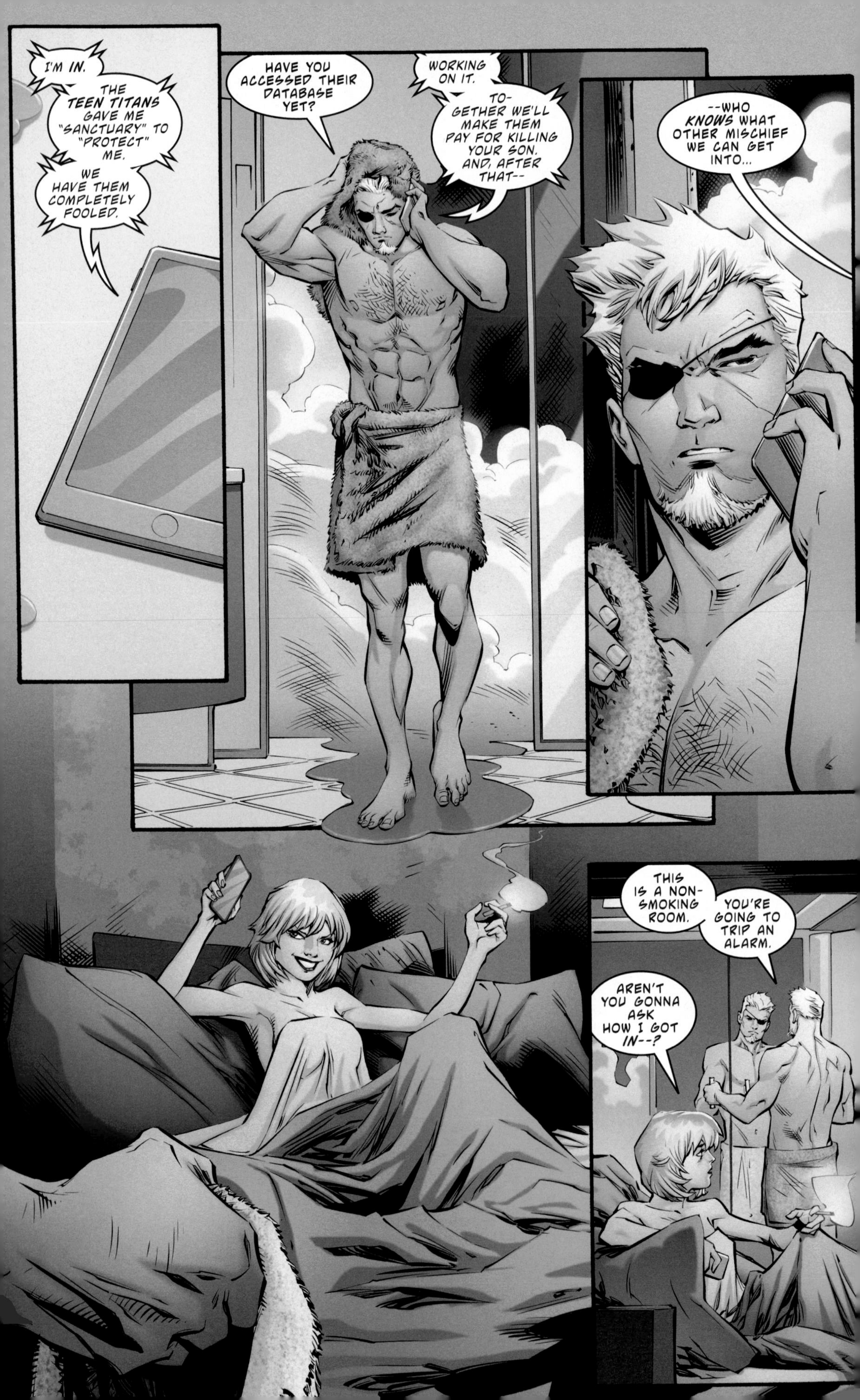
I'M IN.
THE TEEN TITANS GAVE ME "SANCTUARY" TO "PROTECT" ME.
WE HAVE THEM COMPLETELY FOOLED.
HAVE YOU ACCESSED THEIR DATABASE YET?
WORKING ON IT.
TO-GETHER WE'LL MAKE THEM PAY FOR KILLING YOUR SON. AND, AFTER THAT--
--WHO KNOWS WHAT OTHER MISCHIEF WE CAN GET INTO...
THIS IS A NON-SMOKING ROOM.
YOU'RE GOING TO TRIP AN ALARM.
AREN'T YOU GONNA ASK HOW I GOT IN--?

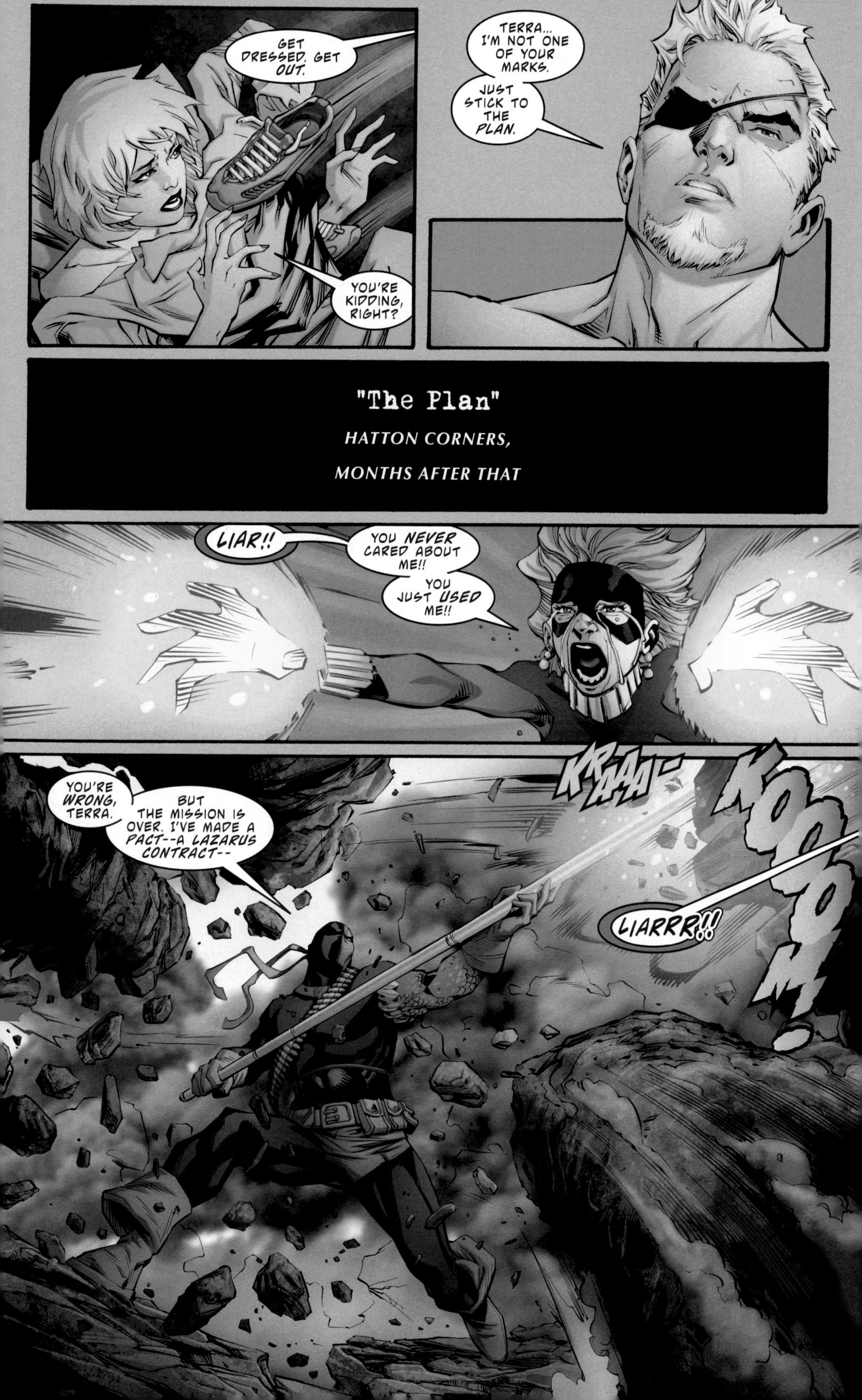
GET DRESSED. GET OUT.
YOU'RE KIDDING, RIGHT?
TERRA... I'M NOT ONE OF YOUR MARKS.
JUST STICK TO THE PLAN.
"The Plan"
HATTON CORNERS,
MONTHS AFTER THAT
LIAR!!
YOU NEVER CARED ABOUT ME!!
YOU JUST USED ME!!
YOU'RE WRONG, TERRA.
BUT THE MISSION IS OVER. I'VE MADE A PACT--A LAZARUS CONTRACT--
KRAAAA-KOOOOM!
LIARRR!!

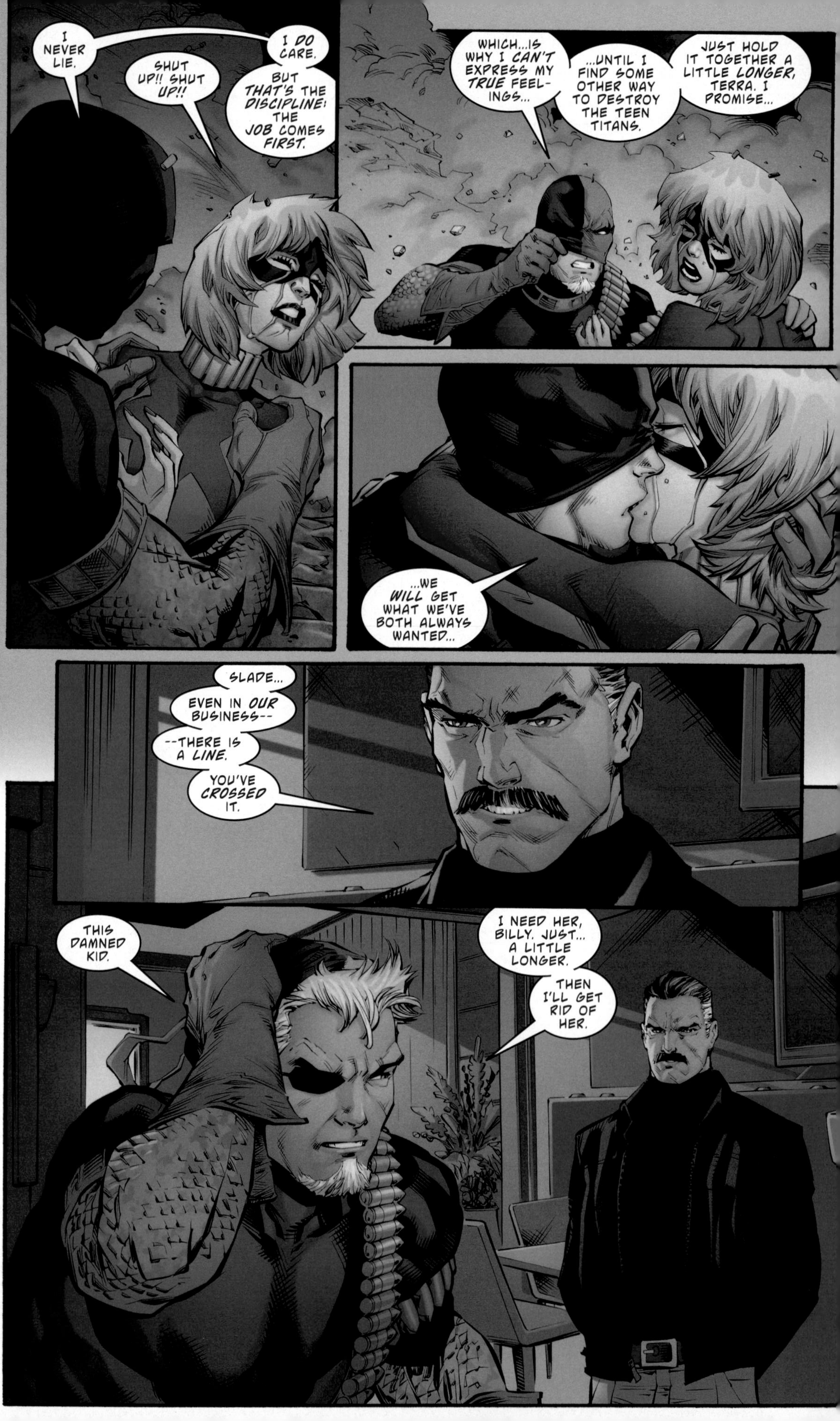
I NEVER LIE.
I DO CARE.
SHUT UP!! SHUT UP!!
BUT THAT'S THE DISCIPLINE: THE JOB COMES FIRST.
WHICH...IS WHY I CAN'T EXPRESS MY TRUE FEEL-INGS...
...UNTIL I FIND SOME OTHER WAY TO DESTROY THE TEEN TITANS.
JUST HOLD IT TOGETHER A LITTLE LONGER, TERRA. I PROMISE...
...WE WILL GET WHAT WE'VE BOTH ALWAYS WANTED...
SLADE...
EVEN IN OUR BUSINESS--
--THERE IS A LINE.
YOU'VE CROSSED IT.
THIS DAMNED KID.
I NEED HER, BILLY. JUST... A LITTLE LONGER.
THEN I'LL GET RID OF HER.

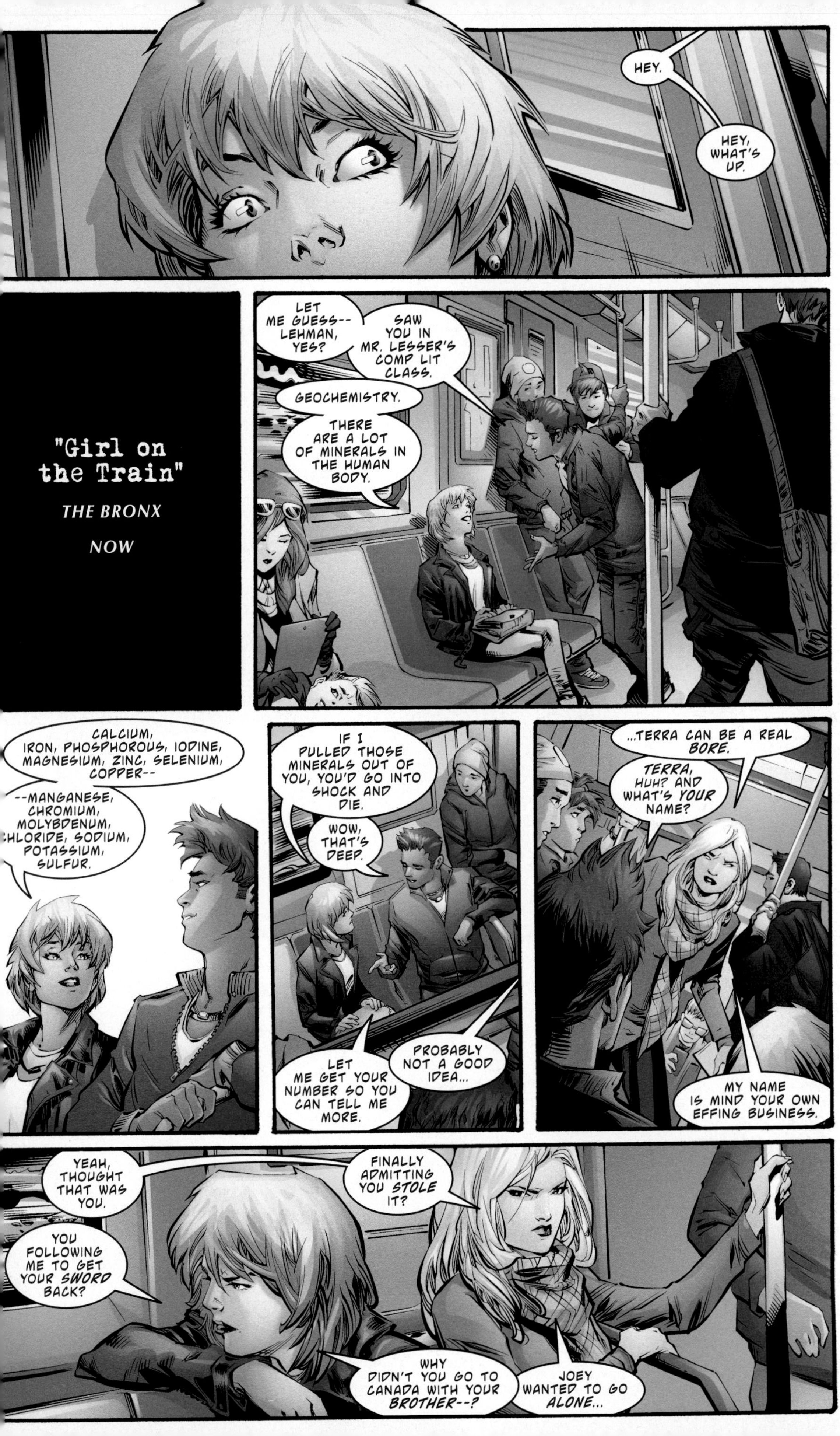
HEY.
HEY, WHAT'S UP.
"Girl on the Train"
THE BRONX
NOW
LET ME GUESS-- LEHMAN, YES?
SAW YOU IN MR. LESSER'S COMP LIT CLASS.
GEOCHEMISTRY.
THERE ARE A LOT OF MINERALS IN THE HUMAN BODY.
CALCIUM, IRON, PHOSPHOROUS, IODINE, MAGNESIUM, ZINC, SELENIUM, COPPER--
--MANGANESE, CHROMIUM, MOLYBDENUM, CHLORIDE, SODIUM, POTASSIUM, SULFUR.
IF I PULLED THOSE MINERALS OUT OF YOU, YOU'D GO INTO SHOCK AND DIE.
WOW, THAT'S DEEP.
LET ME GET YOUR NUMBER SO YOU CAN TELL ME MORE.
PROBABLY NOT A GOOD IDEA...
...TERRA CAN BE A REAL BORE.
TERRA, HUH? AND WHAT'S YOUR NAME?
MY NAME IS MIND YOUR OWN EFFING BUSINESS.
YEAH, THOUGHT THAT WAS YOU.
FINALLY ADMITTING YOU STOLE IT?
YOU FOLLOWING ME TO GET YOUR SWORD BACK?
WHY DIDN'T YOU GO TO CANADA WITH YOUR BROTHER--?
JOEY WANTED TO GO ALONE...

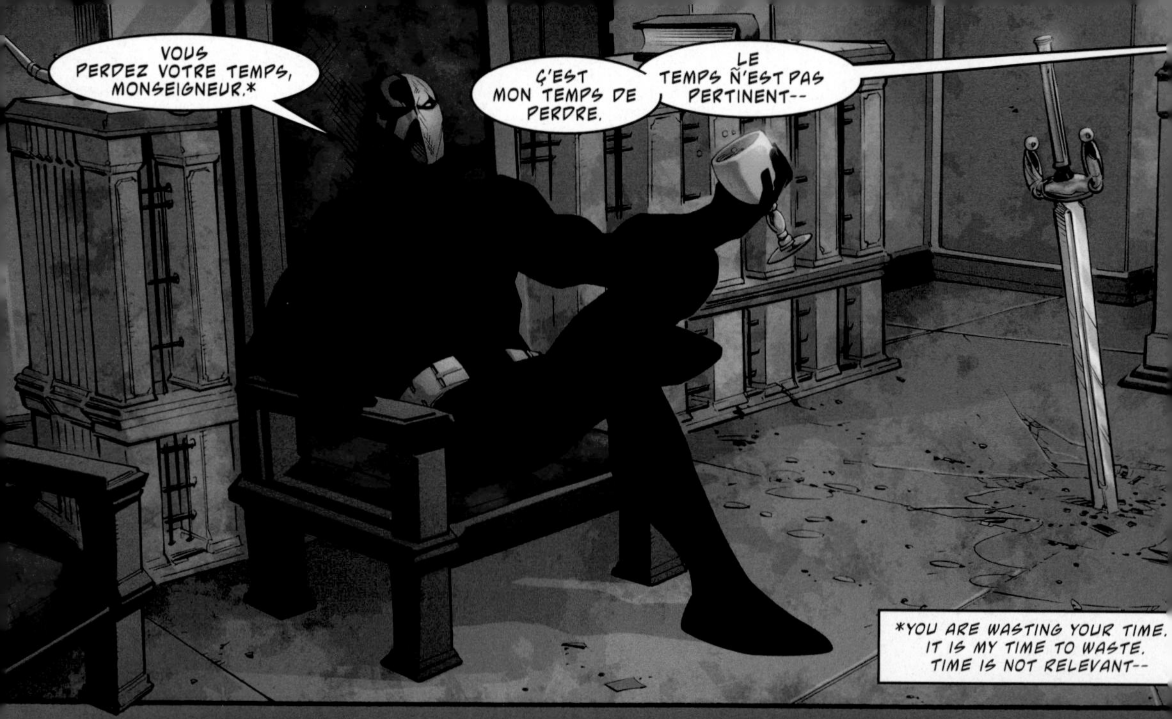
VOUS PERDEZ VOTRE TEMPS, MONSEIGNEUR.*
Ç'EST MON TEMPS DE PERDRE.
LE TEMPS Ñ'EST PAS PERTINENT--
*YOU ARE WASTING YOUR TIME. IT IS MY TIME TO WASTE. TIME IS NOT RELEVANT--

"Magna Dii Curant"

WINDSOR, ONTARIO

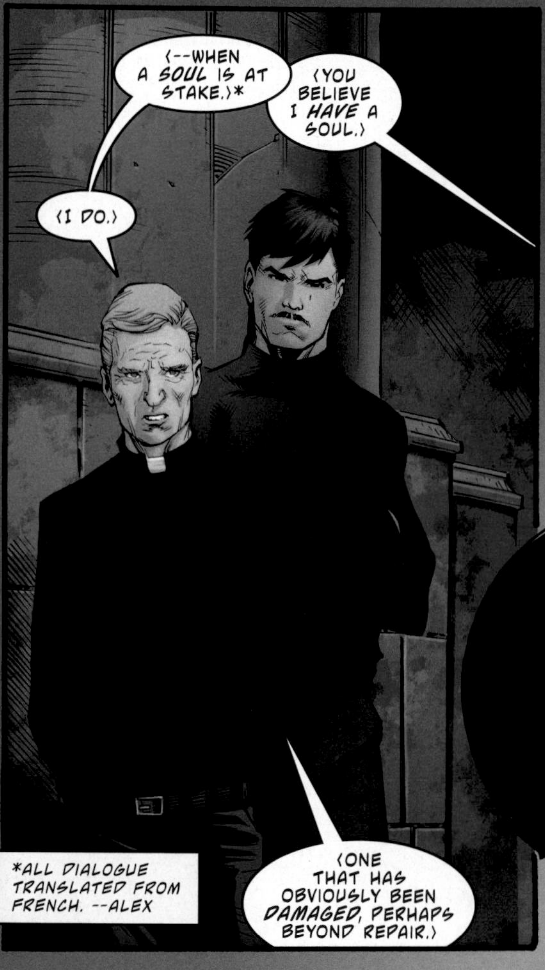
⟨--WHEN A *SOUL* IS AT STAKE.⟩*
⟨YOU BELIEVE I *HAVE* A SOUL.⟩
⟨I DO.⟩
⟨ONE THAT HAS OBVIOUSLY BEEN *DAMAGED*, PERHAPS BEYOND REPAIR.⟩
*ALL DIALOGUE TRANSLATED FROM FRENCH. --ALEX

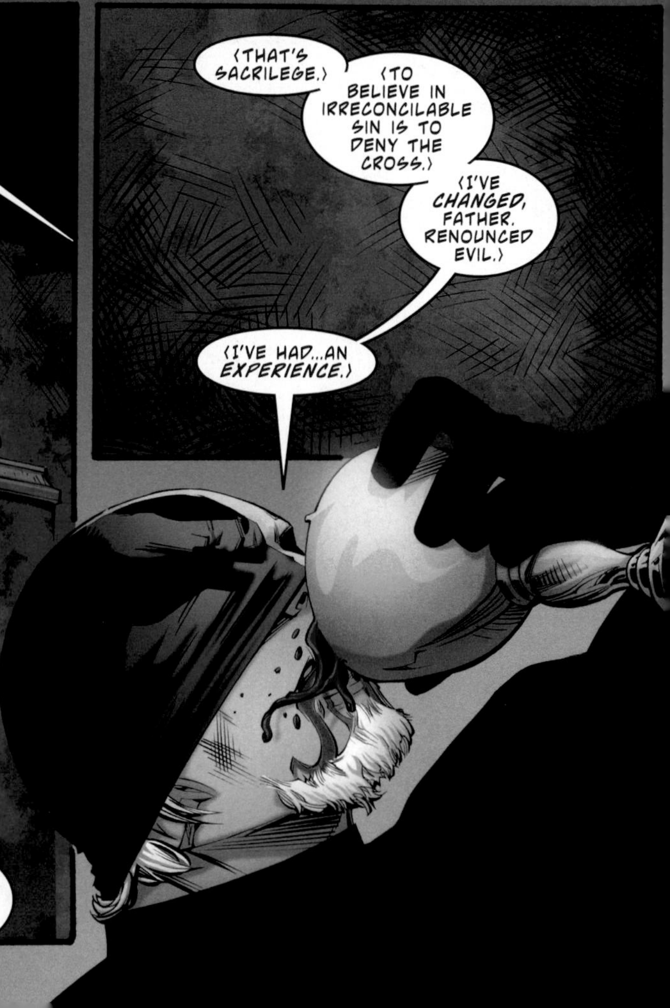
⟨THAT'S SACRILEGE.⟩
⟨TO BELIEVE IN IRRECONCILABLE SIN IS TO DENY THE CROSS.⟩
⟨I'VE *CHANGED*, FATHER. RENOUNCED EVIL.⟩
⟨I'VE HAD...AN *EXPERIENCE*.⟩

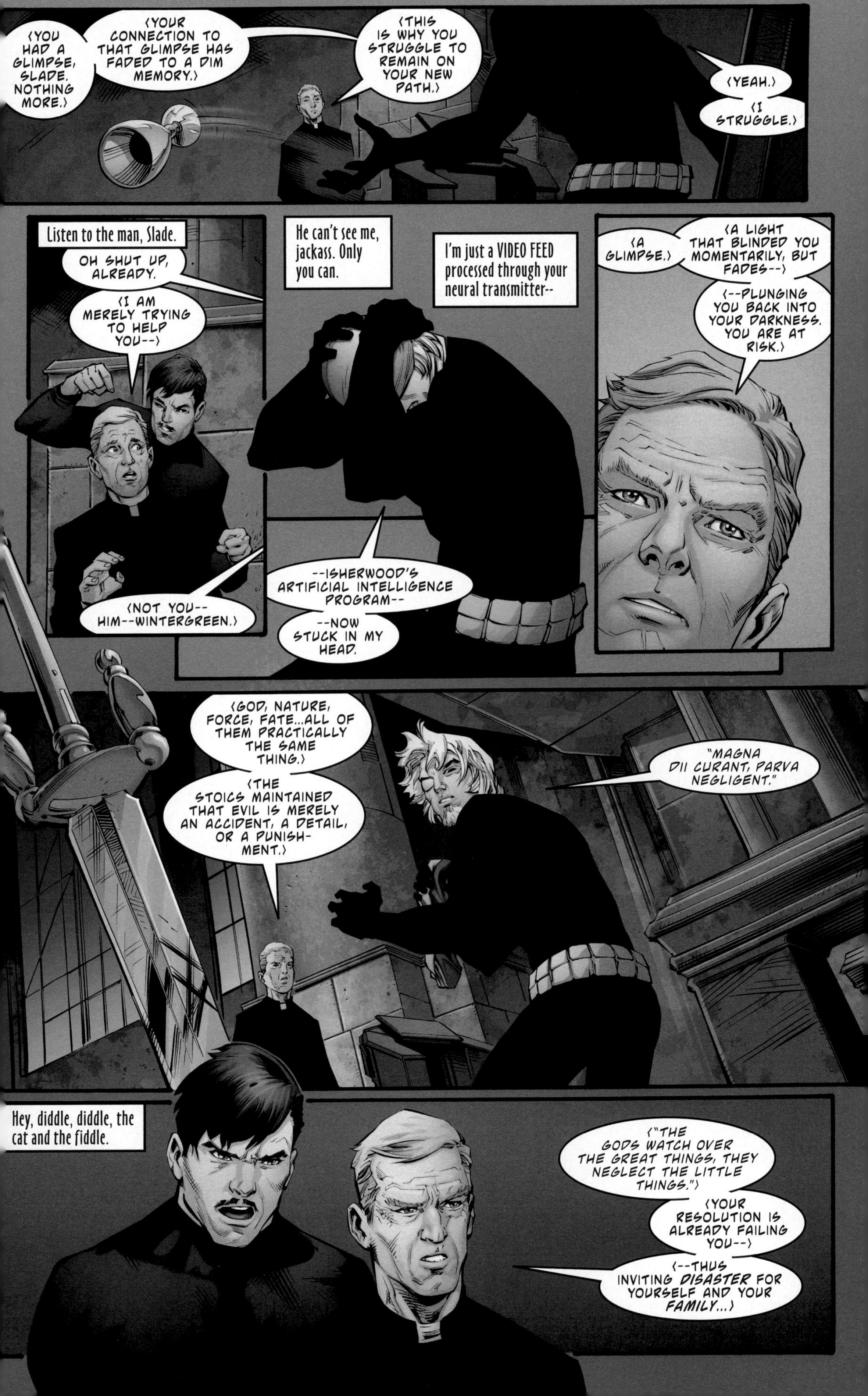
‹YOU HAD A GLIMPSE, SLADE. NOTHING MORE.›
‹YOUR CONNECTION TO THAT GLIMPSE HAS FADED TO A DIM MEMORY.›
‹THIS IS WHY YOU STRUGGLE TO REMAIN ON YOUR NEW PATH.›
‹YEAH.›
‹I STRUGGLE.›
Listen to the man, Slade.
OH SHUT UP, ALREADY.
‹I AM MERELY TRYING TO HELP YOU--›
‹NOT YOU-- HIM--WINTERGREEN.›
He can't see me, jackass. Only you can.
I'm just a VIDEO FEED processed through your neural transmitter--
--ISHERWOOD'S ARTIFICIAL INTELLIGENCE PROGRAM--
--NOW STUCK IN MY HEAD.
‹A GLIMPSE.›
‹A LIGHT THAT BLINDED YOU MOMENTARILY, BUT FADES--›
‹--PLUNGING YOU BACK INTO YOUR DARKNESS. YOU ARE AT RISK.›
‹GOD, NATURE, FORCE, FATE...ALL OF THEM PRACTICALLY THE SAME THING.›
‹THE STOICS MAINTAINED THAT EVIL IS MERELY AN ACCIDENT, A DETAIL, OR A PUNISH-MENT.›
"MAGNA DII CURANT, PARVA NEGLIGENT."
Hey, diddle, diddle, the cat and the fiddle.
‹"THE GODS WATCH OVER THE GREAT THINGS, THEY NEGLECT THE LITTLE THINGS."›
‹YOUR RESOLUTION IS ALREADY FAILING YOU--›
‹--THUS INVITING *DISASTER* FOR YOURSELF AND YOUR *FAMILY*...›

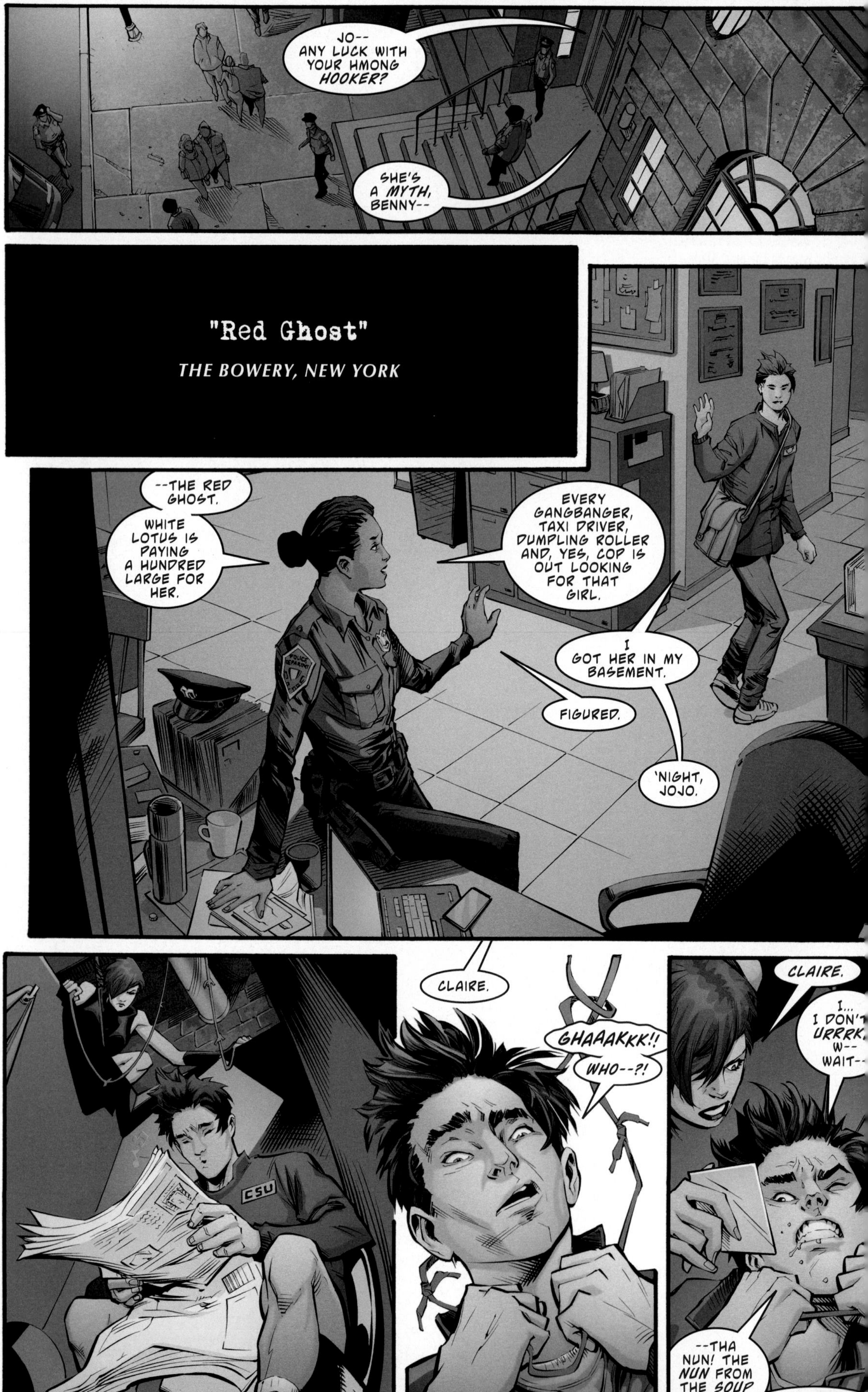
JO--
ANY LUCK WITH YOUR HMONG *HOOKER?*
SHE'S A *MYTH,* BENNY--
"Red Ghost"
THE BOWERY, NEW YORK
--THE RED GHOST.
WHITE LOTUS IS PAYING A HUNDRED LARGE FOR HER.
EVERY GANGBANGER, TAXI DRIVER, DUMPLING ROLLER AND, YES, COP IS OUT LOOKING FOR THAT GIRL.
I GOT HER IN MY BASEMENT.
FIGURED.
'NIGHT, JOJO.
CSU
CLAIRE.
GHAAAKKK!!
WHO--?!
CLAIRE.
I... I DON'
URRRK
W-- WAIT--
--THA NUN! THE *NUN* FROM THE *SOUP KITCH--*
SOME-BODY...*GRABBE*
HER--?!?

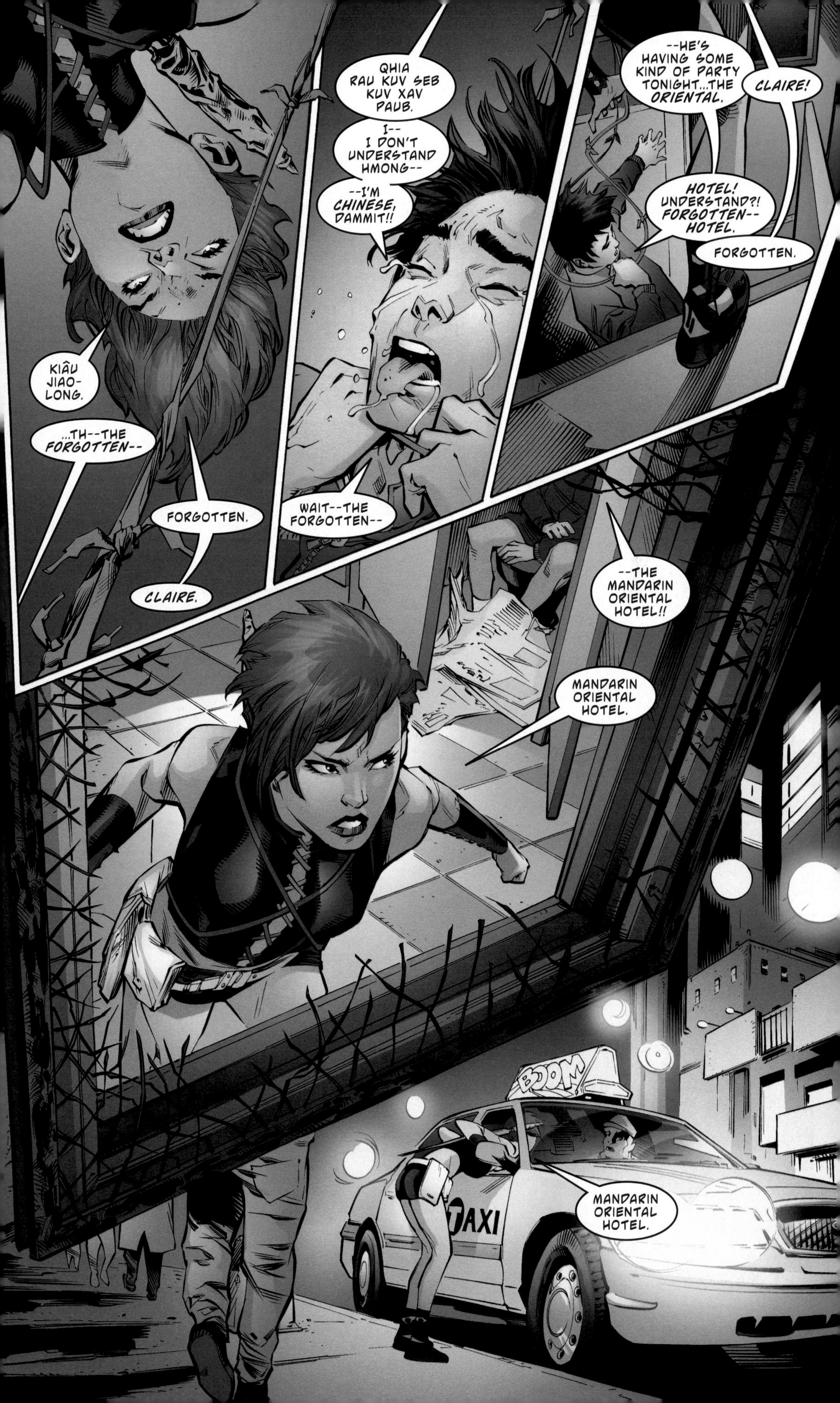
QHIA RAU KUV SEB KUV XAV PAUB.
I-- I DON'T UNDERSTAND HMONG--
--I'M CHINESE, DAMMIT!!
--HE'S HAVING SOME KIND OF PARTY TONIGHT...THE ORIENTAL.
CLAIRE!
HOTEL! UNDERSTAND?! FORGOTTEN--HOTEL.
FORGOTTEN.
KIÂU JIAO-LONG.
...TH--THE FORGOTTEN--
FORGOTTEN.
CLAIRE.
WAIT--THE FORGOTTEN--
--THE MANDARIN ORIENTAL HOTEL!!
MANDARIN ORIENTAL HOTEL.
BOOM
TAXI
MANDARIN ORIENTAL HOTEL.

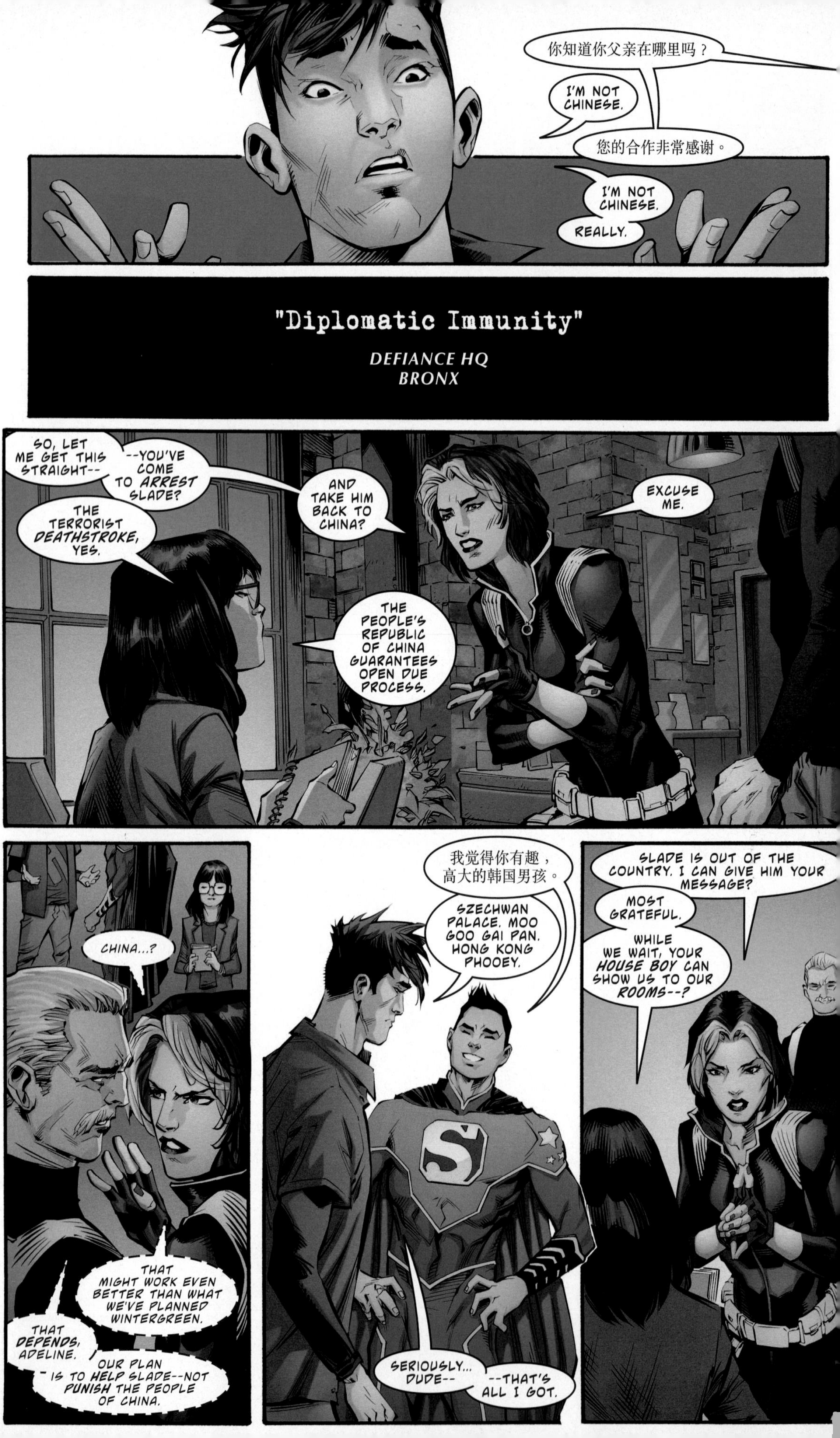
你知道你父亲在哪里吗？
I'M NOT CHINESE.
您的合作非常感谢。
I'M NOT CHINESE.
REALLY.
"Diplomatic Immunity"
DEFIANCE HQ
BRONX
SO, LET ME GET THIS STRAIGHT--
--YOU'VE COME TO ARREST SLADE?
THE TERRORIST DEATHSTROKE, YES.
AND TAKE HIM BACK TO CHINA?
THE PEOPLE'S REPUBLIC OF CHINA GUARANTEES OPEN DUE PROCESS.
EXCUSE ME.
CHINA...?
THAT MIGHT WORK EVEN BETTER THAN WHAT WE'VE PLANNED WINTERGREEN.
THAT DEPENDS, ADELINE.
OUR PLAN IS TO HELP SLADE--NOT PUNISH THE PEOPLE OF CHINA.
我觉得你有趣，
高大的韩国男孩。
SZECHWAN PALACE. MOO GOO GAI PAN. HONG KONG PHOOEY.
SERIOUSLY... DUDE--
--THAT'S ALL I GOT.
SLADE IS OUT OF THE COUNTRY. I CAN GIVE HIM YOUR MESSAGE?
MOST GRATEFUL.
WHILE WE WAIT, YOUR HOUSE BOY CAN SHOW US TO OUR ROOMS--?

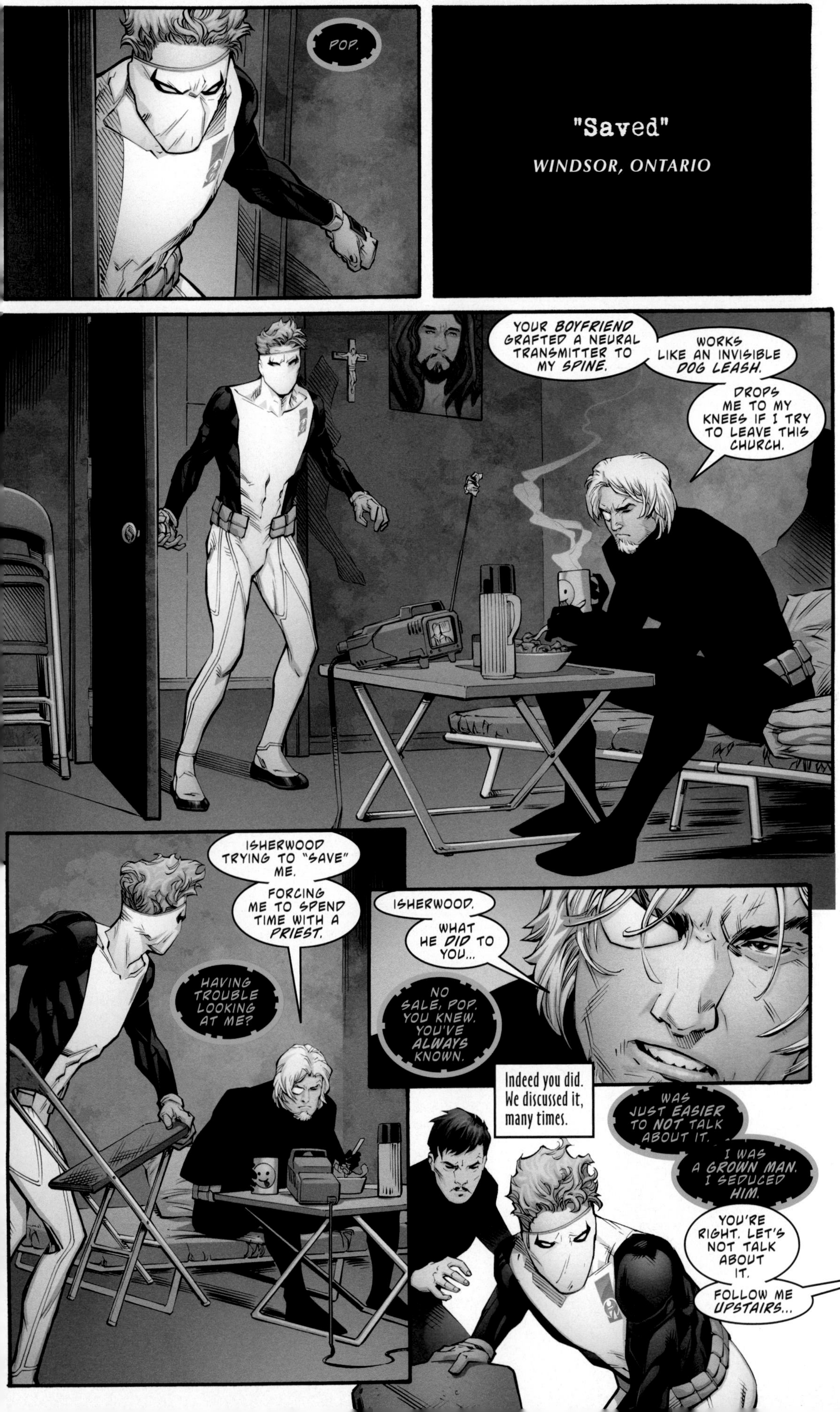
POP.
"Saved"
WINDSOR, ONTARIO
YOUR BOYFRIEND GRAFTED A NEURAL TRANSMITTER TO MY SPINE.
WORKS LIKE AN INVISIBLE DOG LEASH.
DROPS ME TO MY KNEES IF I TRY TO LEAVE THIS CHURCH.
ISHERWOOD TRYING TO "SAVE" ME.
FORCING ME TO SPEND TIME WITH A PRIEST.
HAVING TROUBLE LOOKING AT ME?
ISHERWOOD.
WHAT HE DID TO YOU...
NO SALE, POP. YOU KNEW. YOU'VE ALWAYS KNOWN.
Indeed you did. We discussed it, many times.
WAS JUST EASIER TO NOT TALK ABOUT IT.
I WAS A GROWN MAN. I SEDUCED HIM.
YOU'RE RIGHT. LET'S NOT TALK ABOUT IT.
FOLLOW ME UPSTAIRS...

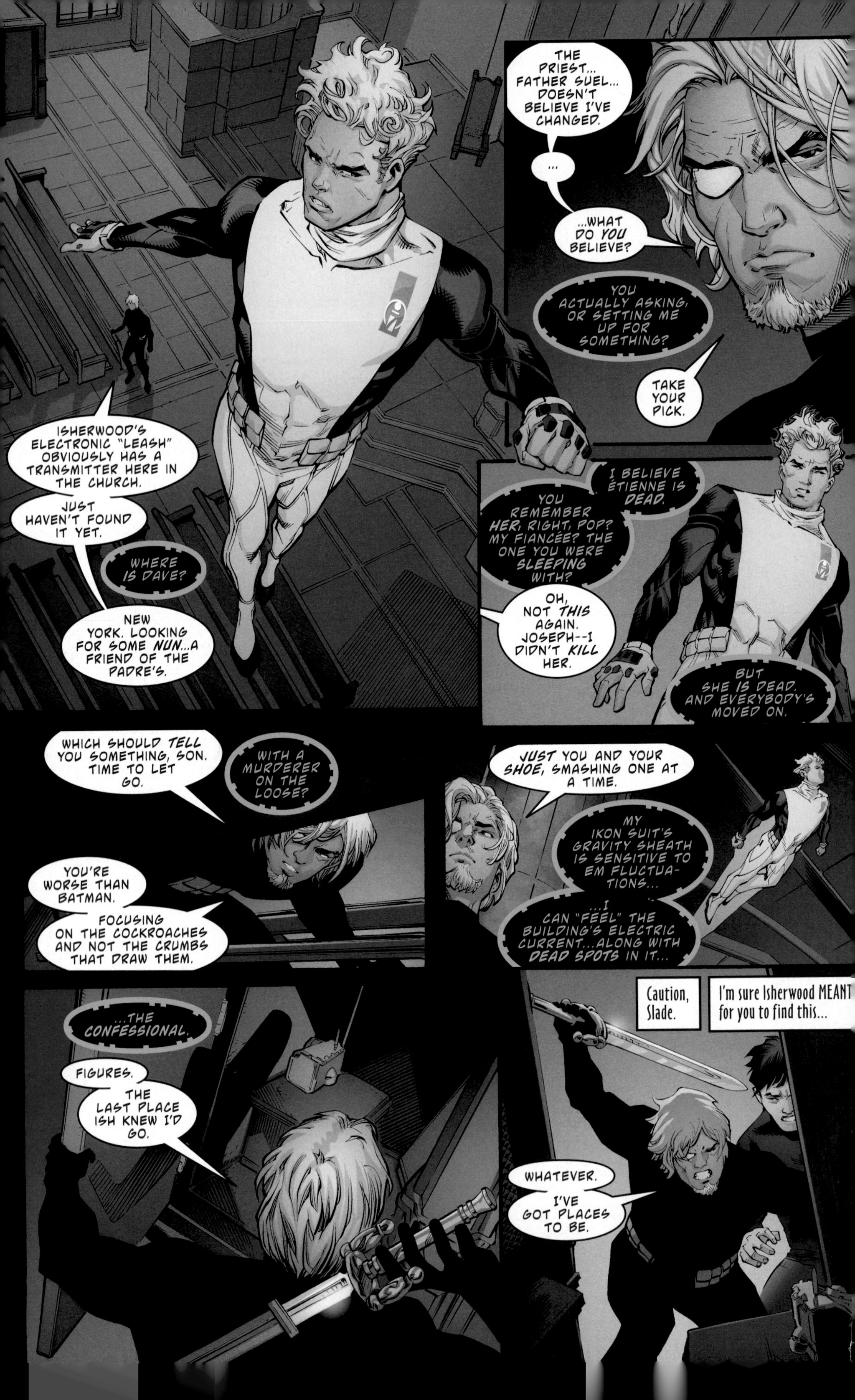

ISHERWOOD'S ELECTRONIC "LEASH" OBVIOUSLY HAS A TRANSMITTER HERE IN THE CHURCH.
JUST HAVEN'T FOUND IT YET.
WHERE IS DAVE?
NEW YORK. LOOKING FOR SOME NUN...A FRIEND OF THE PADRE'S.
THE PRIEST... FATHER SUEL... DOESN'T BELIEVE I'VE CHANGED.
...
...WHAT DO YOU BELIEVE?
YOU ACTUALLY ASKING, OR SETTING ME UP FOR SOMETHING?
TAKE YOUR PICK.
I BELIEVE ÉTIENNE IS DEAD.
YOU REMEMBER HER, RIGHT, POP? MY FIANCÉE? THE ONE YOU WERE SLEEPING WITH?
OH, NOT THIS AGAIN. JOSEPH--I DIDN'T KILL HER.
BUT SHE IS DEAD. AND EVERYBODY'S MOVED ON.
WHICH SHOULD TELL YOU SOMETHING, SON. TIME TO LET GO.
WITH A MURDERER ON THE LOOSE?
YOU'RE WORSE THAN BATMAN.
FOCUSING ON THE COCKROACHES AND NOT THE CRUMBS THAT DRAW THEM.
JUST YOU AND YOUR SHOE, SMASHING ONE AT A TIME.
MY IKON SUIT'S GRAVITY SHEATH IS SENSITIVE TO EM FLUCTUATIONS...
...I CAN "FEEL" THE BUILDING'S ELECTRIC CURRENT...ALONG WITH DEAD SPOTS IN IT...
...THE CONFESSIONAL.
FIGURES.
THE LAST PLACE ISH KNEW I'D GO.
Caution, Slade.
I'm sure Isherwood MEANT for you to find this...
WHATEVER.
I'VE GOT PLACES TO BE.

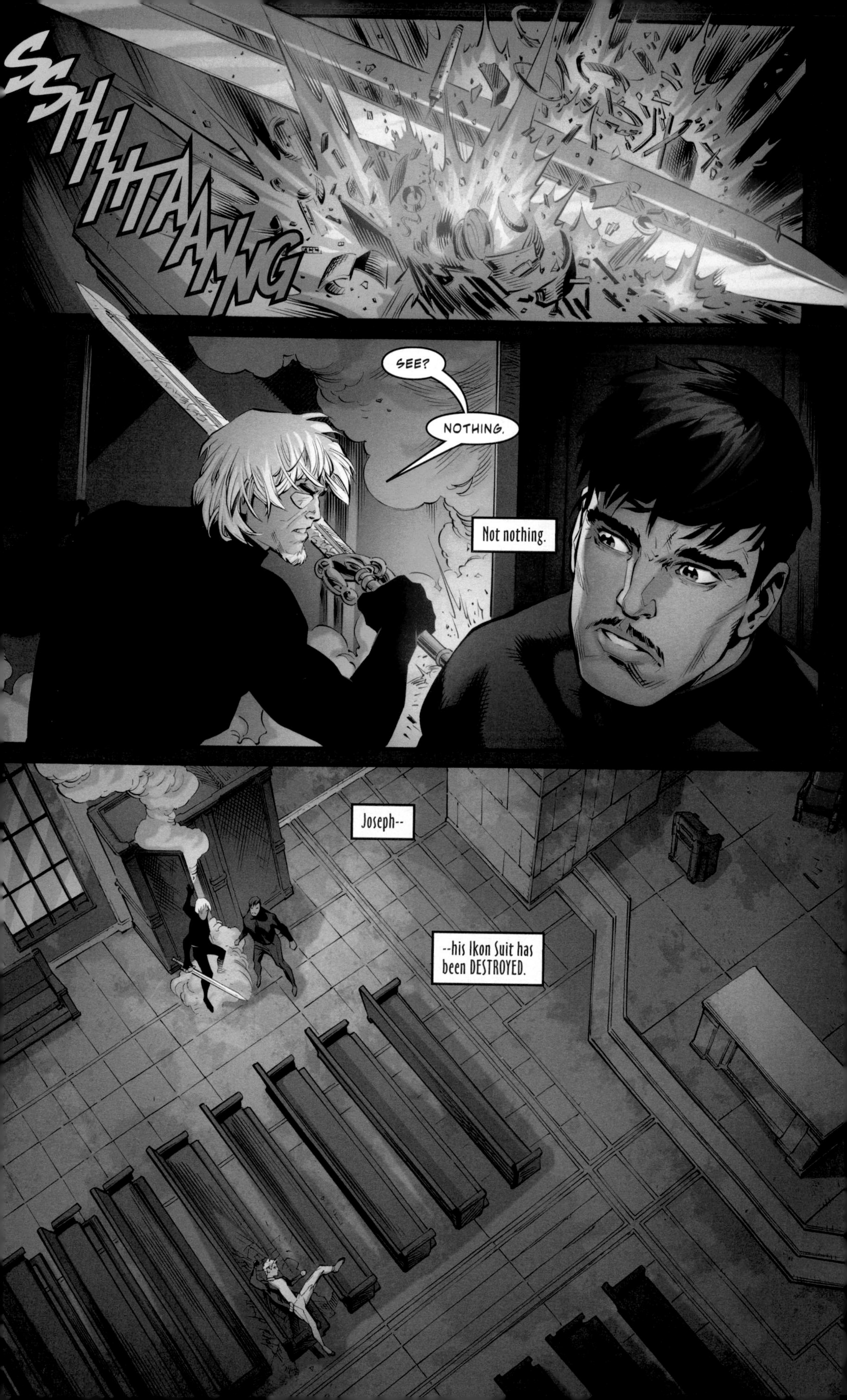
SSHHHTAANNG
SEE?
NOTHING.
Not nothing.
Joseph--
--his Ikon Suit has been DESTROYED.

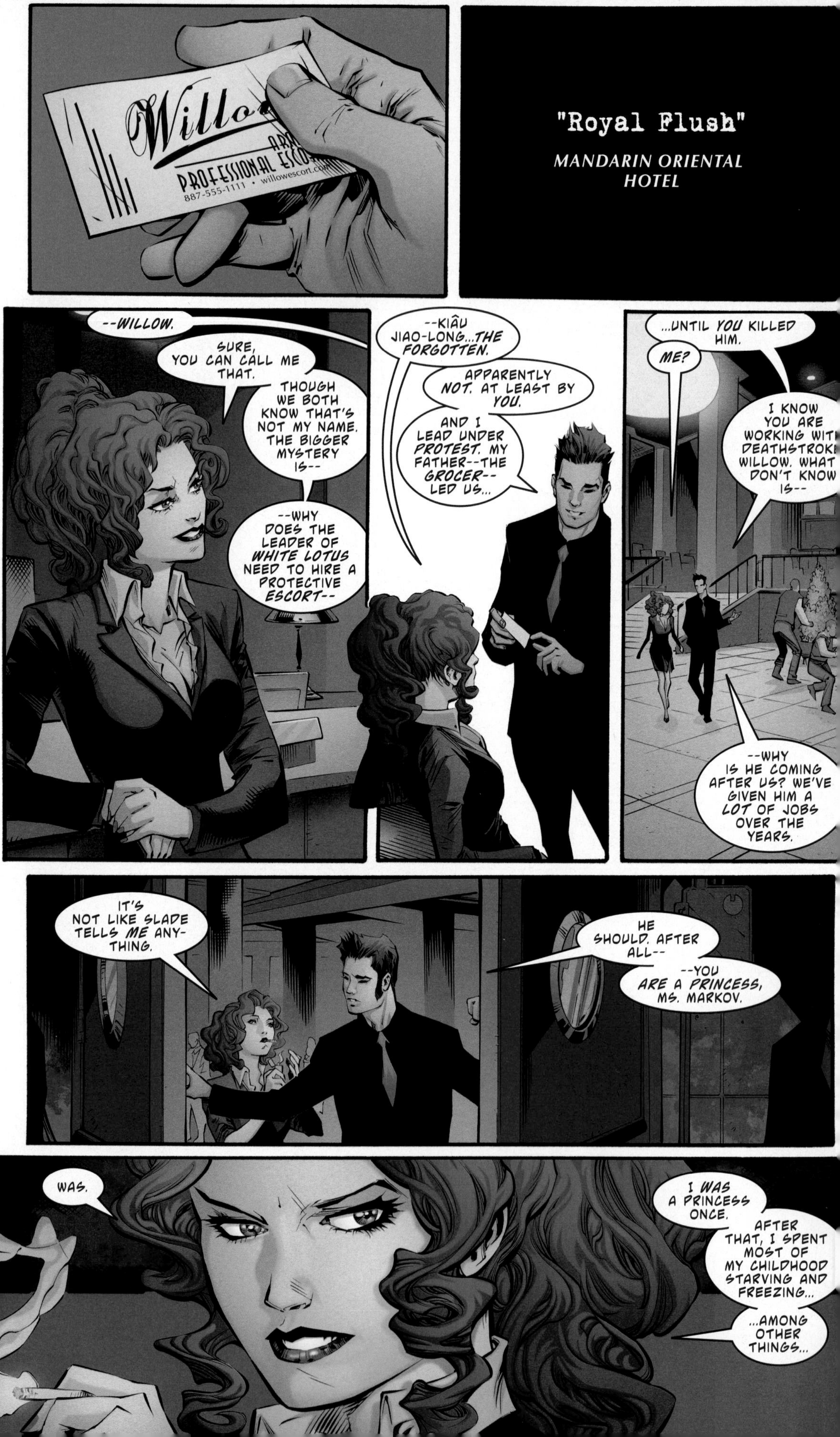
887-555-1111 • willowescort.com
"Royal Flush"
MANDARIN ORIENTAL HOTEL
--WILLOW.
SURE, YOU CAN CALL ME THAT.
THOUGH WE BOTH KNOW THAT'S NOT MY NAME. THE BIGGER MYSTERY IS--
--WHY DOES THE LEADER OF WHITE LOTUS NEED TO HIRE A PROTECTIVE ESCORT--
--KIÂU JIAO-LONG...THE FORGOTTEN.
APPARENTLY NOT. AT LEAST BY YOU.
AND I LEAD UNDER PROTEST. MY FATHER--THE GROCER--LED US...
...UNTIL YOU KILLED HIM.
ME?
I KNOW YOU ARE WORKING WITH DEATHSTROKE, WILLOW. WHAT I DON'T KNOW IS--
--WHY IS HE COMING AFTER US? WE'VE GIVEN HIM A LOT OF JOBS OVER THE YEARS.
IT'S NOT LIKE SLADE TELLS ME ANYTHING.
HE SHOULD. AFTER ALL--
--YOU ARE A PRINCESS, MS. MARKOV.
WAS.
I WAS A PRINCESS ONCE.
AFTER THAT, I SPENT MOST OF MY CHILDHOOD STARVING AND FREEZING...
...AMONG OTHER THINGS...

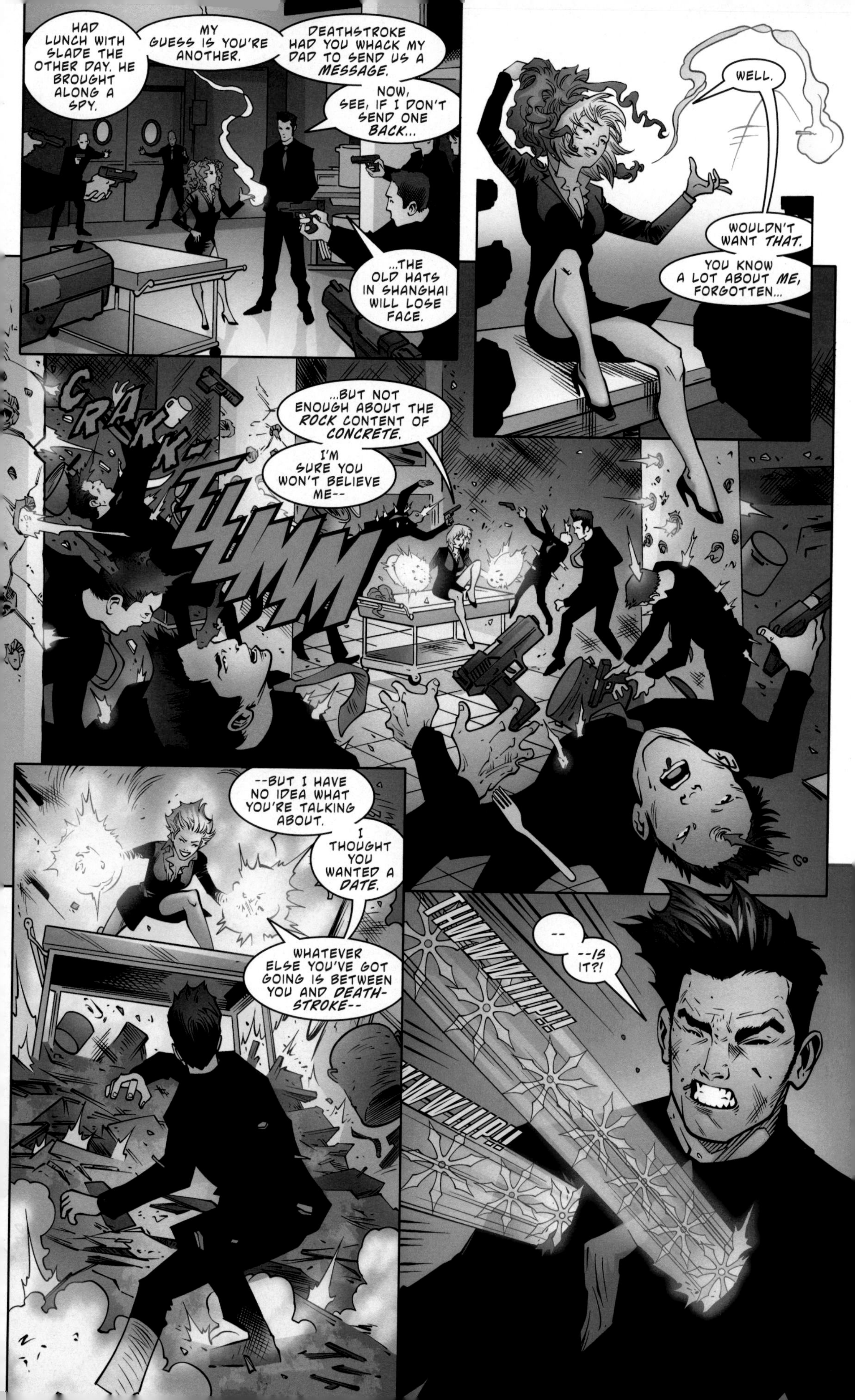
HAD LUNCH WITH SLADE THE OTHER DAY. HE BROUGHT ALONG A SPY.
MY GUESS IS YOU'RE ANOTHER.
DEATHSTROKE HAD YOU WHACK MY DAD TO SEND US A MESSAGE.
NOW, SEE, IF I DON'T SEND ONE BACK...
...THE OLD HATS IN SHANGHAI WILL LOSE FACE.
WELL.
WOULDN'T WANT THAT.
YOU KNOW A LOT ABOUT ME, FORGOTTEN...
CRAKK-
...BUT NOT ENOUGH ABOUT THE ROCK CONTENT OF CONCRETE.
I'M SURE YOU WON'T BELIEVE ME--
THUMM
--BUT I HAVE NO IDEA WHAT YOU'RE TALKING ABOUT.
I THOUGHT YOU WANTED A DATE.
WHATEVER ELSE YOU'VE GOT GOING IS BETWEEN YOU AND DEATH-STROKE--
--
--IS IT?!
THWWWVVHIP!!
VVVHIP!!

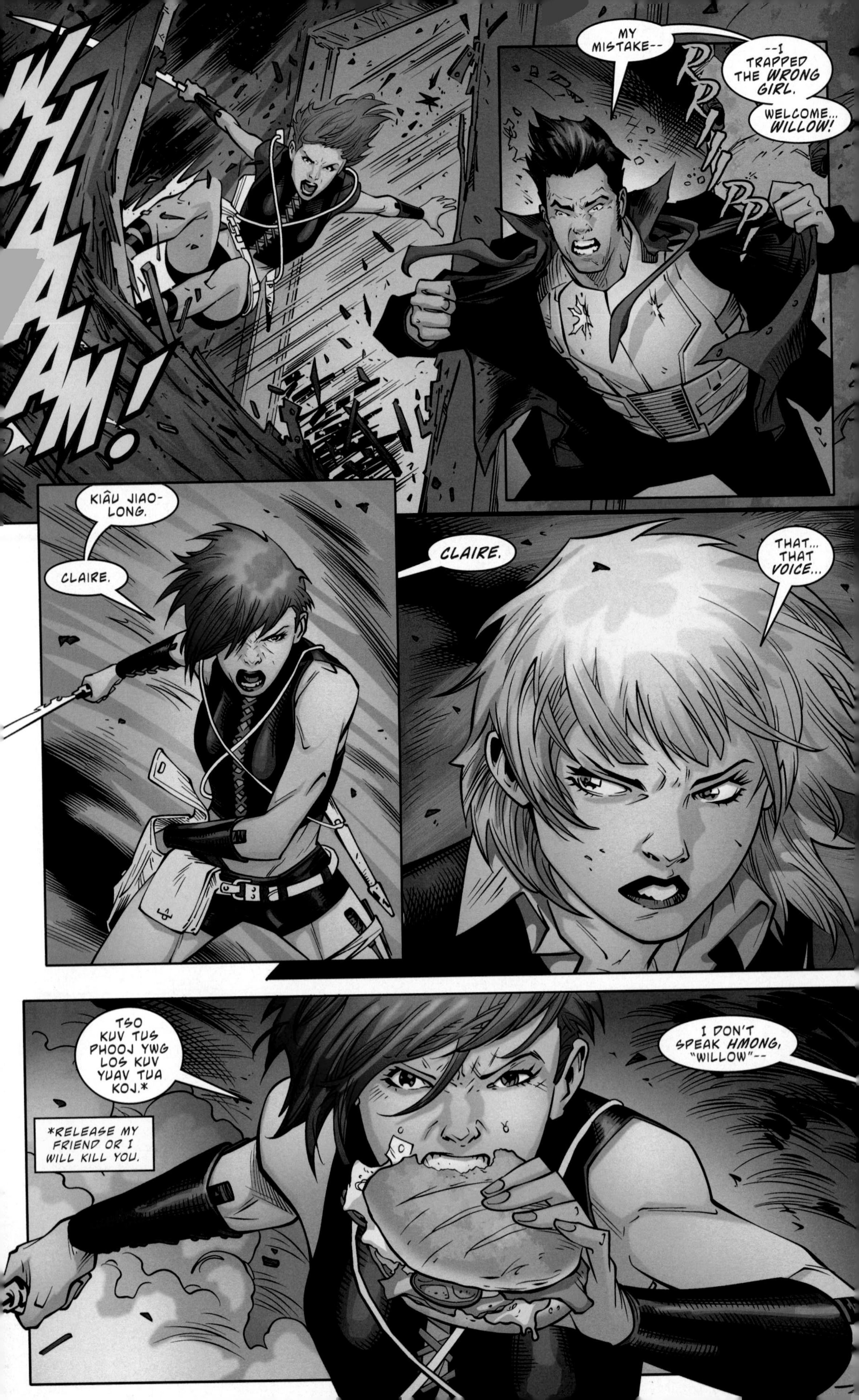
WHAAAM!
MY MISTAKE--
RRRIIIPP!
--I TRAPPED THE WRONG GIRL.
WELCOME... WILLOW!
KIÂU JIAO-LONG.
CLAIRE.
CLAIRE.
THAT... THAT VOICE...
TSO KUV TUS PHOOJ YWG LOS KUV YUAV TUA KOJ.*
*RELEASE MY FRIEND OR I WILL KILL YOU.
I DON'T SPEAK HMONG, "WILLOW"--

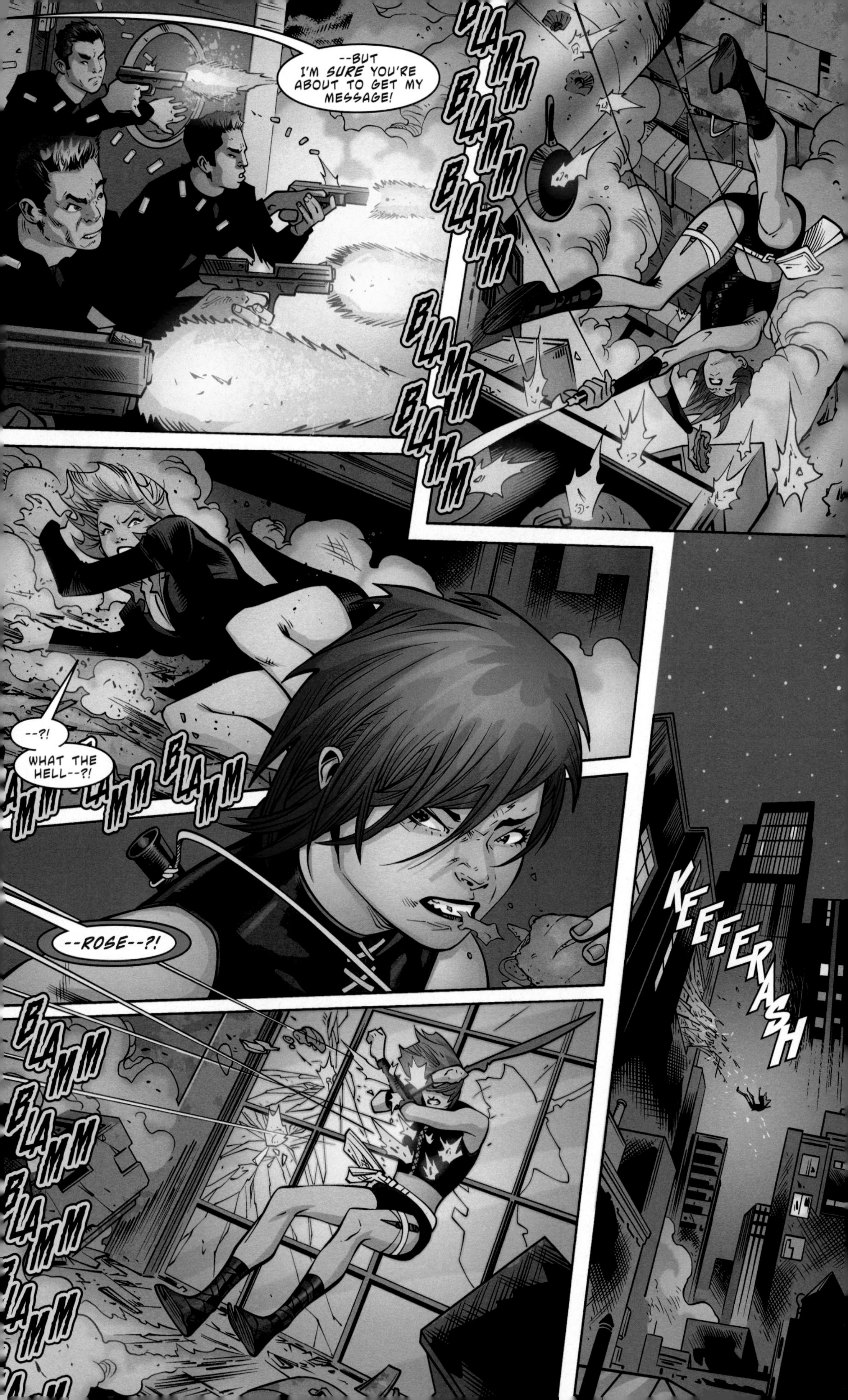
--BUT I'M SURE YOU'RE ABOUT TO GET MY MESSAGE!
BLAMM BLAMM BLAMM BLAMM
BLAMM BLAMM
--?!
WHAT THE HELL--?!
BLAMM
--ROSE--?!
KEEEERASH
BLAMM BLAMM BLAMM

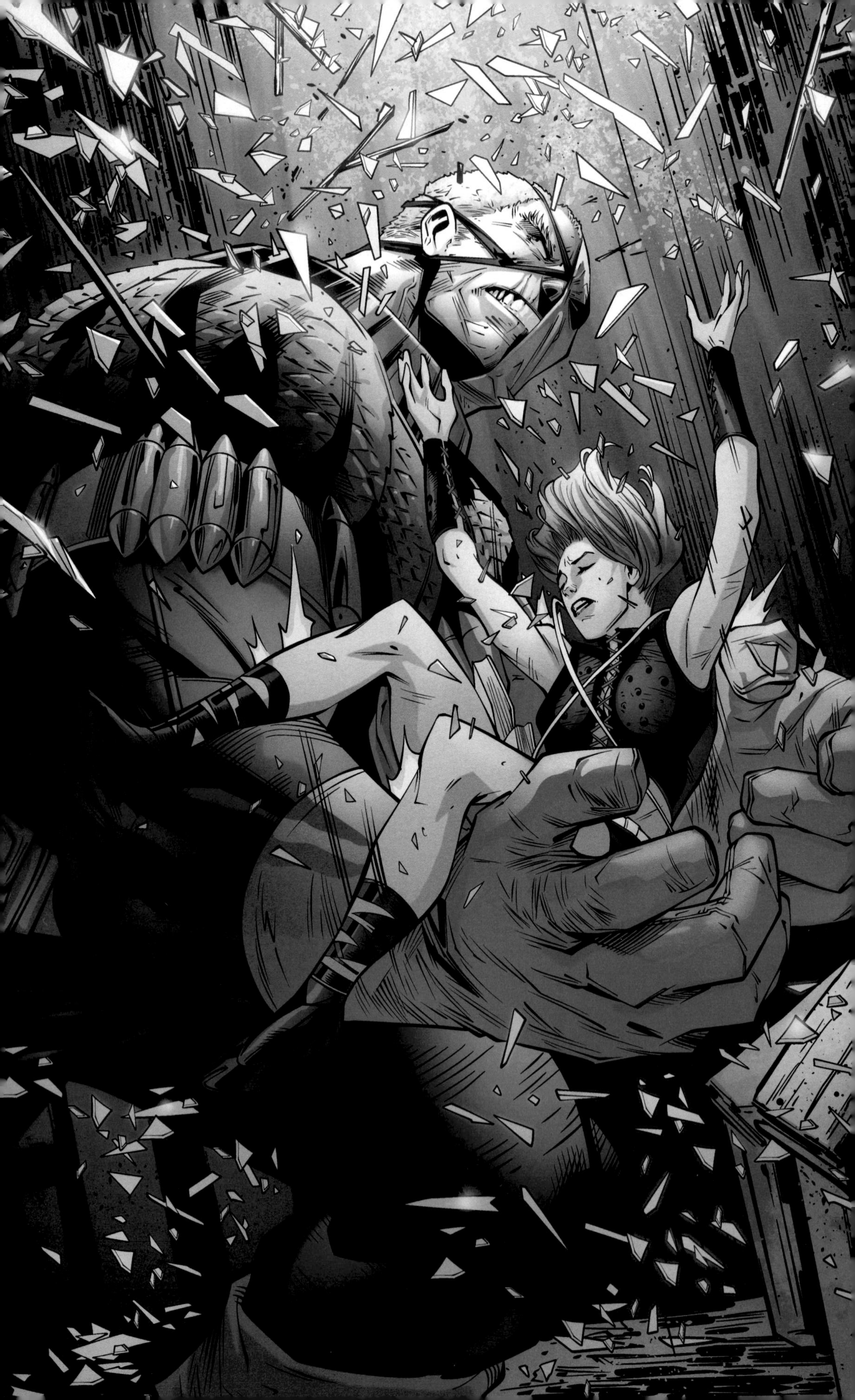

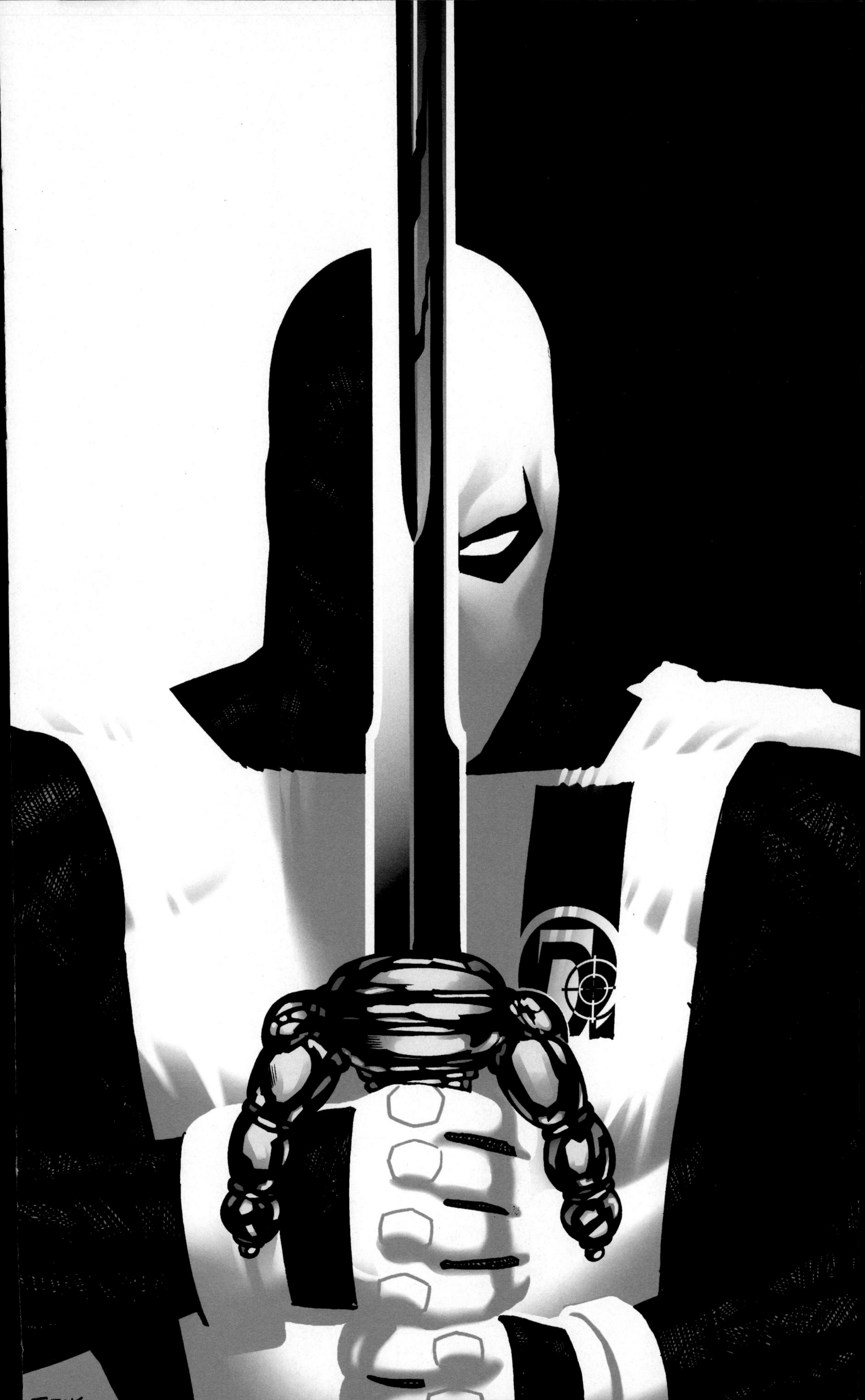

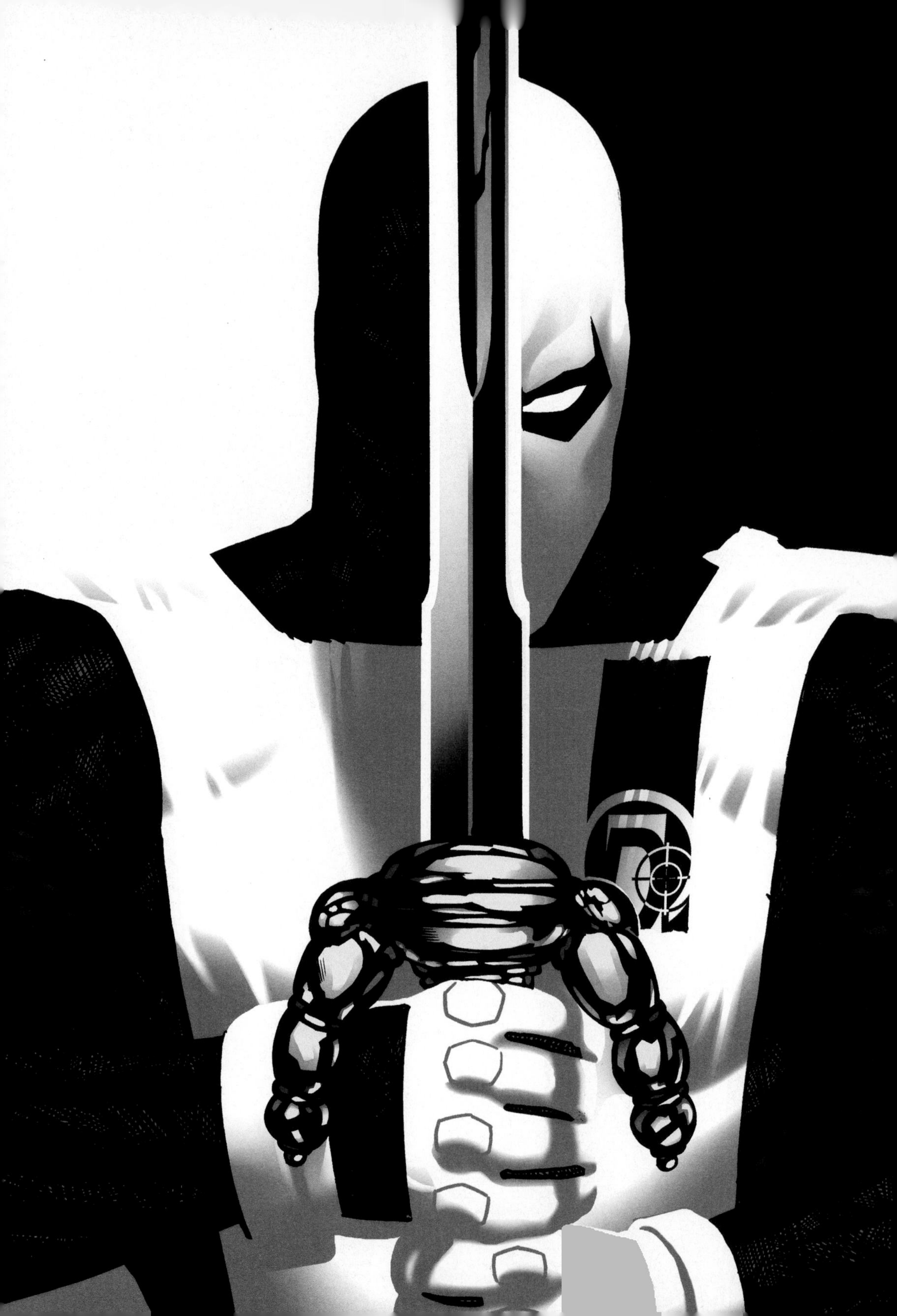

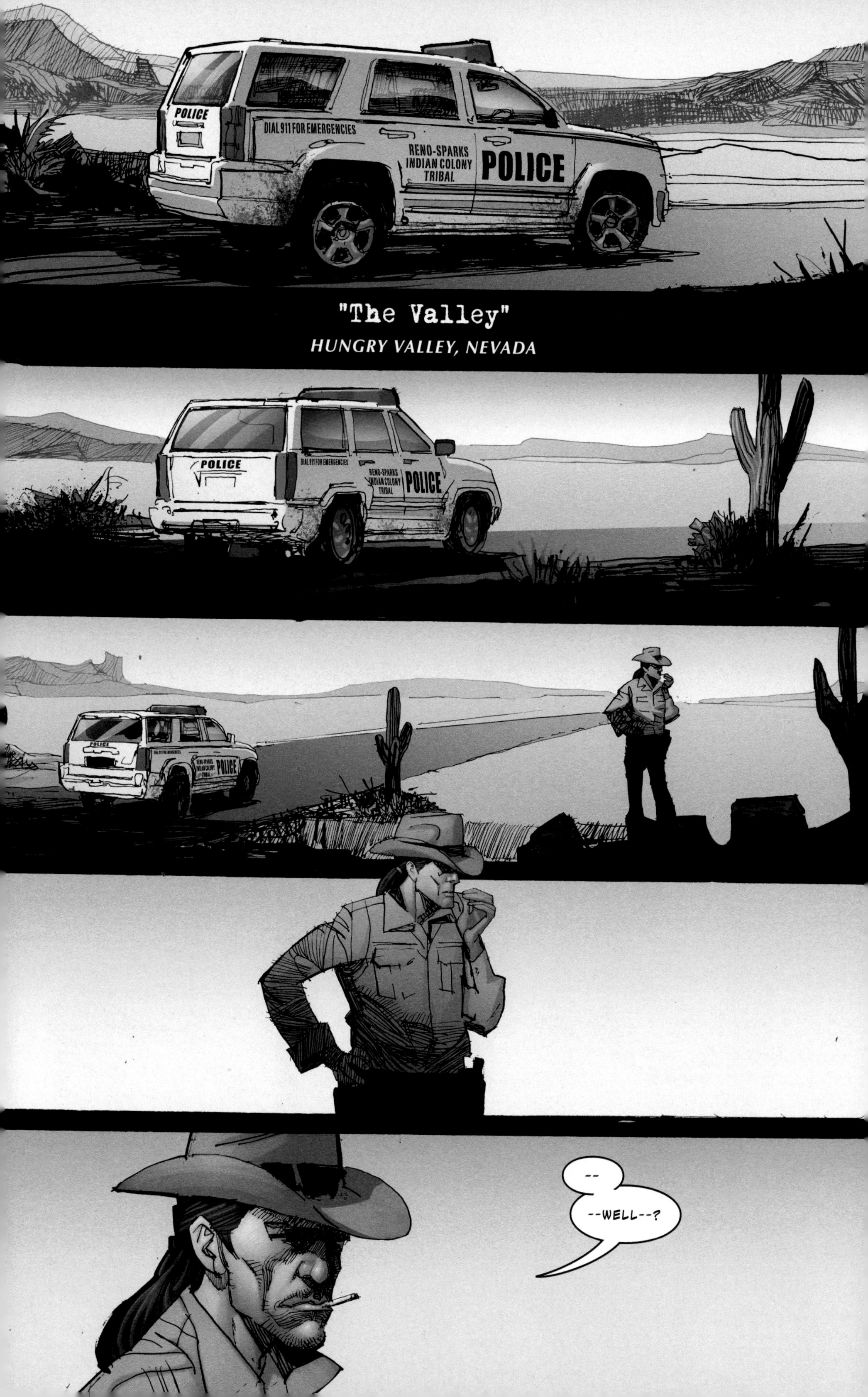
POLICE
DIAL 911 FOR EMERGENCIES
RENO-SPARKS INDIAN COLONY TRIBAL
POLICE
"The Valley"
HUNGRY VALLEY, NEVADA
--
--WELL--?

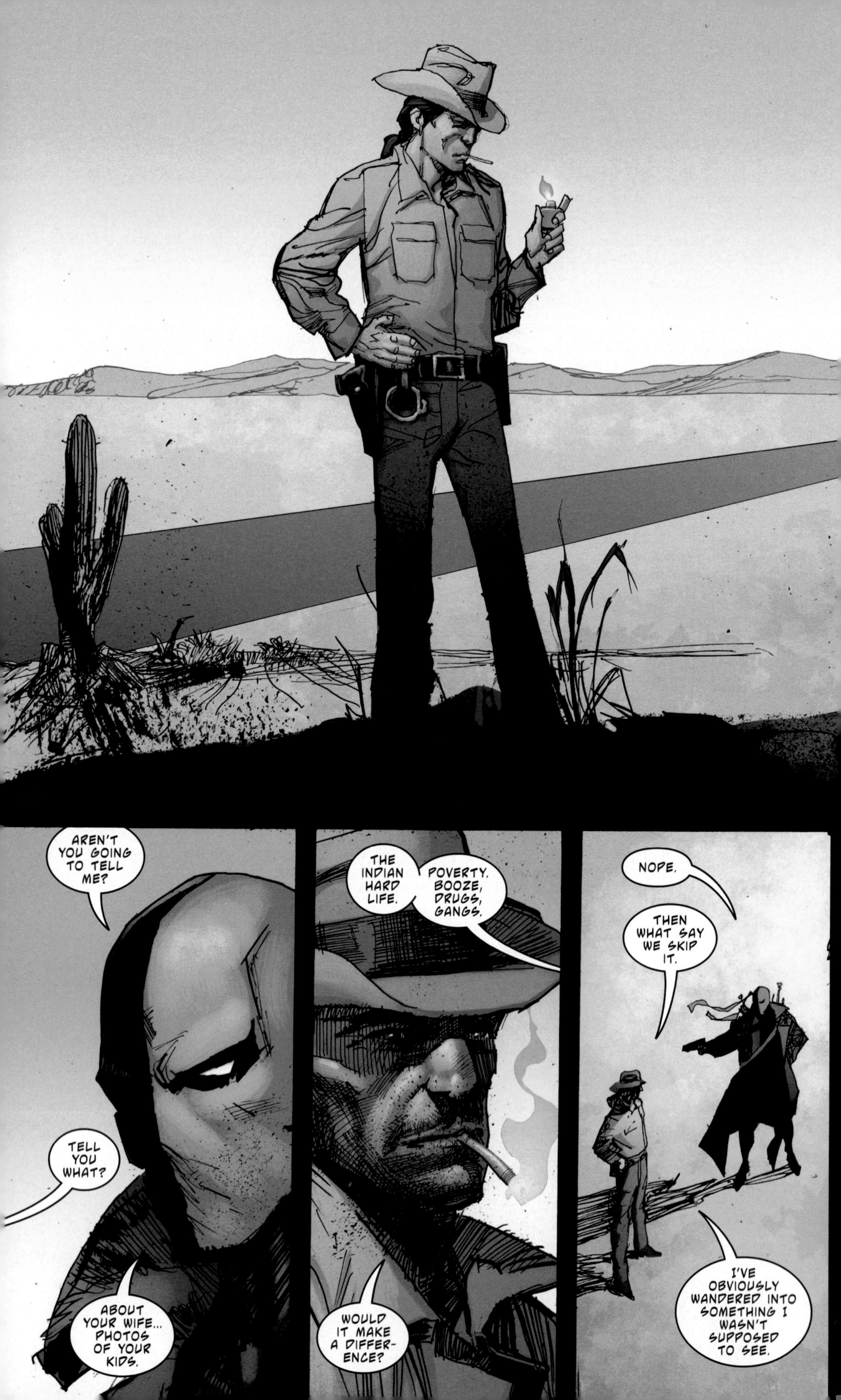
AREN'T YOU GOING TO TELL ME?
TELL YOU WHAT?
ABOUT YOUR WIFE... PHOTOS OF YOUR KIDS.
THE INDIAN HARD LIFE.
POVERTY. BOOZE, DRUGS, GANGS.
WOULD IT MAKE A DIFFERENCE?
NOPE.
THEN WHAT SAY WE SKIP IT.
I'VE OBVIOUSLY WANDERED INTO SOMETHING I WASN'T SUPPOSED TO SEE.

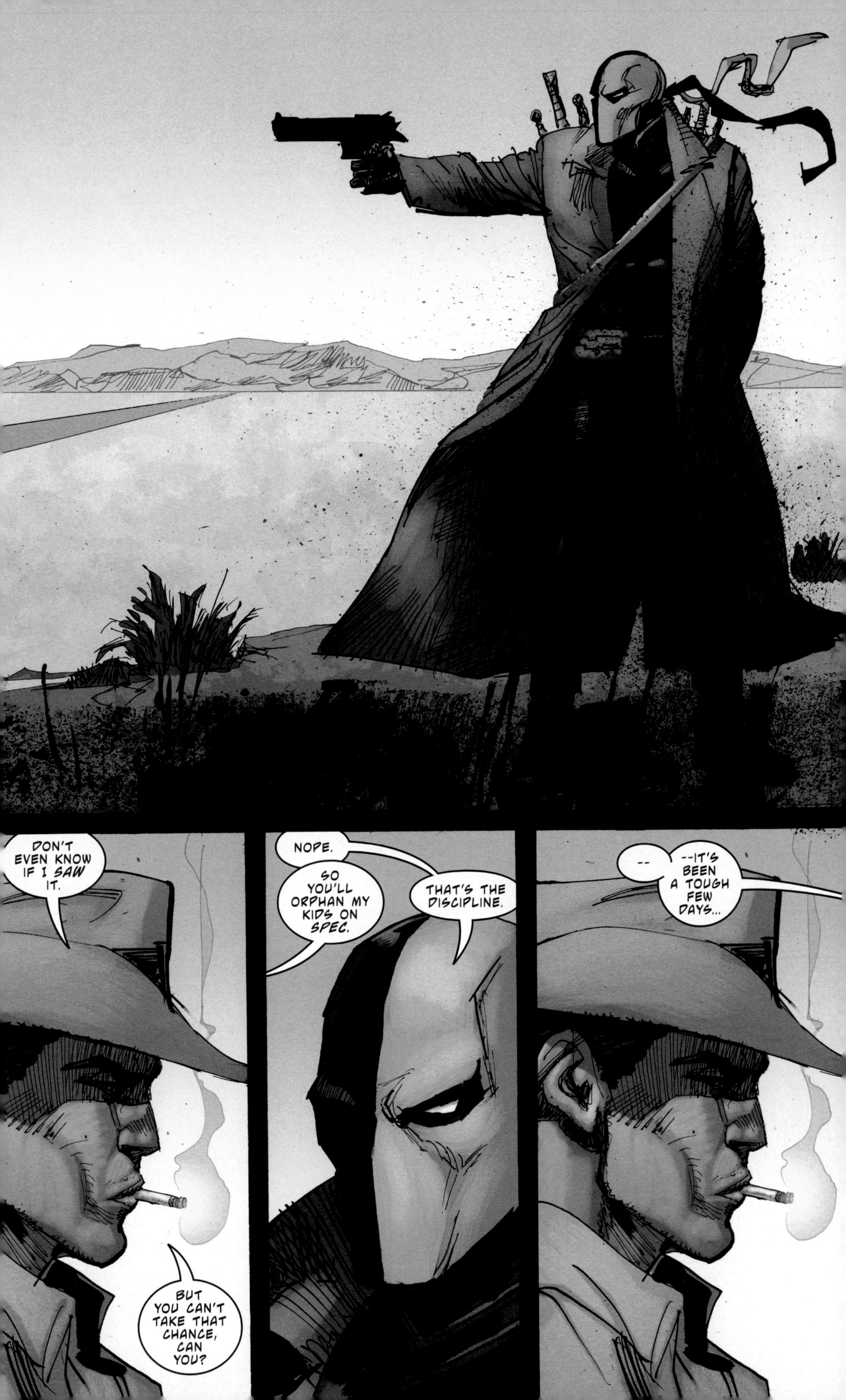
DON'T EVEN KNOW IF I SAW IT.
BUT YOU CAN'T TAKE THAT CHANCE, CAN YOU?
NOPE.
SO YOU'LL ORPHAN MY KIDS ON SPEC.
THAT'S THE DISCIPLINE.
--
--IT'S BEEN A TOUGH FEW DAYS...

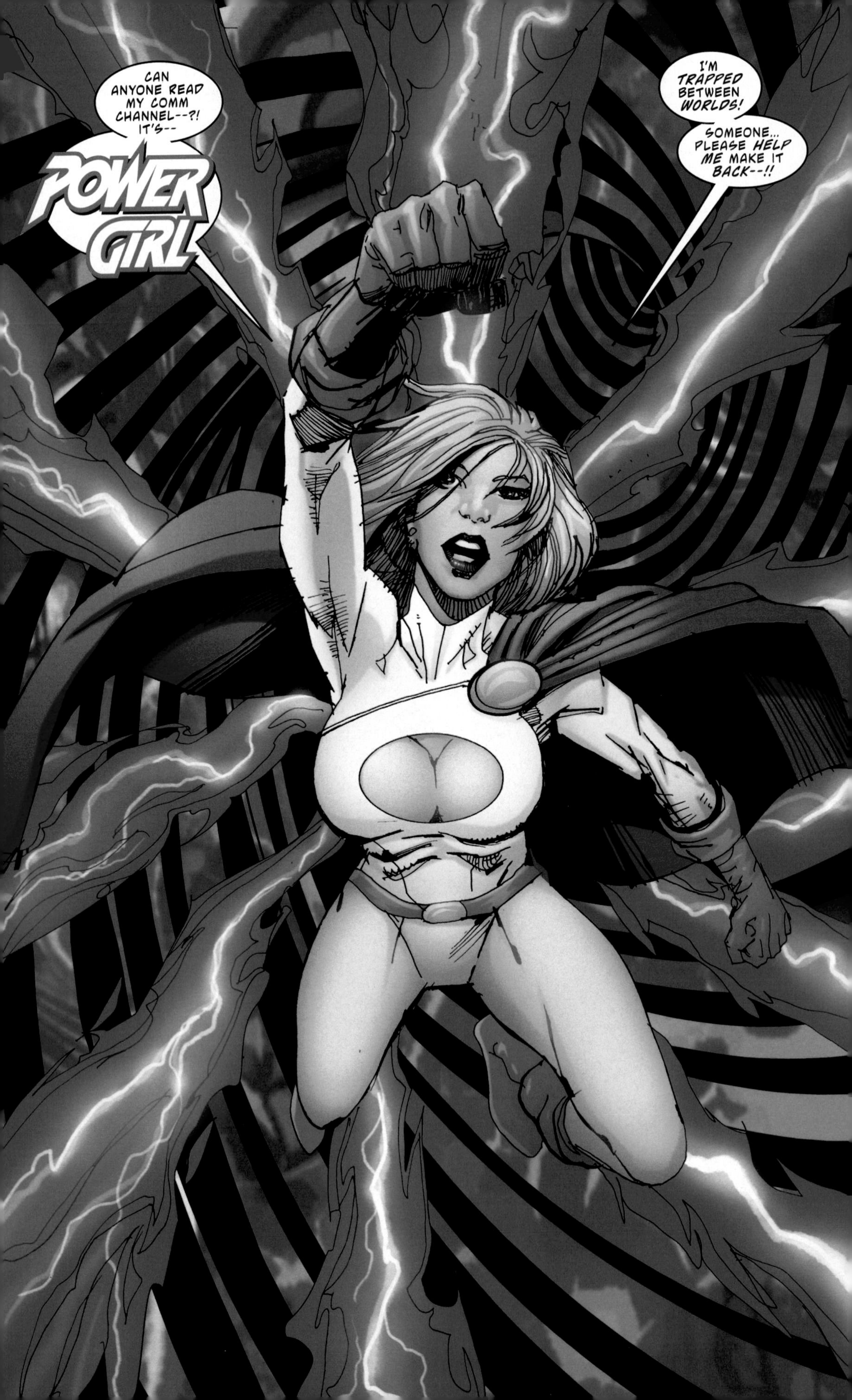
CAN ANYONE READ MY COMM CHANNEL--?! IT'S--
POWER GIRL
I'M TRAPPED BETWEEN WORLDS!
SOMEONE... PLEASE HELP ME MAKE IT BACK--!!

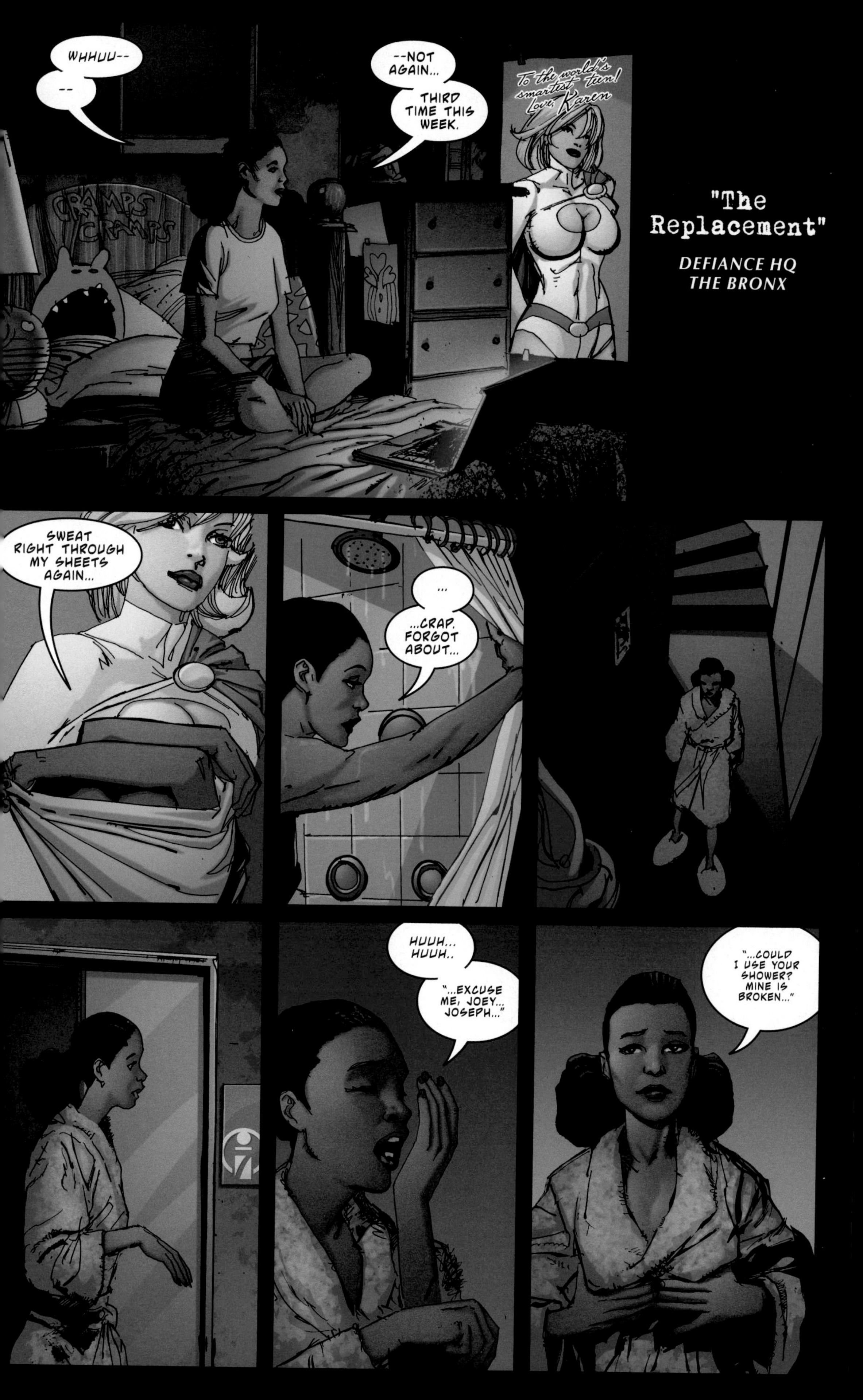
WHHUU--
--
--NOT AGAIN...
THIRD TIME THIS WEEK.
To the world's smartest teen! Love, Karen
"The Replacement"
DEFIANCE HQ THE BRONX
SWEAT RIGHT THROUGH MY SHEETS AGAIN...
...
...CRAP. FORGOT ABOUT...
HUUH... HUUH..
"...EXCUSE ME, JOEY... JOSEPH..."
"...COULD I USE YOUR SHOWER? MINE IS BROKEN..."

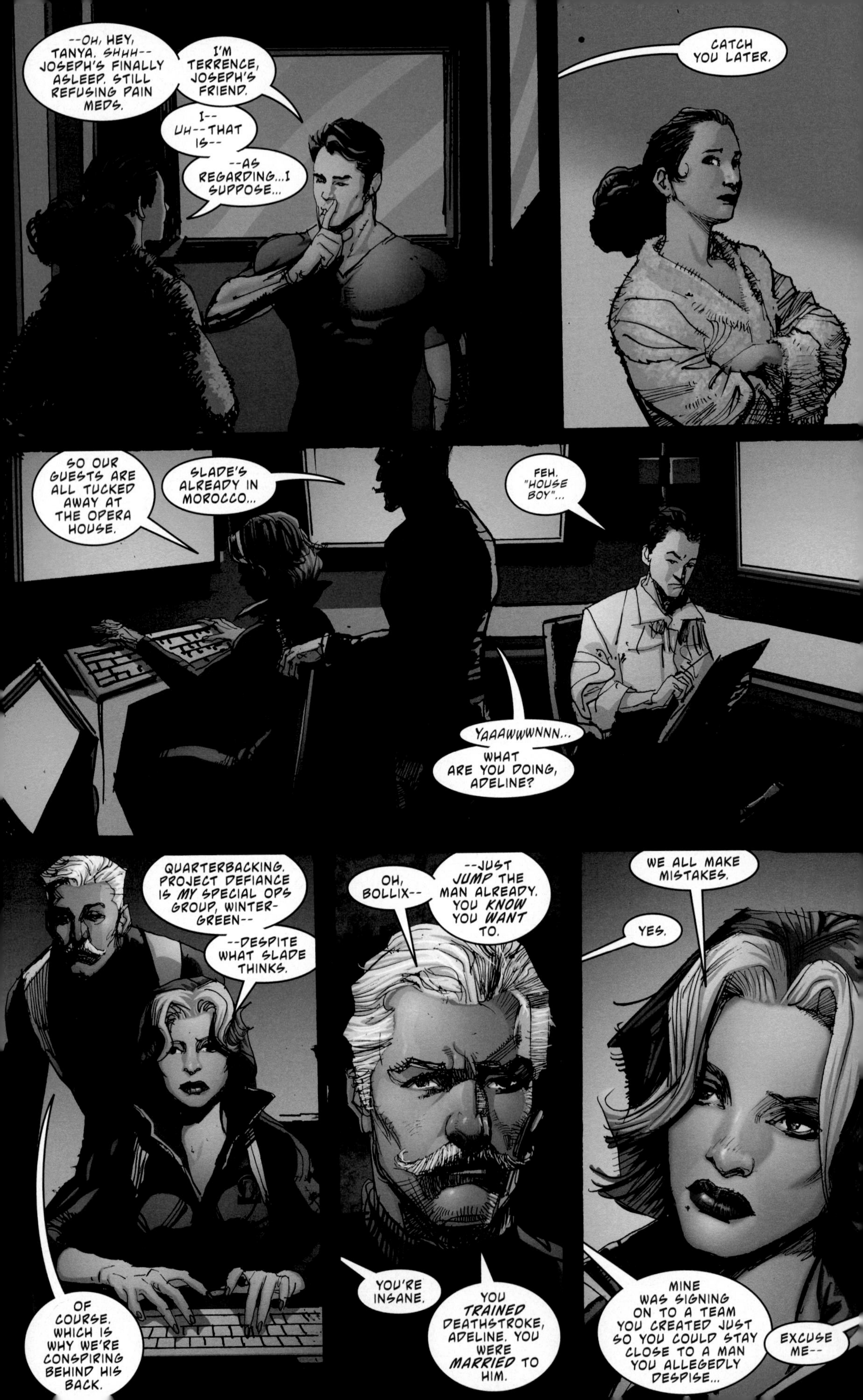
--OH, HEY, TANYA. SHHH-- JOSEPH'S FINALLY ASLEEP. STILL REFUSING PAIN MEDS.
I'M TERRENCE, JOSEPH'S FRIEND.
I-- UH--THAT IS--
--AS REGARDING...I SUPPOSE...
CATCH YOU LATER.
SO OUR GUESTS ARE ALL TUCKED AWAY AT THE OPERA HOUSE.
SLADE'S ALREADY IN MOROCCO...
FEH. "HOUSE BOY"...
YAAAWWWNNN... WHAT ARE YOU DOING, ADELINE?
QUARTERBACKING. PROJECT DEFIANCE IS MY SPECIAL OPS GROUP, WINTER-GREEN--
--DESPITE WHAT SLADE THINKS.
OF COURSE. WHICH IS WHY WE'RE CONSPIRING BEHIND HIS BACK.
OH, BOLLIX--
--JUST JUMP THE MAN ALREADY. YOU KNOW YOU WANT TO.
YOU'RE INSANE.
YOU TRAINED DEATHSTROKE, ADELINE. YOU WERE MARRIED TO HIM.
WE ALL MAKE MISTAKES.
YES.
MINE WAS SIGNING ON TO A TEAM YOU CREATED JUST SO YOU COULD STAY CLOSE TO A MAN YOU ALLEGEDLY DESPISE...
EXCUSE ME--

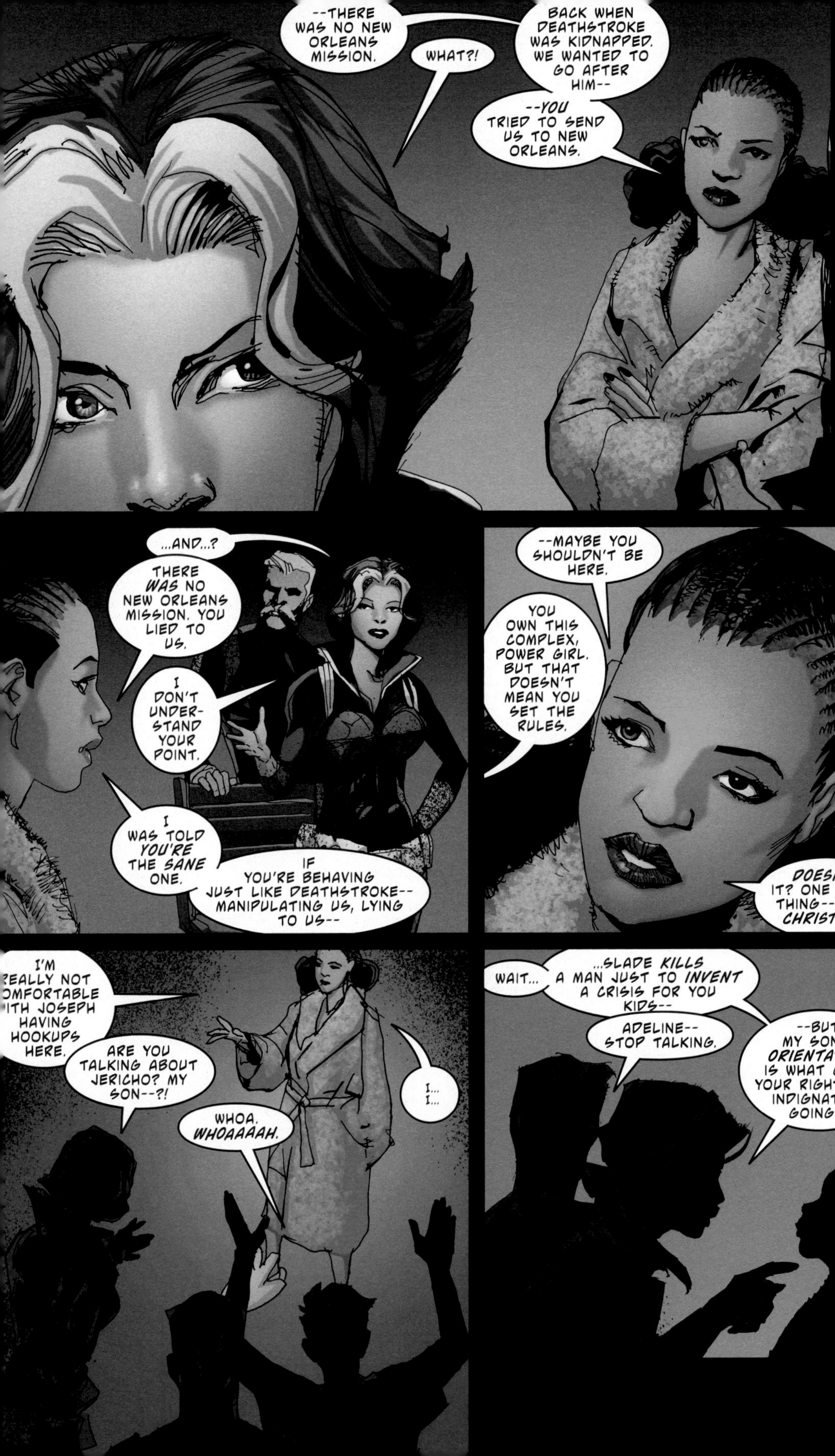
--THERE WAS NO NEW ORLEANS MISSION.
WHAT?!
BACK WHEN DEATHSTROKE WAS KIDNAPPED, WE WANTED TO GO AFTER HIM--
--YOU TRIED TO SEND US TO NEW ORLEANS.
...AND...?
THERE WAS NO NEW ORLEANS MISSION. YOU LIED TO US.
I DON'T UNDERSTAND YOUR POINT.
I WAS TOLD YOU'RE THE SANE ONE.
IF YOU'RE BEHAVING JUST LIKE DEATHSTROKE-- MANIPULATING US, LYING TO US--
--MAYBE YOU SHOULDN'T BE HERE.
YOU OWN THIS COMPLEX, POWER GIRL, BUT THAT DOESN'T MEAN YOU SET THE RULES.
DOESN'T IT? ONE MORE THING--I'M A CHRISTIAN.
I'M REALLY NOT COMFORTABLE WITH JOSEPH HAVING HOOKUPS HERE.
ARE YOU TALKING ABOUT JERICHO? MY SON--?!
WHOA. WHOAAAAAH.
I... I...
WAIT...
...SLADE KILLS A MAN JUST TO INVENT A CRISIS FOR YOU KIDS--
ADELINE-- STOP TALKING.
--BUT MY SON'S ORIENTATION IS WHAT GETS YOUR RIGHTEOUS INDIGNATION GOING?!

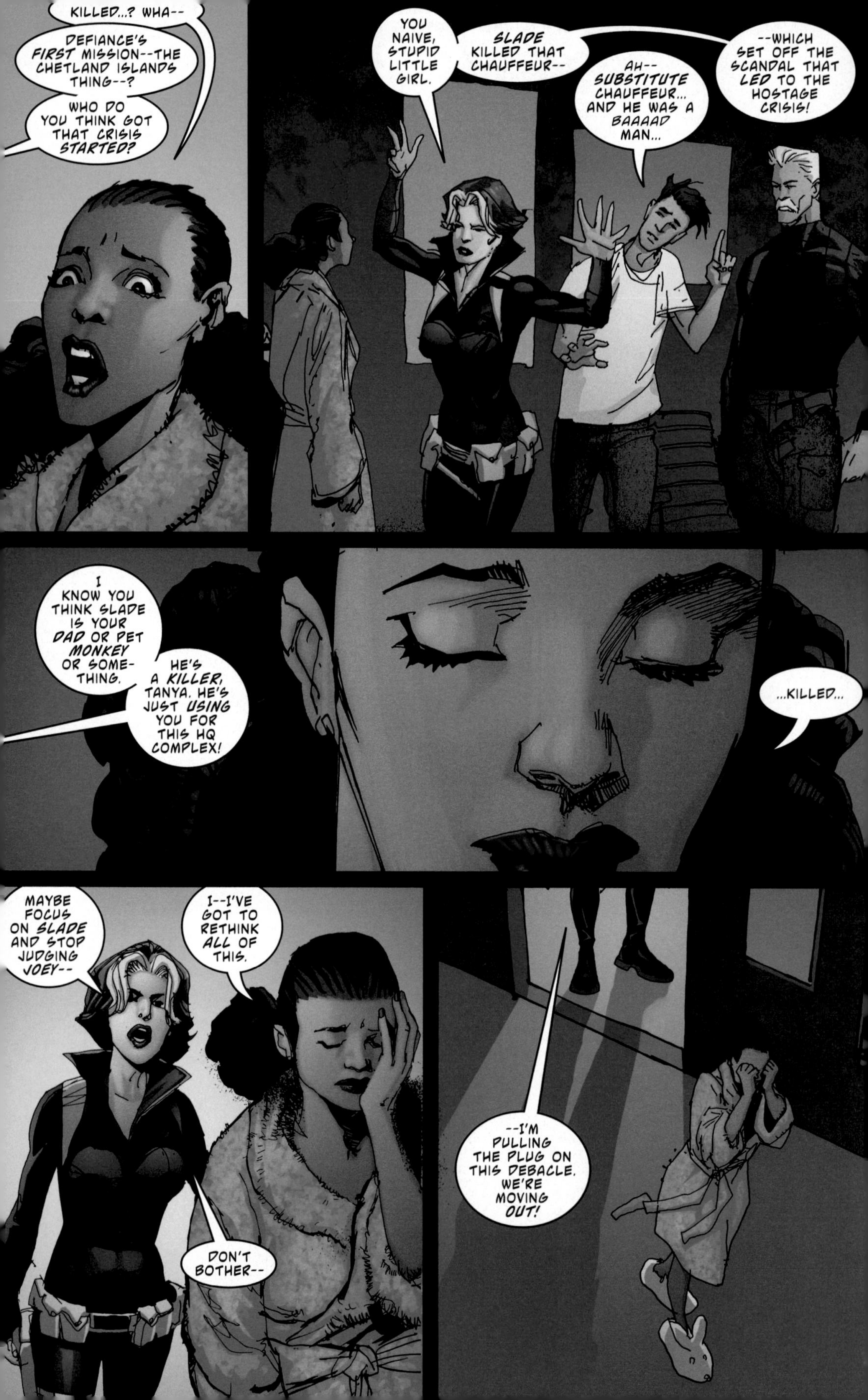
KILLED...? WHA--
DEFIANCE'S FIRST MISSION--THE CHETLAND ISLANDS THING--?
WHO DO YOU THINK GOT THAT CRISIS STARTED?
YOU NAIVE, STUPID LITTLE GIRL.
SLADE KILLED THAT CHAUFFEUR--
AH-- SUBSTITUTE CHAUFFEUR... AND HE WAS A BAAAAD MAN...
--WHICH SET OFF THE SCANDAL THAT LED TO THE HOSTAGE CRISIS!
I KNOW YOU THINK SLADE IS YOUR DAD OR PET MONKEY OR SOMETHING.
HE'S A KILLER, TANYA. HE'S JUST USING YOU FOR THIS HQ COMPLEX!
...KILLED...
MAYBE FOCUS ON SLADE AND STOP JUDGING JOEY--
I--I'VE GOT TO RETHINK ALL OF THIS.
DON'T BOTHER--
--I'M PULLING THE PLUG ON THIS DEBACLE. WE'RE MOVING OUT!

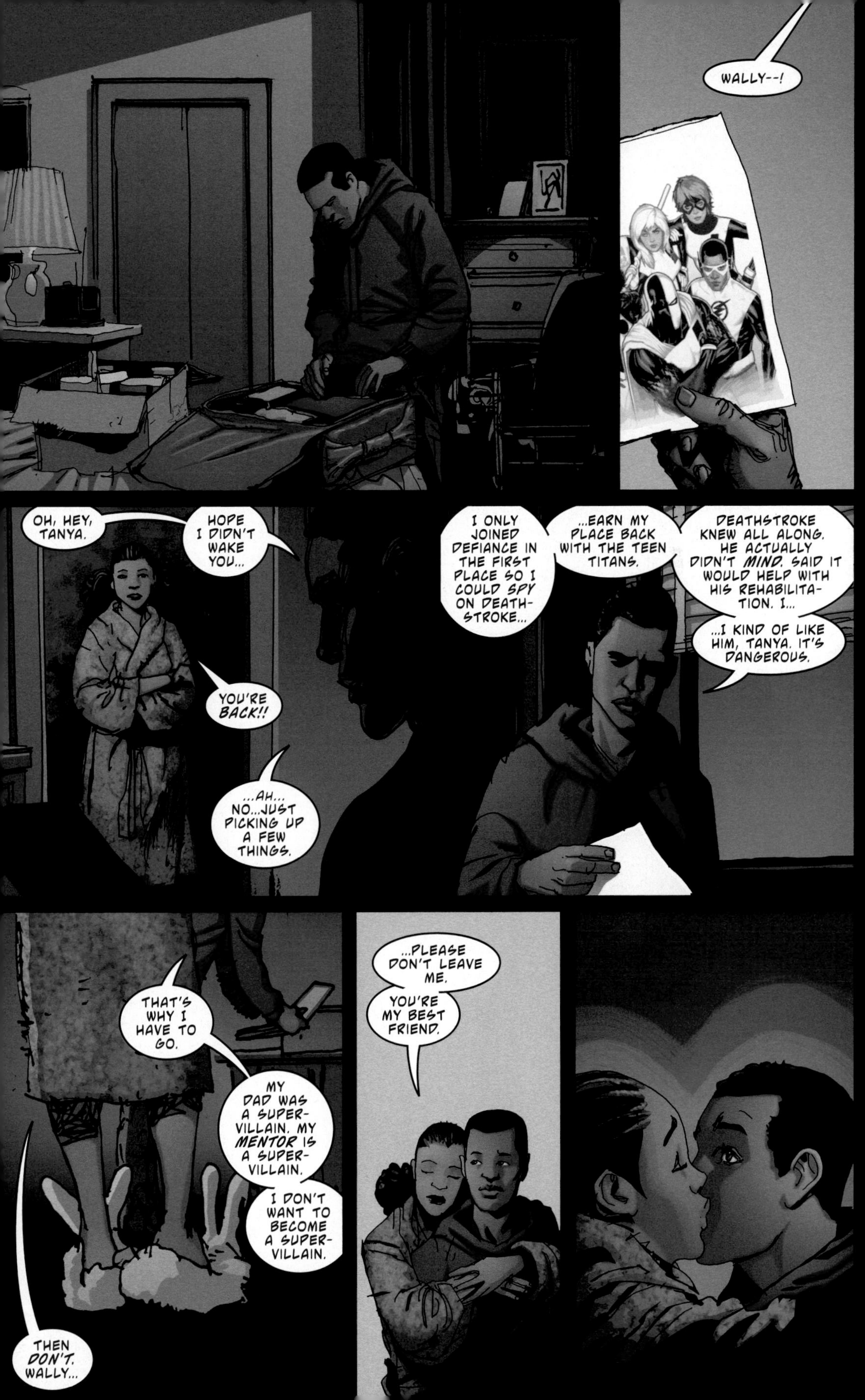
WALLY--!
OH, HEY, TANYA.
HOPE I DIDN'T WAKE YOU...
YOU'RE BACK!!
...AH... NO...JUST PICKING UP A FEW THINGS.
I ONLY JOINED DEFIANCE IN THE FIRST PLACE SO I COULD SPY ON DEATH-STROKE...
...EARN MY PLACE BACK WITH THE TEEN TITANS.
DEATHSTROKE KNEW ALL ALONG. HE ACTUALLY DIDN'T MIND. SAID IT WOULD HELP WITH HIS REHABILITA-TION. I...
...I KIND OF LIKE HIM, TANYA. IT'S DANGEROUS.
THAT'S WHY I HAVE TO GO.
MY DAD WAS A SUPER-VILLAIN. MY MENTOR IS A SUPER-VILLAIN.
I DON'T WANT TO BECOME A SUPER-VILLAIN.
THEN DON'T. WALLY...
...PLEASE DON'T LEAVE ME.
YOU'RE MY BEST FRIEND.

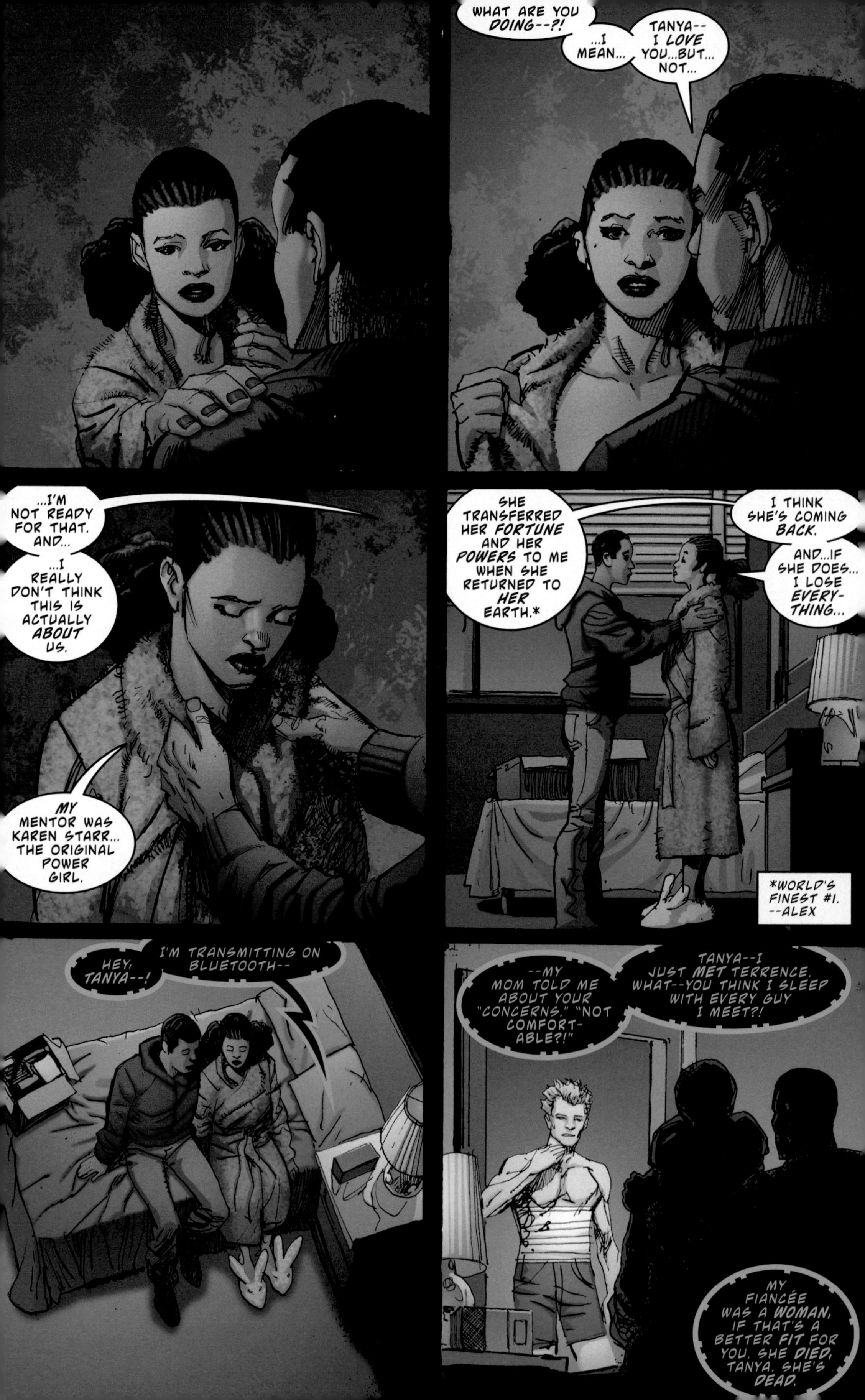
WHAT ARE YOU DOING--?!
...I MEAN...
TANYA-- I LOVE YOU...BUT... NOT...
...I'M NOT READY FOR THAT. AND...
...I REALLY DON'T THINK THIS IS ACTUALLY ABOUT US.
MY MENTOR WAS KAREN STARR... THE ORIGINAL POWER GIRL.
SHE TRANSFERRED HER FORTUNE AND HER POWERS TO ME WHEN SHE RETURNED TO HER EARTH.*
I THINK SHE'S COMING BACK.
AND...IF SHE DOES... I LOSE EVERY-THING...
*WORLD'S FINEST #1. --ALEX
HEY, TANYA--!
I'M TRANSMITTING ON BLUETOOTH--
--MY MOM TOLD ME ABOUT YOUR "CONCERNS." "NOT COMFORT-ABLE?!"
TANYA--I JUST MET TERRENCE. WHAT--YOU THINK I SLEEP WITH EVERY GUY I MEET?!
MY FIANCÉE WAS A WOMAN, IF THAT'S A BETTER FIT FOR YOU. SHE DIED, TANYA. SHE'S DEAD.

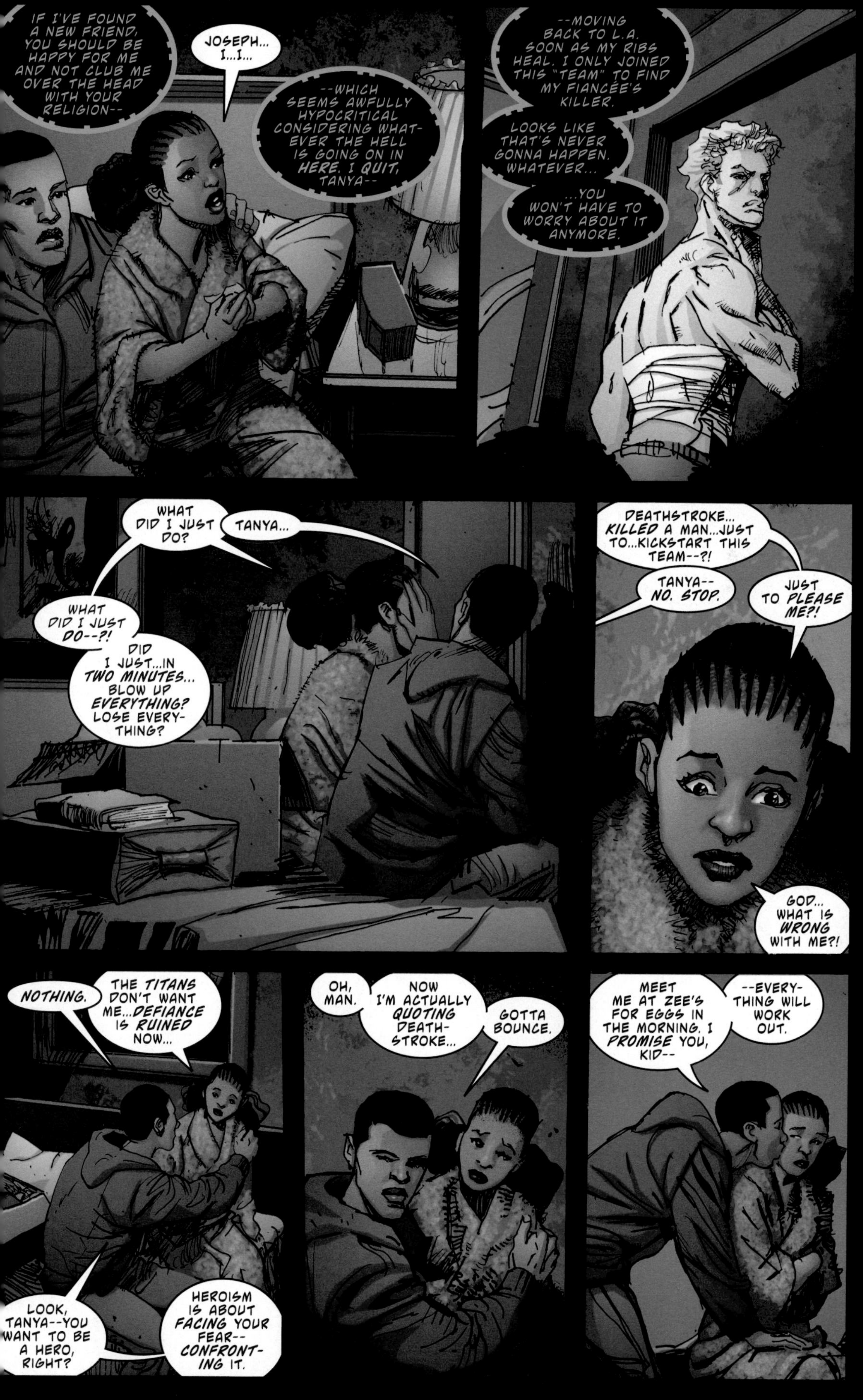
IF I'VE FOUND A NEW FRIEND, YOU SHOULD BE HAPPY FOR ME AND NOT CLUB ME OVER THE HEAD WITH YOUR RELIGION--
JOSEPH... I...I...
--WHICH SEEMS AWFULLY HYPOCRITICAL CONSIDERING WHAT-EVER THE HELL IS GOING ON IN HERE. I QUIT, TANYA--
--MOVING BACK TO L.A. SOON AS MY RIBS HEAL. I ONLY JOINED THIS "TEAM" TO FIND MY FIANCÉE'S KILLER.
LOOKS LIKE THAT'S NEVER GONNA HAPPEN. WHATEVER...
...YOU WON'T HAVE TO WORRY ABOUT IT ANYMORE.
WHAT DID I JUST DO?
TANYA...
WHAT DID I JUST DO--?!
DID I JUST...IN TWO MINUTES... BLOW UP EVERYTHING? LOSE EVERY-THING?
DEATHSTROKE... KILLED A MAN...JUST TO...KICKSTART THIS TEAM--?!
TANYA-- NO. STOP.
JUST TO PLEASE ME?!
GOD... WHAT IS WRONG WITH ME?!
NOTHING.
THE TITANS DON'T WANT ME...DEFIANCE IS RUINED NOW...
LOOK, TANYA--YOU WANT TO BE A HERO, RIGHT?
HEROISM IS ABOUT FACING YOUR FEAR-- CONFRONT-ING IT.
OH, MAN.
NOW I'M ACTUALLY QUOTING DEATH-STROKE...
GOTTA BOUNCE.
MEET ME AT ZEE'S FOR EGGS IN THE MORNING. I PROMISE YOU, KID--
--EVERY-THING WILL WORK OUT.

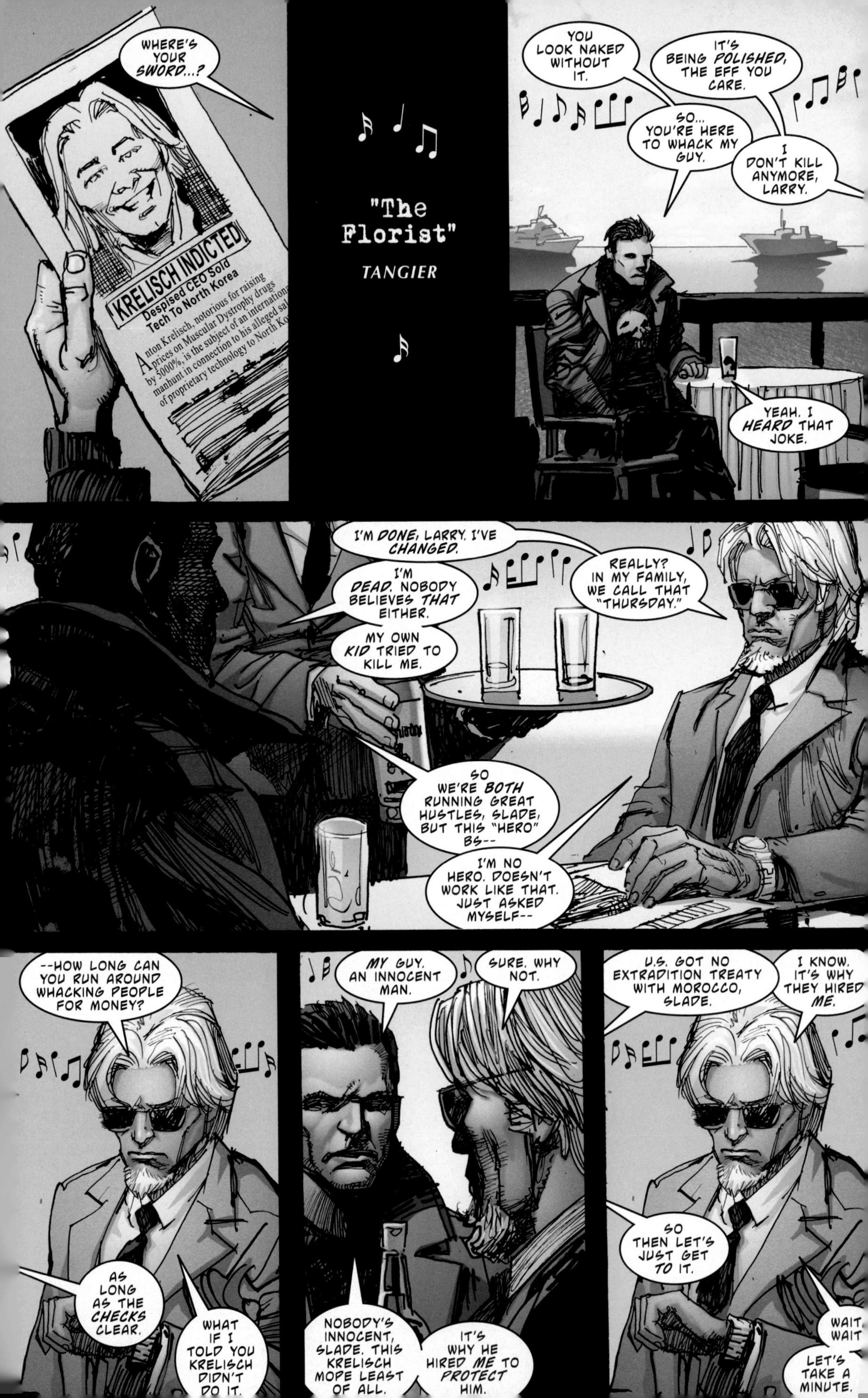
WHERE'S YOUR SWORD...?
KRELISCH INDICTED
Despised CEO Sold Tech To North Korea
Anton Krelisch, notorious for raising prices on Muscular Dystrophy drugs by 5000%, is the subject of an international manhunt in connection to his alleged sale of proprietary technology to North Ko
"The Florist"
TANGIER
YOU LOOK NAKED WITHOUT IT.
IT'S BEING POLISHED, THE EFF YOU CARE.
SO... YOU'RE HERE TO WHACK MY GUY.
I DON'T KILL ANYMORE, LARRY.
YEAH. I HEARD THAT JOKE.
I'M DONE, LARRY. I'VE CHANGED.
I'M DEAD. NOBODY BELIEVES THAT EITHER.
MY OWN KID TRIED TO KILL ME.
REALLY? IN MY FAMILY, WE CALL THAT "THURSDAY."
SO WE'RE BOTH RUNNING GREAT HUSTLES, SLADE, BUT THIS "HERO" BS--
I'M NO HERO. DOESN'T WORK LIKE THAT. JUST ASKED MYSELF--
--HOW LONG CAN YOU RUN AROUND WHACKING PEOPLE FOR MONEY?
AS LONG AS THE CHECKS CLEAR.
WHAT IF I TOLD YOU KRELISCH DIDN'T DO IT.
MY GUY. AN INNOCENT MAN.
SURE. WHY NOT.
NOBODY'S INNOCENT, SLADE. THIS KRELISCH MOPE LEAST OF ALL.
IT'S WHY HE HIRED ME TO PROTECT HIM.
U.S. GOT NO EXTRADITION TREATY WITH MOROCCO, SLADE.
I KNOW. IT'S WHY THEY HIRED ME.
SO THEN LET'S JUST GET TO IT.
WAIT WAIT
LET'S TAKE A MINUTE.

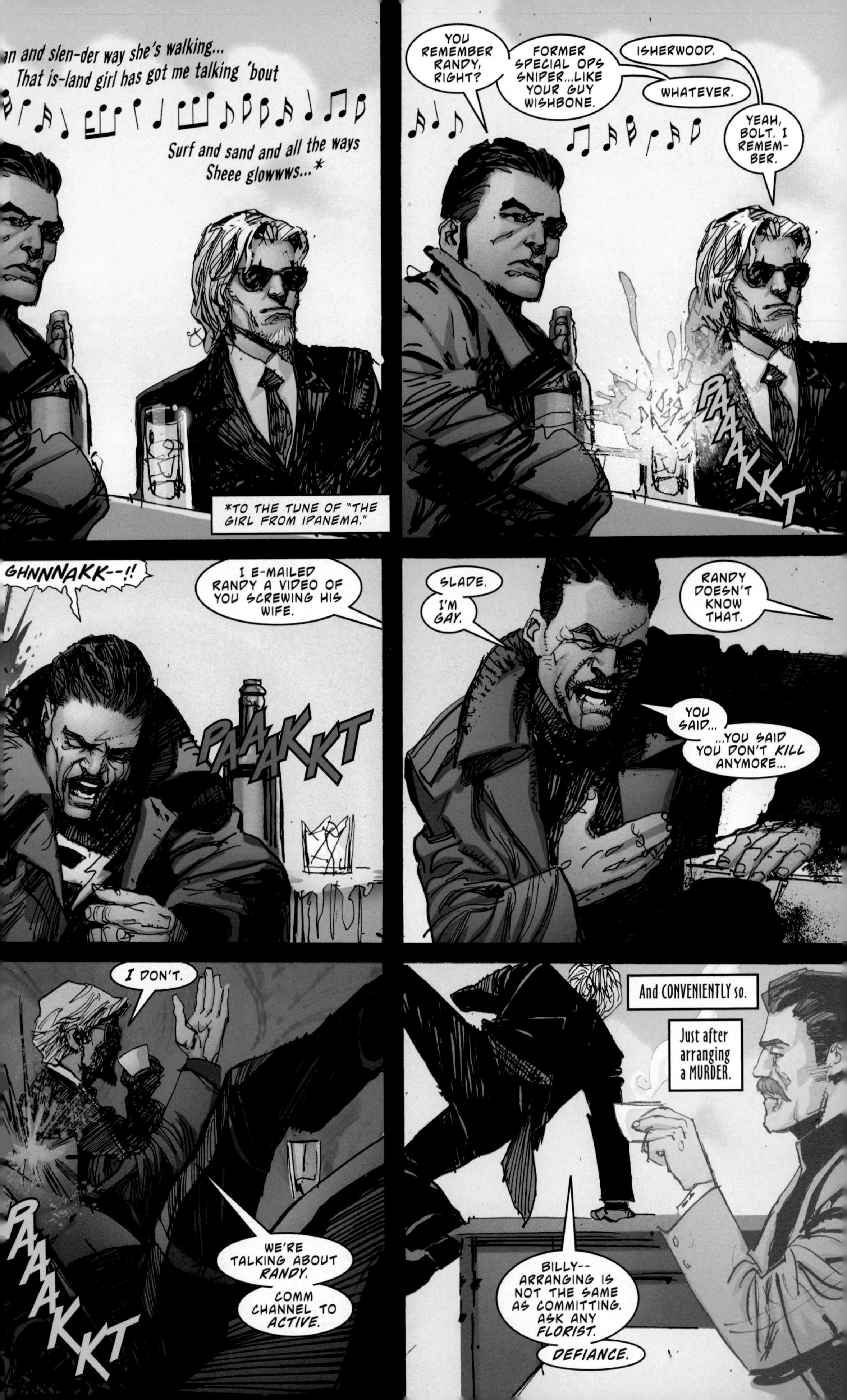

...an and slen-der way she's walking...
That is-land girl has got me talking 'bout
Surf and sand and all the ways
Sheee glowwws...*
*TO THE TUNE OF "THE GIRL FROM IPANEMA."
YOU REMEMBER RANDY, RIGHT?
FORMER SPECIAL OPS SNIPER...LIKE YOUR GUY WISHBONE.
ISHERWOOD.
WHATEVER.
YEAH, BOLT. I REMEM-BER.
PAAAKKT
GHNNNAKK--!!
I E-MAILED RANDY A VIDEO OF YOU SCREWING HIS WIFE.
PAAAKKT
SLADE.
I'M GAY.
RANDY DOESN'T KNOW THAT.
YOU SAID...
...YOU SAID YOU DON'T KILL ANYMORE...
I DON'T.
PAAAKKT
WE'RE TALKING ABOUT RANDY.
COMM CHANNEL TO ACTIVE.
And CONVENIENTLY so.
Just after arranging a MURDER.
BILLY-- ARRANGING IS NOT THE SAME AS COMMITTING. ASK ANY FLORIST.
DEFIANCE.

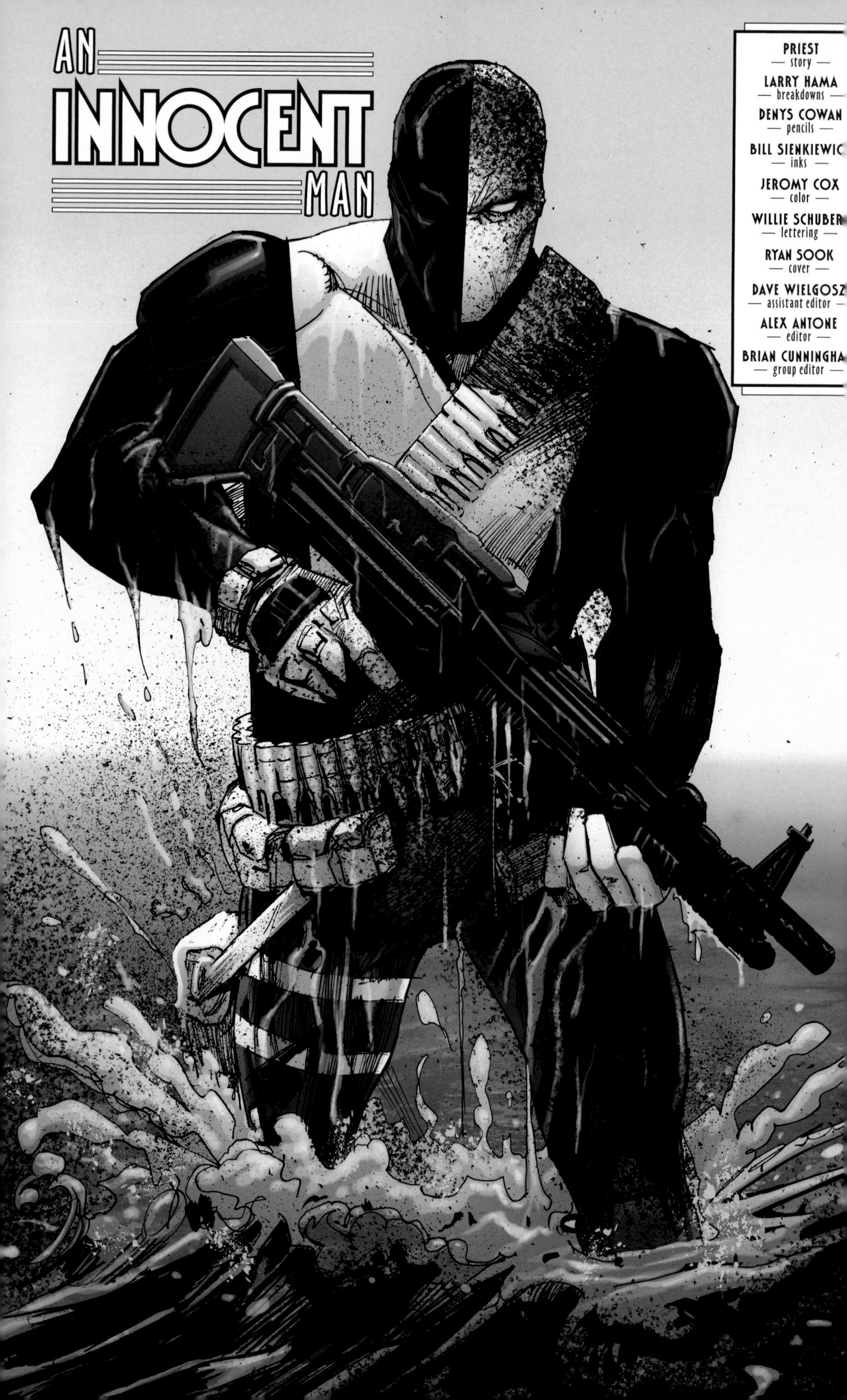
AN INNOCENT MAN
PRIEST
— story —
LARRY HAMA
— breakdowns —
DENYS COWAN
— pencils —
BILL SIENKIEWIC
— inks —
JEROMY COX
— color —
WILLIE SCHUBER
— lettering —
RYAN SOOK
— cover —
DAVE WIELGOSZ
— assistant editor —
ALEX ANTONE
— editor —
BRIAN CUNNINGHA
— group editor —

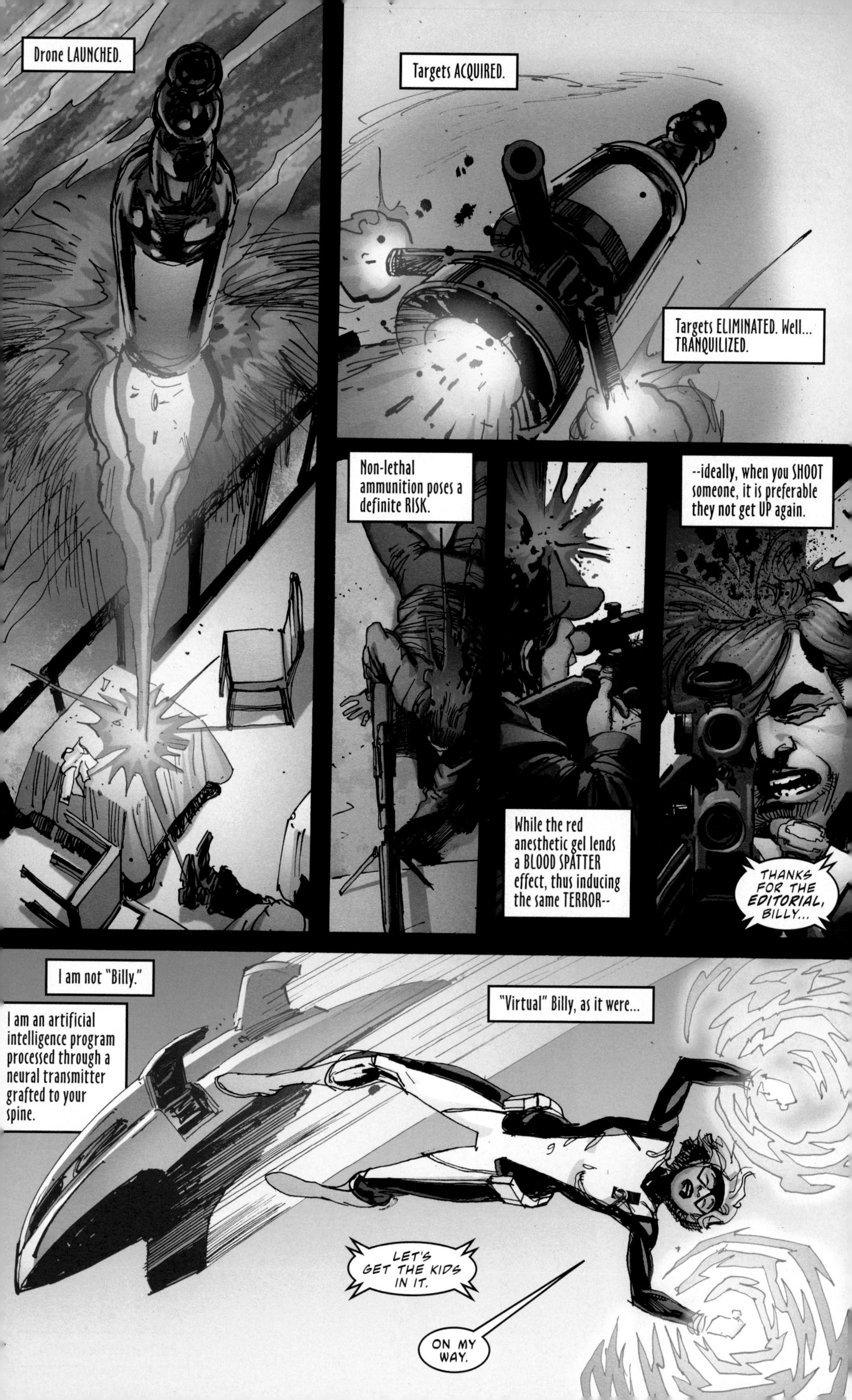
Drone LAUNCHED.
Targets ACQUIRED.
Targets ELIMINATED. Well... TRANQUILIZED.
Non-lethal ammunition poses a definite RISK.
While the red anesthetic gel lends a BLOOD SPATTER effect, thus inducing the same TERROR--
--ideally, when you SHOOT someone, it is preferable they not get UP again.
THANKS FOR THE EDITORIAL, BILLY...
I am not "Billy."
I am an artificial intelligence program processed through a neural transmitter grafted to your spine.
"Virtual" Billy, as it were...
LET'S GET THE KIDS IN IT.
ON MY WAY.

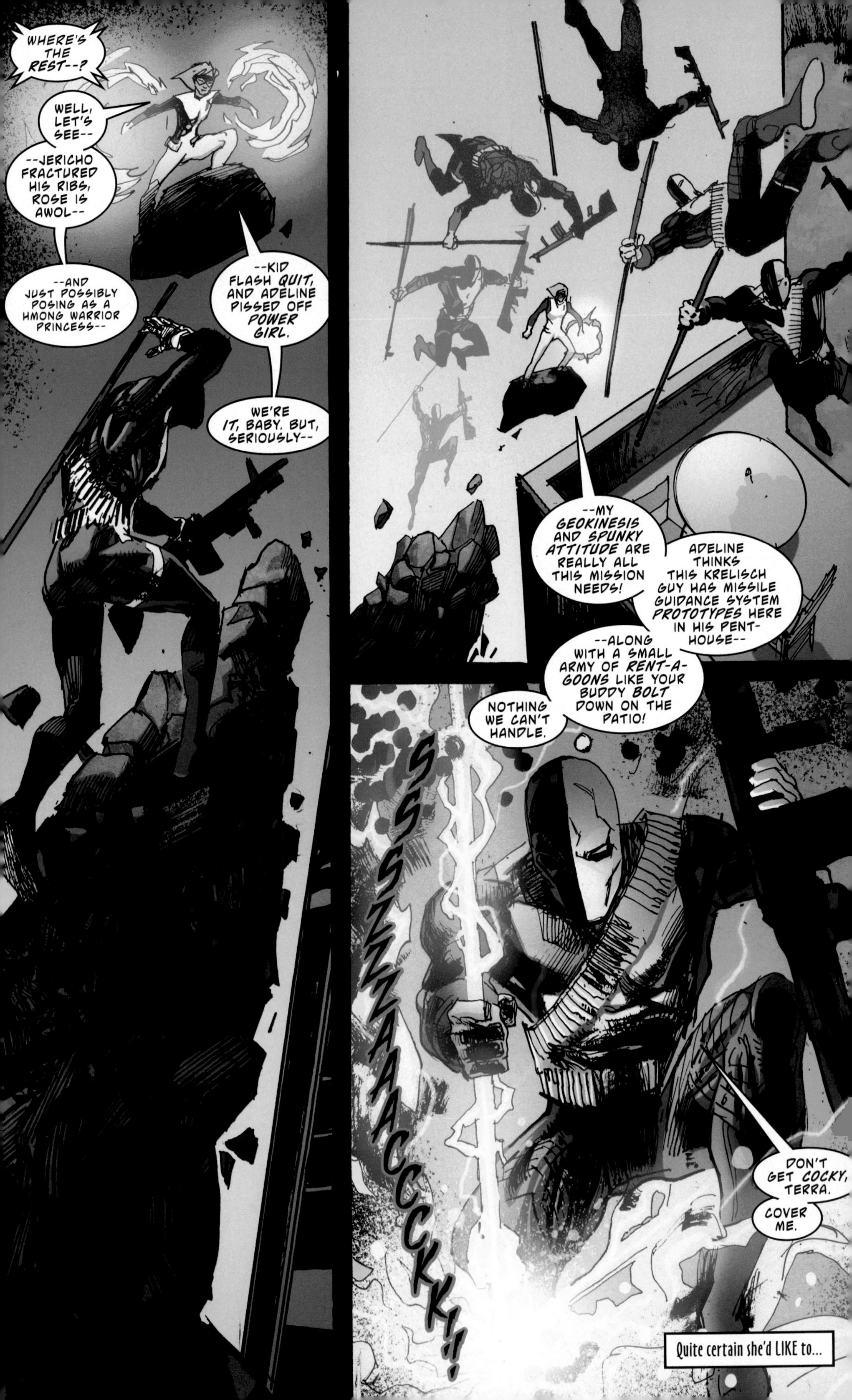
WHERE'S THE REST--?
WELL, LET'S SEE--
--JERICHO FRACTURED HIS RIBS, ROSE IS AWOL--
--AND JUST POSSIBLY POSING AS A HMONG WARRIOR PRINCESS--
--KID FLASH QUIT, AND ADELINE PISSED OFF POWER GIRL.
WE'RE IT, BABY. BUT, SERIOUSLY--
--MY GEOKINESIS AND SPUNKY ATTITUDE ARE REALLY ALL THIS MISSION NEEDS!
ADELINE THINKS THIS KRELISCH GUY HAS MISSILE GUIDANCE SYSTEM PROTOTYPES HERE IN HIS PENT-HOUSE--
--ALONG WITH A SMALL ARMY OF RENT-A-GOONS LIKE YOUR BUDDY BOLT DOWN ON THE PATIO!
NOTHING WE CAN'T HANDLE.
SSSZZZAAACCCKK!!
DON'T GET COCKY, TERRA.
COVER ME.
Quite certain she'd LIKE to...

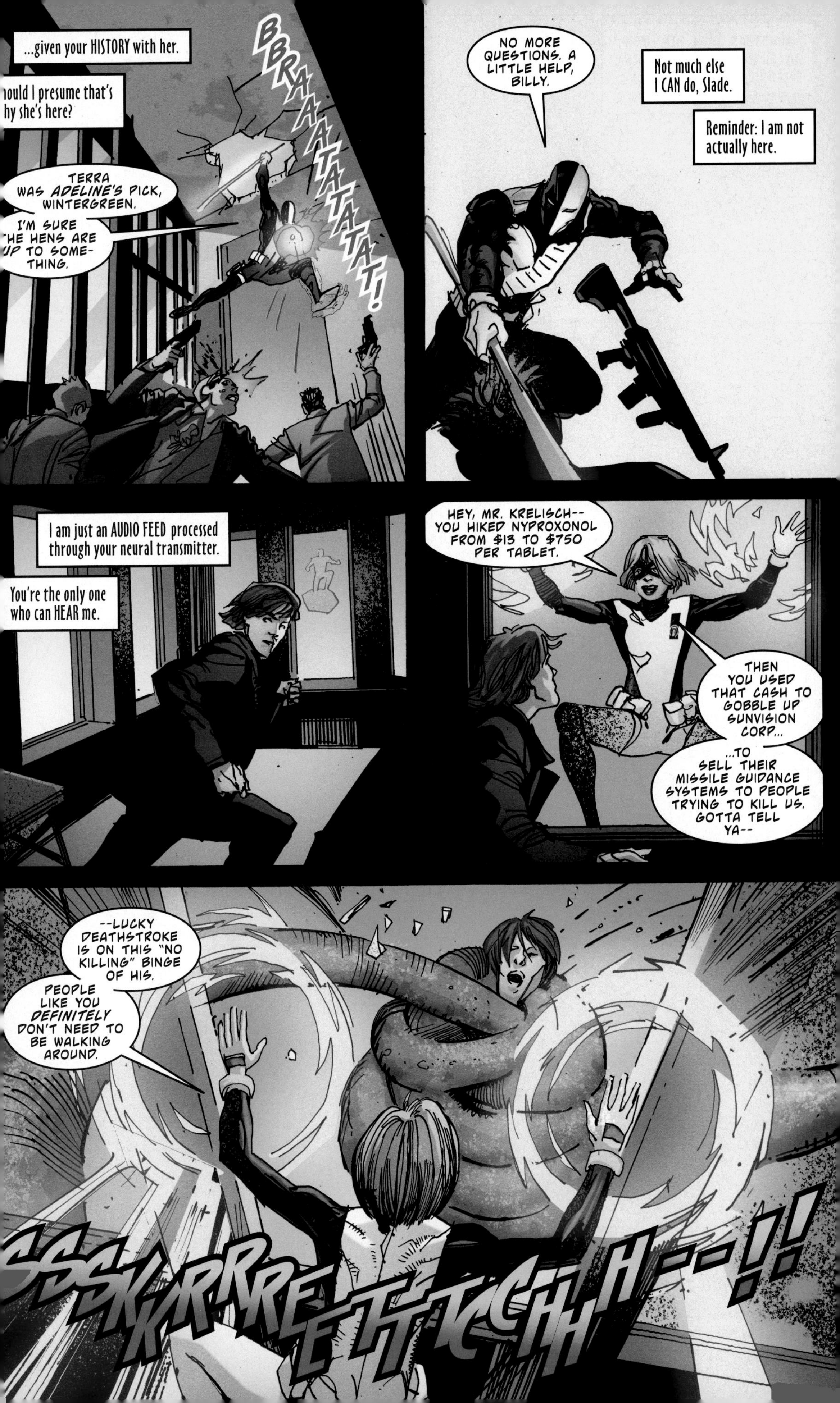
...given your HISTORY with her.
hould I presume that's
hy she's here?
TERRA WAS ADELINE'S PICK, WINTERGREEN.
I'M SURE HE HENS ARE UP TO SOME-THING.
BBRAAAATATATATAT!
NO MORE QUESTIONS. A LITTLE HELP, BILLY.
Not much else I CAN do, Slade.
Reminder: I am not actually here.
I am just an AUDIO FEED processed through your neural transmitter.
You're the only one who can HEAR me.
HEY, MR. KRELISCH--YOU HIKED NYPROXONOL FROM $13 TO $750 PER TABLET.
THEN YOU USED THAT CASH TO GOBBLE UP SUNVISION CORP...
...TO SELL THEIR MISSILE GUIDANCE SYSTEMS TO PEOPLE TRYING TO KILL US. GOTTA TELL YA--
--LUCKY DEATHSTROKE IS ON THIS "NO KILLING" BINGE OF HIS.
PEOPLE LIKE YOU DEFINITELY DON'T NEED TO BE WALKING AROUND.
SSKRRREETTCHH--!!

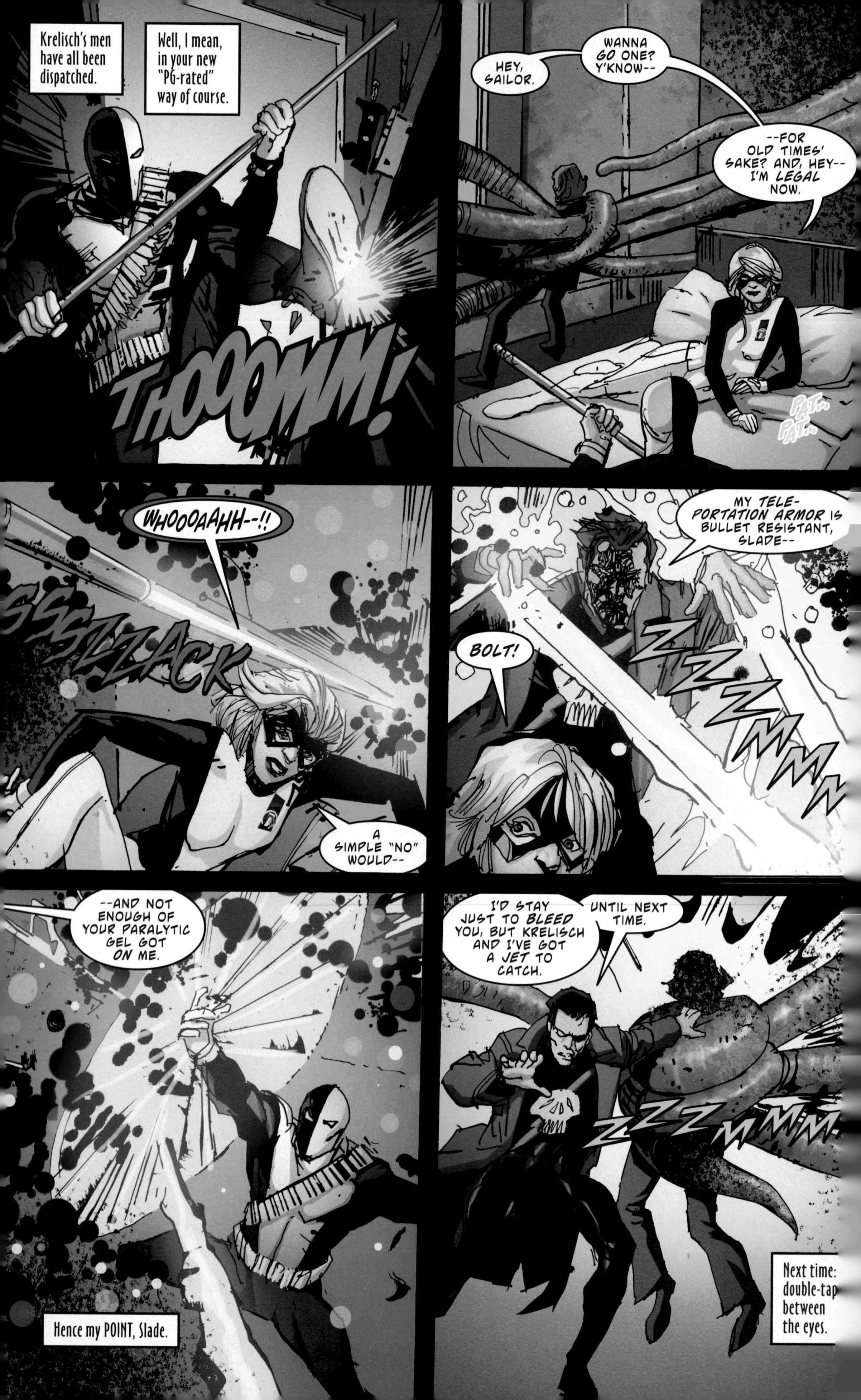

Krelisch's men have all been dispatched.
Well, I mean, in your new "PG-rated" way of course.
THOOOMM!
HEY, SAILOR.
WANNA GO ONE? Y'KNOW--
--FOR OLD TIMES' SAKE? AND, HEY-- I'M LEGAL NOW.
PAT... PAT...
WHOOOAAHH--!!
SSSZZZACK
A SIMPLE "NO" WOULD--
MY TELE-PORTATION ARMOR IS BULLET RESISTANT, SLADE--
BOLT!
ZZZZMMMN
--AND NOT ENOUGH OF YOUR PARALYTIC GEL GOT ON ME.
Hence my POINT, Slade.
I'D STAY JUST TO BLEED YOU, BUT KRELISCH AND I'VE GOT A JET TO CATCH.
UNTIL NEXT TIME.
ZZZZMMMM-
Next time: double-tap between the eyes.

ZZZMMM

WHAT THE--

BOLT--HE'S MATERIALIZED RIGHT IN THE PATH OF--

--DAMMIT--BOLT'S TELEPORTED ON BOARD!

ZZZZZZMMMMMMMMMMMM

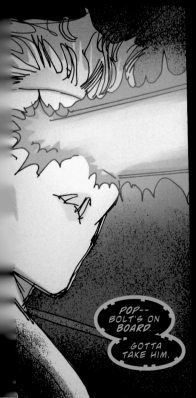

POP--BOLT'S ON BOARD.

GOTTA TAKE HIM.

TRANS-FERRING MY CONSCIOUSNESS TO BOLT--

--BUT HE'S FIGHTING ME--!

--HE'S TRIGGERED HIS TELEPORTATION ARMOR--

ZZZMMMM

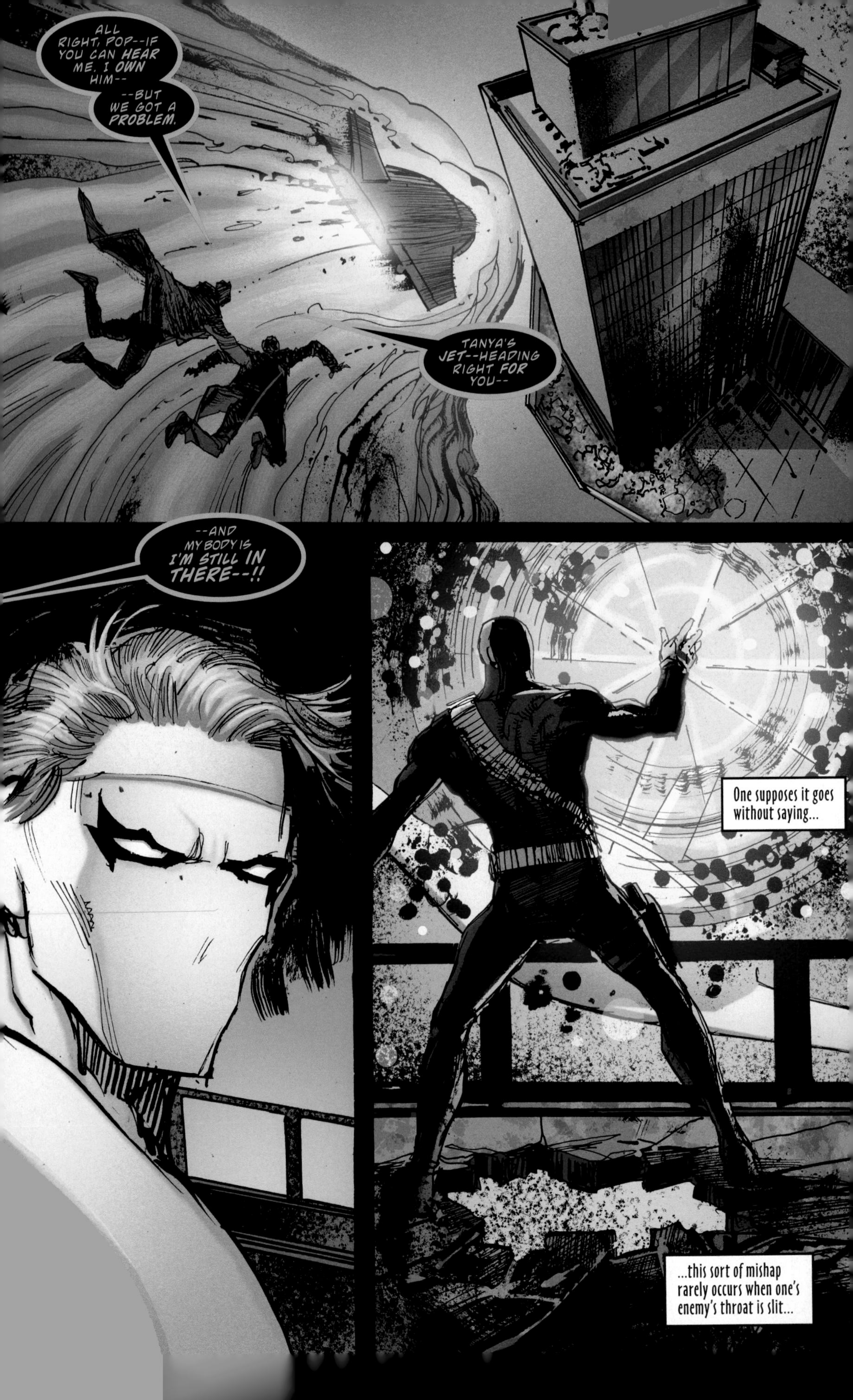
ALL RIGHT, POP--IF YOU CAN HEAR ME. I OWN HIM--
--BUT WE GOT A PROBLEM.
TANYA'S JET--HEADING RIGHT FOR YOU--
--AND MY BODY IS I'M STILL IN THERE--!!
One supposes it goes without saying...
...this sort of mishap rarely occurs when one's enemy's throat is slit...

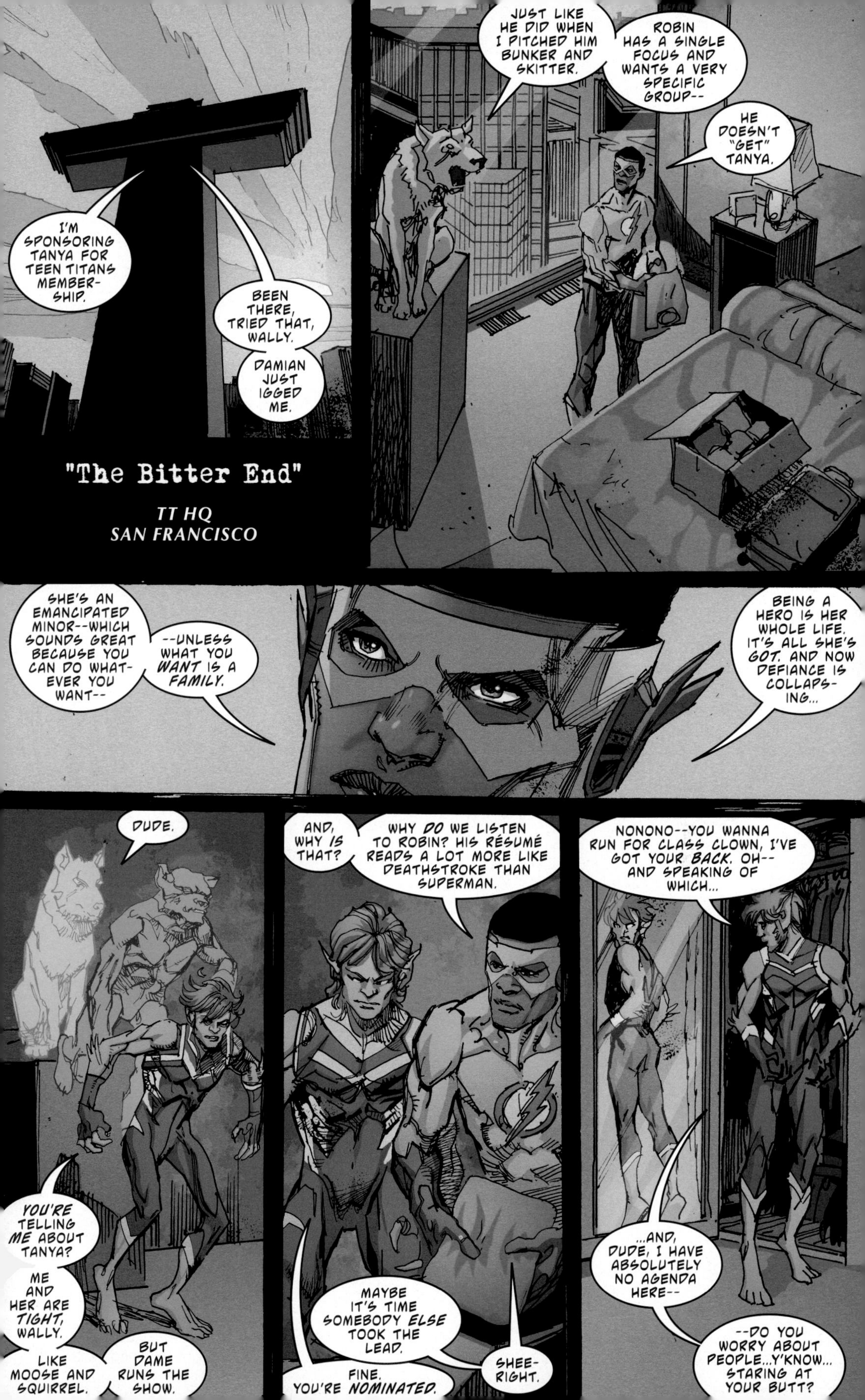
I'M SPONSORING TANYA FOR TEEN TITANS MEMBERSHIP.
BEEN THERE, TRIED THAT, WALLY.
DAMIAN JUST IGGED ME.
"The Bitter End"
TT HQ
SAN FRANCISCO
JUST LIKE HE DID WHEN I PITCHED HIM BUNKER AND SKITTER.
ROBIN HAS A SINGLE FOCUS AND WANTS A VERY SPECIFIC GROUP--
HE DOESN'T "GET" TANYA.
SHE'S AN EMANCIPATED MINOR--WHICH SOUNDS GREAT BECAUSE YOU CAN DO WHATEVER YOU WANT--
--UNLESS WHAT YOU *WANT* IS A *FAMILY*.
BEING A HERO IS HER WHOLE LIFE. IT'S ALL SHE'S *GOT*. AND NOW DEFIANCE IS COLLAPSING...
DUDE.
YOU'RE TELLING *ME* ABOUT TANYA?
ME AND HER ARE *TIGHT*, WALLY.
LIKE MOOSE AND SQUIRREL.
BUT DAME RUNS THE SHOW.
AND, WHY *IS* THAT?
WHY *DO* WE LISTEN TO ROBIN? HIS RÉSUMÉ READS A LOT MORE LIKE DEATHSTROKE THAN SUPERMAN.
MAYBE IT'S TIME SOMEBODY *ELSE* TOOK THE LEAD.
SHEE-RIGHT.
FINE. YOU'RE *NOMINATED*.
NONONO--YOU WANNA RUN FOR CLASS CLOWN, I'VE GOT YOUR *BACK*. OH--AND SPEAKING OF WHICH...
...AND, DUDE, I HAVE ABSOLUTELY NO AGENDA HERE--
--DO YOU WORRY ABOUT PEOPLE...Y'KNOW... STARING AT YOUR BUTT?

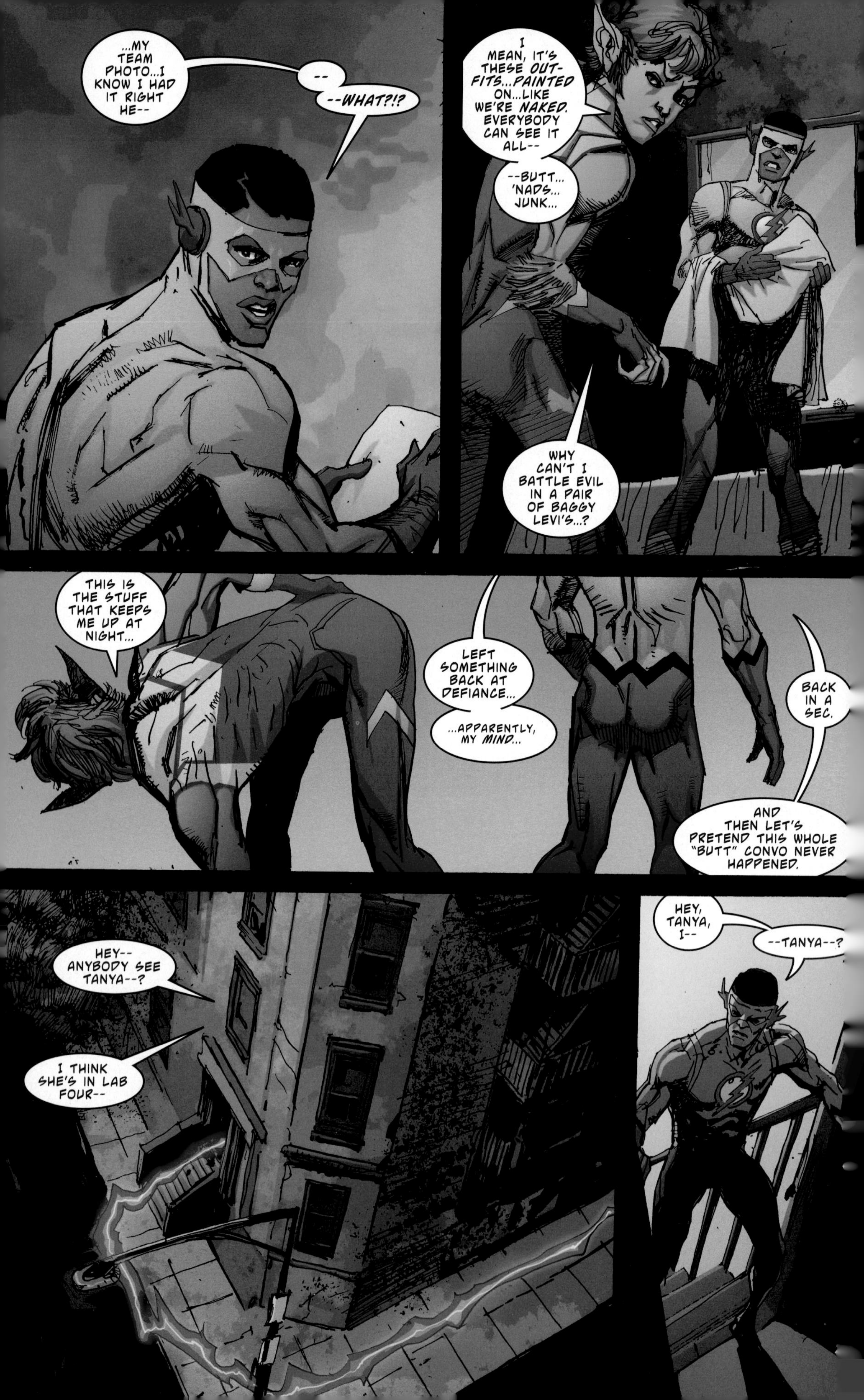
...MY TEAM PHOTO...I KNOW I HAD IT RIGHT HE--
--
--WHAT?!?
I MEAN, IT'S THESE *OUT-FITS*...*PAINTED* ON...LIKE WE'RE *NAKED*. EVERYBODY CAN SEE IT ALL--
--BUTT... 'NADS... JUNK...
WHY CAN'T I BATTLE EVIL IN A PAIR OF BAGGY LEVI'S...?
THIS IS THE STUFF THAT KEEPS ME UP AT NIGHT...
LEFT SOMETHING BACK AT DEFIANCE...
...APPARENTLY, MY *MIND*...
BACK IN A SEC.
AND THEN LET'S PRETEND THIS WHOLE "BUTT" CONVO NEVER HAPPENED.
HEY-- ANYBODY SEE TANYA--?
I THINK SHE'S IN LAB FOUR--
HEY, TANYA, I--
--TANYA--?

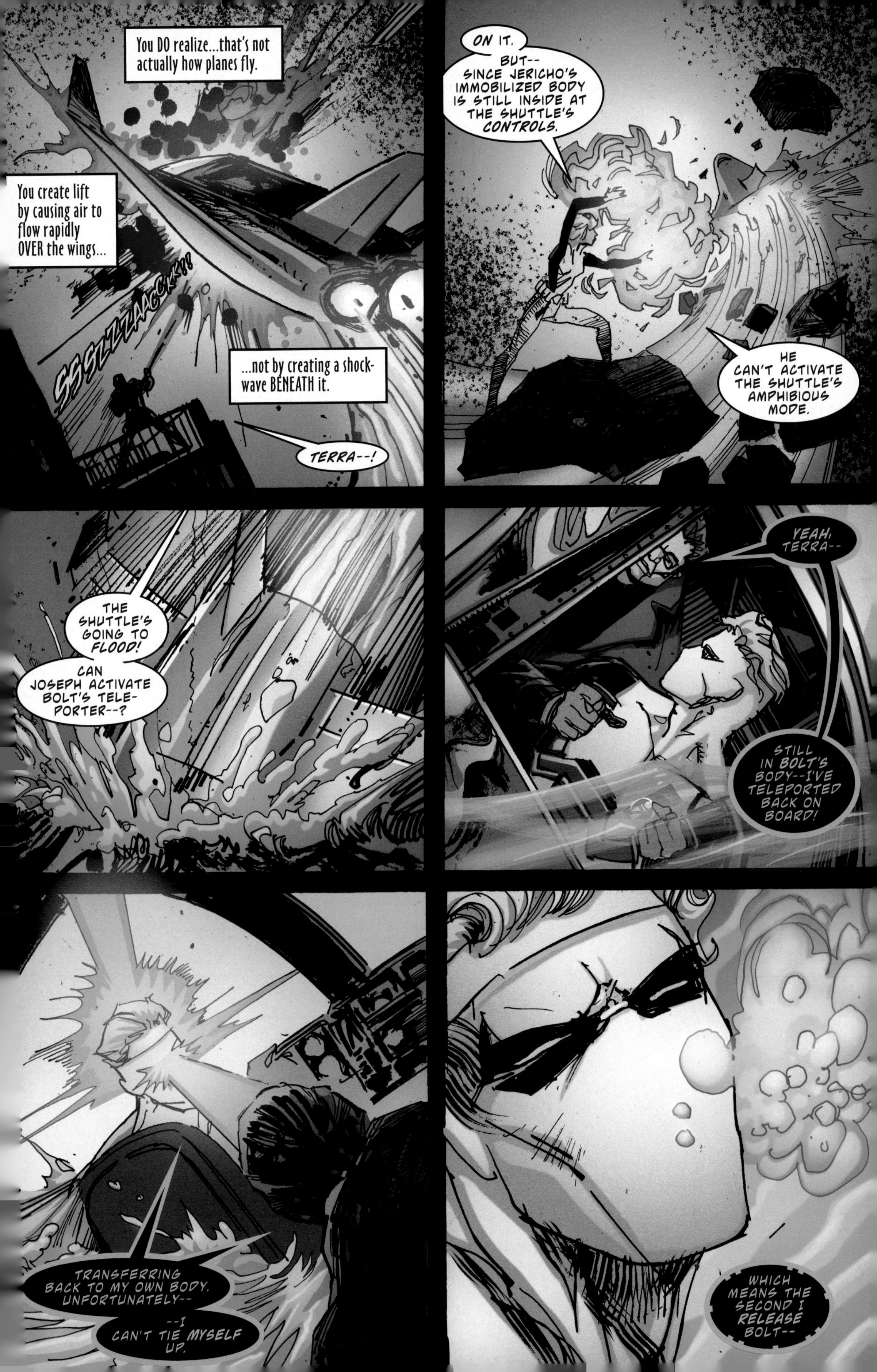
You DO realize...that's not actually how planes fly.
You create lift by causing air to flow rapidly OVER the wings...
SSSZZZZAACK!!
...not by creating a shock-wave BENEATH it.
TERRA--!
ON IT.
BUT-- SINCE JERICHO'S IMMOBILIZED BODY IS STILL INSIDE AT THE SHUTTLE'S CONTROLS,
HE CAN'T ACTIVATE THE SHUTTLE'S AMPHIBIOUS MODE.
THE SHUTTLE'S GOING TO FLOOD!
CAN JOSEPH ACTIVATE BOLT'S TELE-PORTER--?
YEAH, TERRA--
STILL IN BOLT'S BODY--I'VE TELEPORTED BACK ON BOARD!
TRANSFERRING BACK TO MY OWN BODY. UNFORTUNATELY--
--I CAN'T TIE MYSELF UP.
WHICH MEANS THE SECOND I RELEASE BOLT--

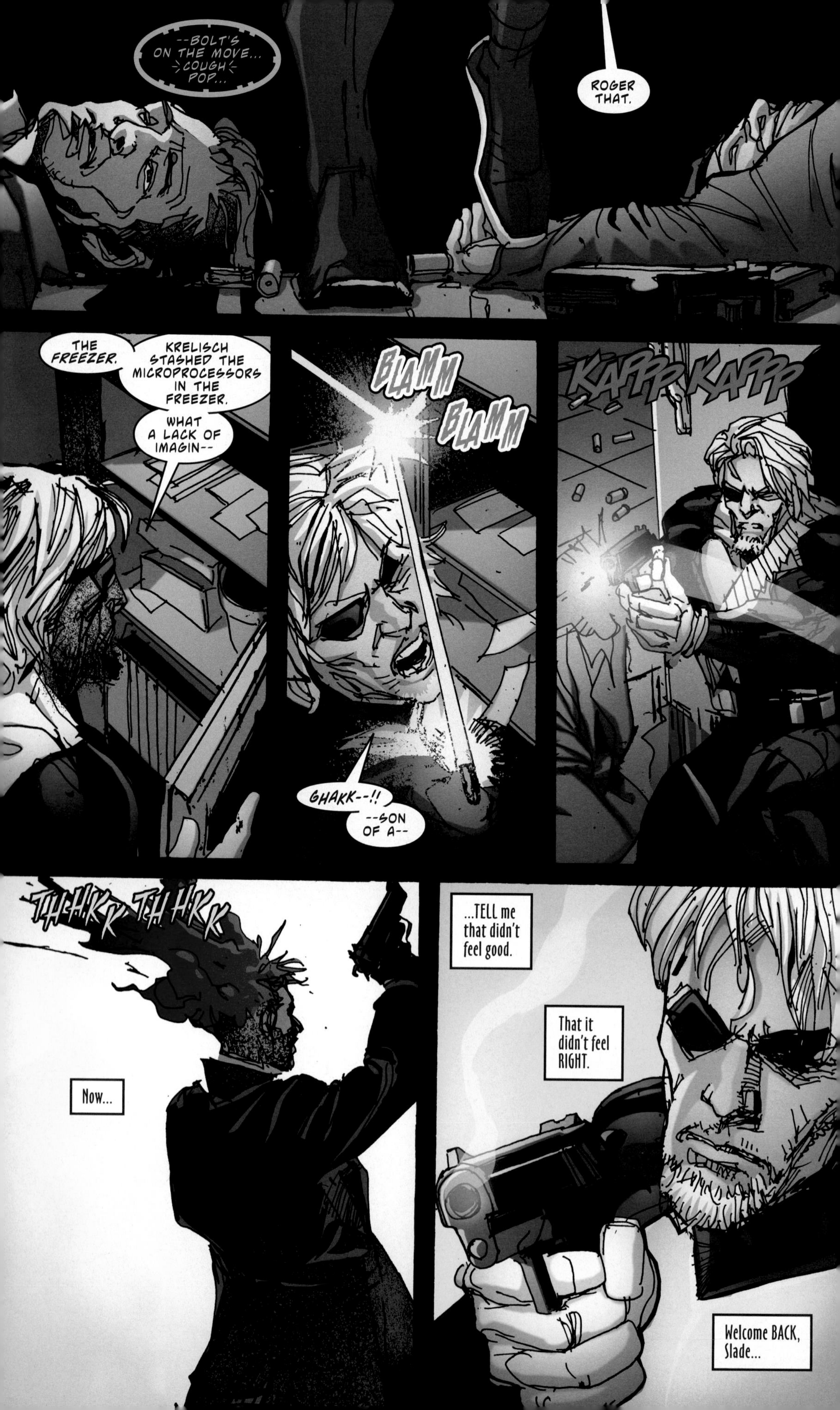
--BOLT'S ON THE MOVE... COUGH POP...
ROGER THAT.
THE FREEZER.
KRELISCH STASHED THE MICROPROCESSORS IN THE FREEZER.
WHAT A LACK OF IMAGIN--
BLAMM
BLAMM
GHAKK--!!
--SON OF A--
KAPPP KAPPP
THHKK THHKK
Now...
...TELL me that didn't feel good.
That it didn't feel RIGHT.
Welcome BACK, Slade...

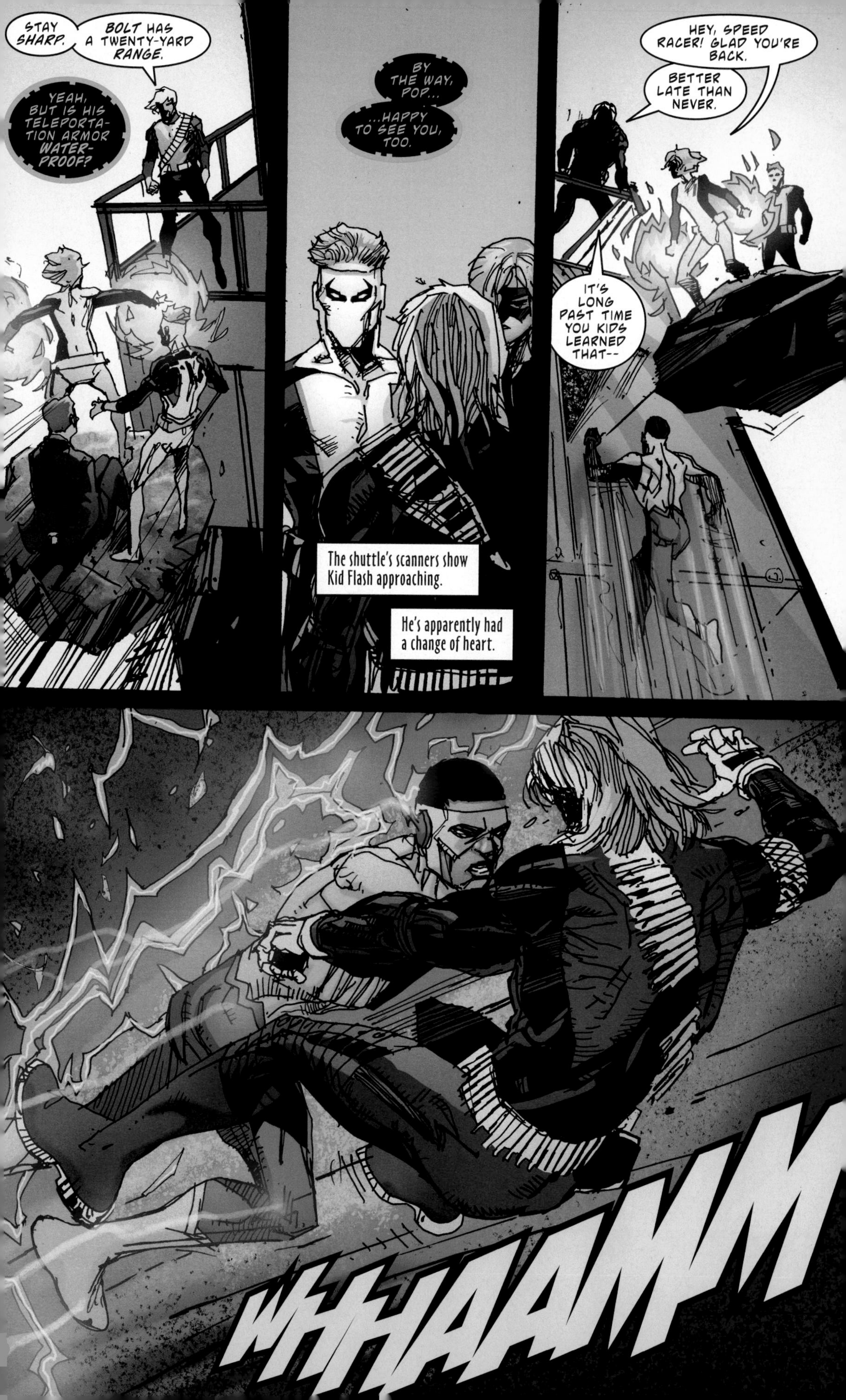

STAY SHARP.
BOLT HAS A TWENTY-YARD RANGE.
YEAH, BUT IS HIS TELEPORTATION ARMOR WATERPROOF?
BY THE WAY, POP...
...HAPPY TO SEE YOU, TOO.
The shuttle's scanners show Kid Flash approaching.
He's apparently had a change of heart.
HEY, SPEED RACER! GLAD YOU'RE BACK.
BETTER LATE THAN NEVER.
IT'S LONG PAST TIME YOU KIDS LEARNED THAT--
WHAAMM

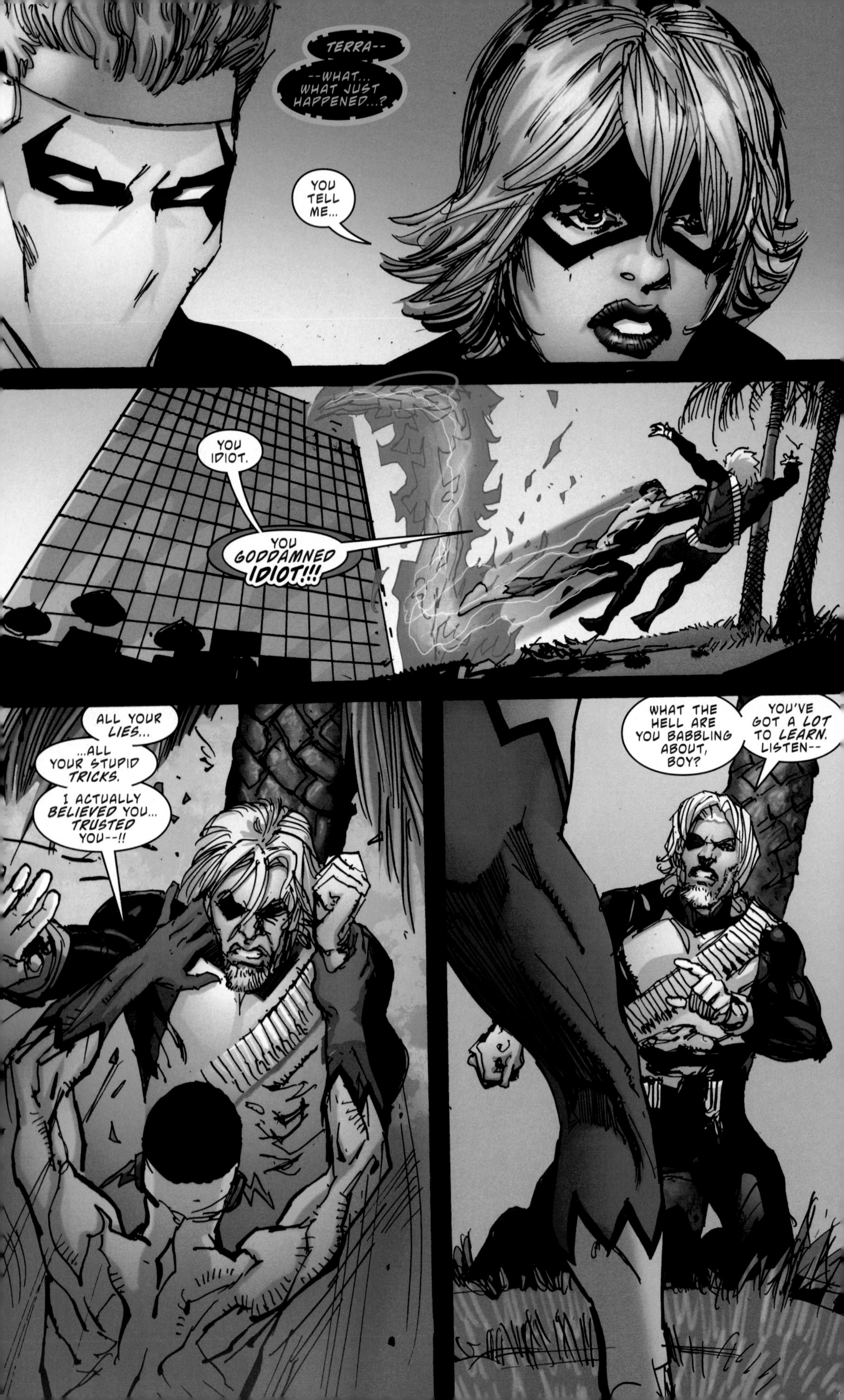
TERRA--
--WHAT... WHAT JUST HAPPENED...?
YOU TELL ME...
YOU IDIOT.
YOU GODDAMNED IDIOT!!!
ALL YOUR LIES...
...ALL YOUR STUPID TRICKS.
I ACTUALLY BELIEVED YOU... TRUSTED YOU--!!
WHAT THE HELL ARE YOU BABBLING ABOUT, BOY?
YOU'VE GOT A LOT TO LEARN. LISTEN--

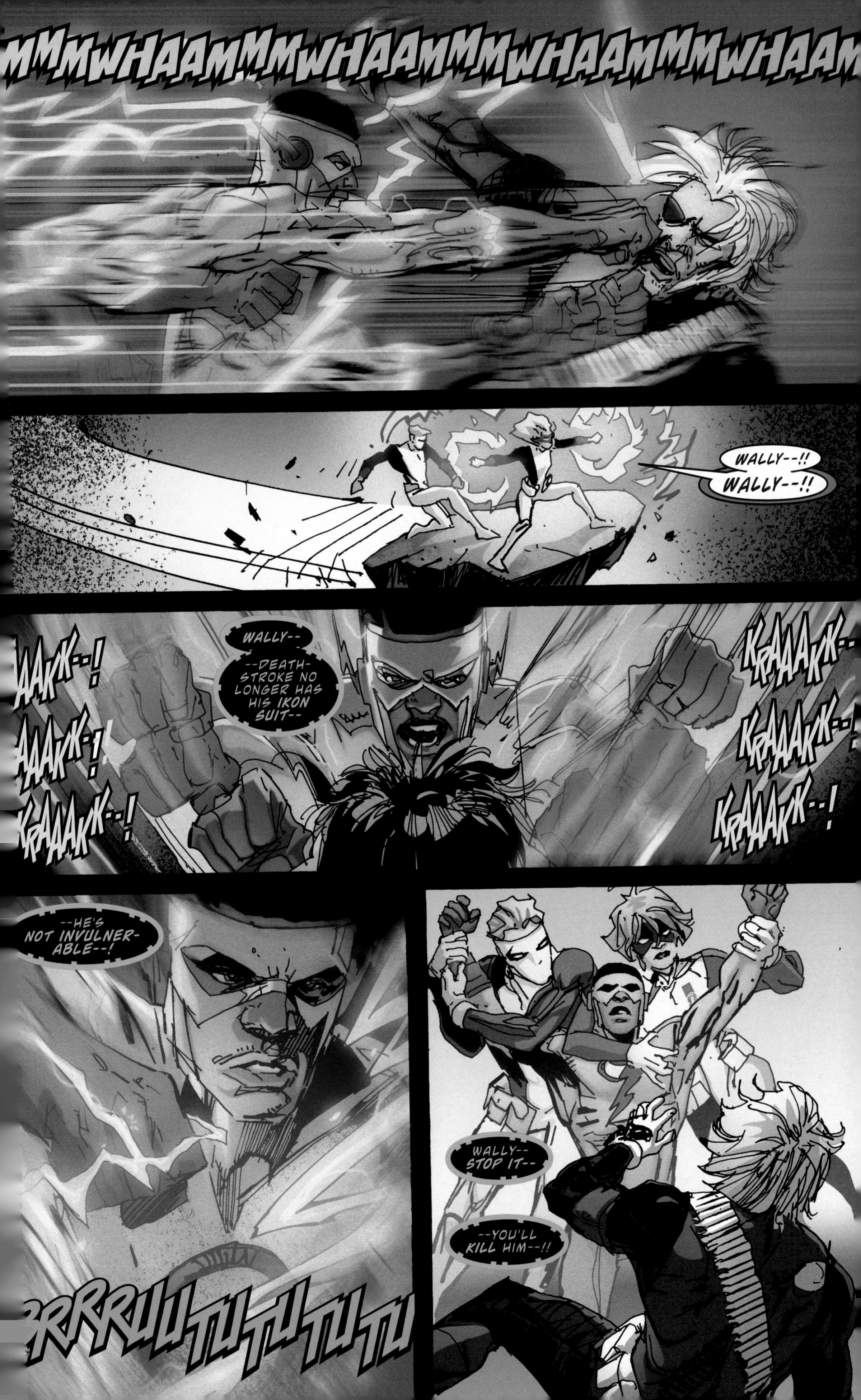
MMMWHAAMMMWHAAMMMWHAAMMMWHAAM
WALLY--!!
WALLY--!!
AAKK--!
AAAKK--!
KRAAAKK--!
WALLY--
--DEATH-STROKE NO LONGER HAS HIS IKON SUIT--
KRAAAKK--
KRAAAKK--!
KRAAAKK--!
--HE'S NOT INVULNERABLE--!
RRRUUTUTUTUTU
WALLY-- STOP IT--
--YOU'LL KILL HIM--!!

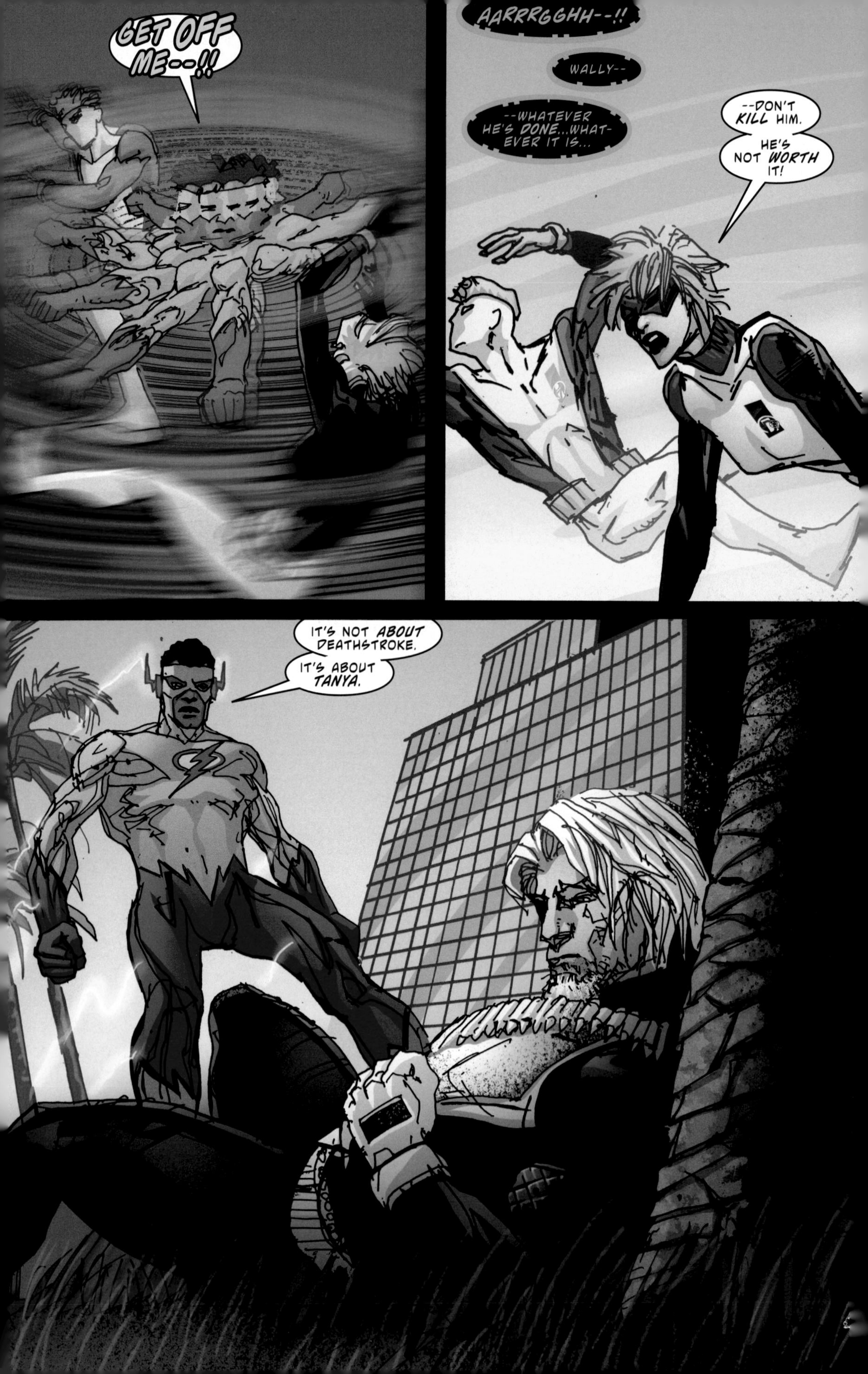
GET OFF ME--!!
AARRRGGHH--!!
WALLY--
--WHATEVER HE'S DONE...WHATEVER IT IS...
--DON'T KILL HIM.
HE'S NOT WORTH IT!
IT'S NOT ABOUT DEATHSTROKE.
IT'S ABOUT TANYA.

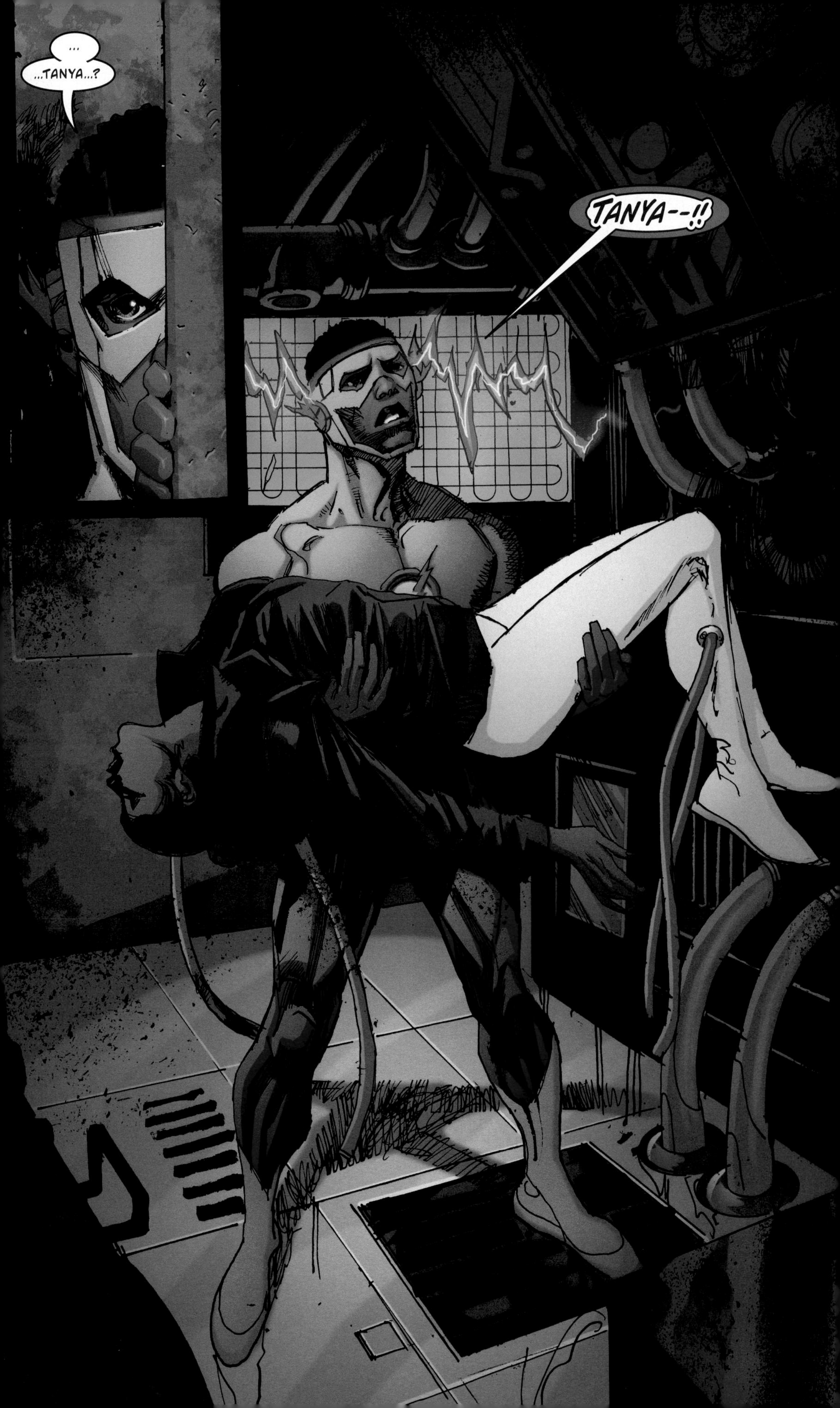
...
...TANYA...?
TANYA--!!

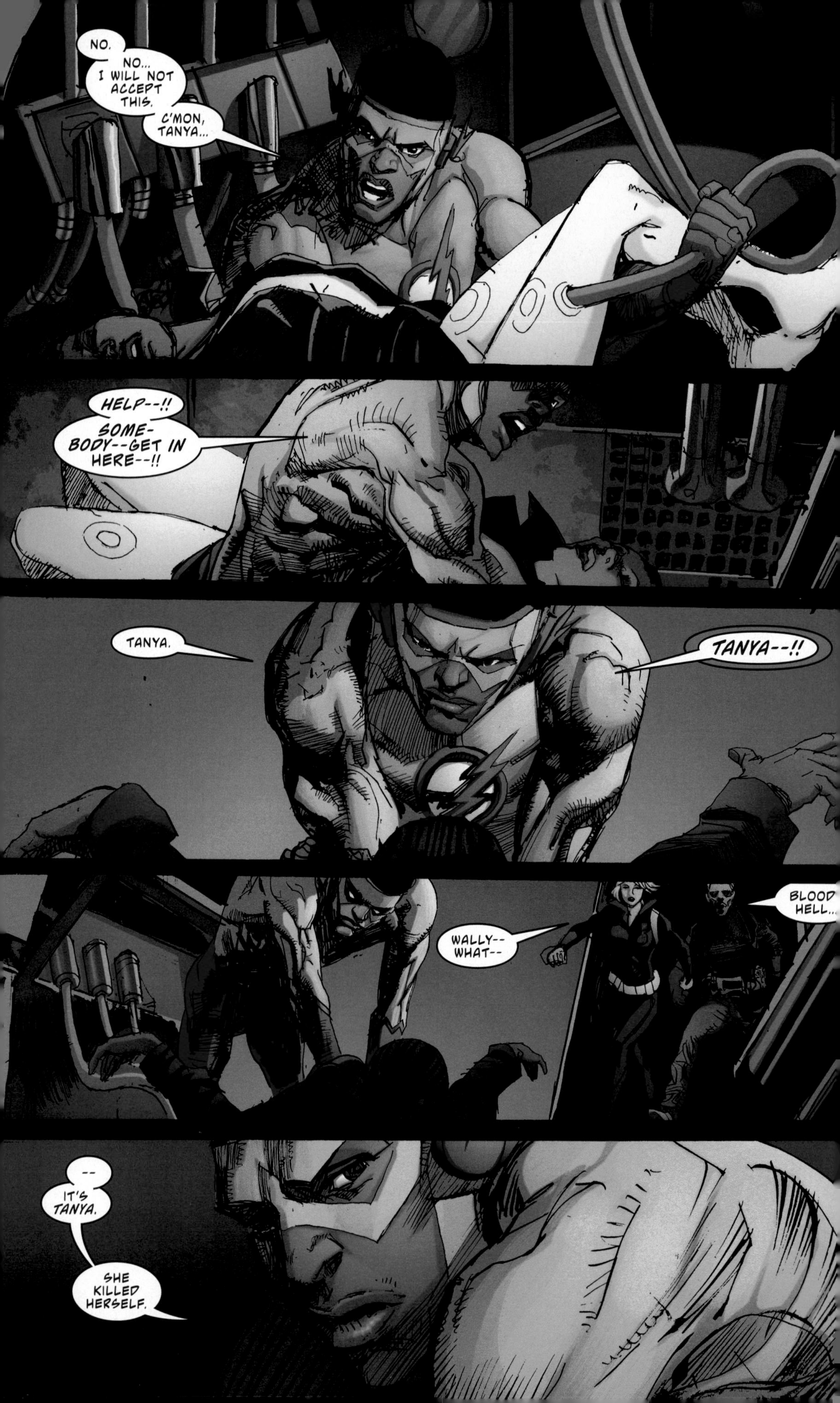
NO.
NO... I WILL NOT ACCEPT THIS.
C'MON, TANYA...
HELP--!! SOME-BODY--GET IN HERE--!!
TANYA.
TANYA--!!
WALLY-- WHAT--
BLOOD HELL...
-- IT'S TANYA.
SHE KILLED HERSELF.

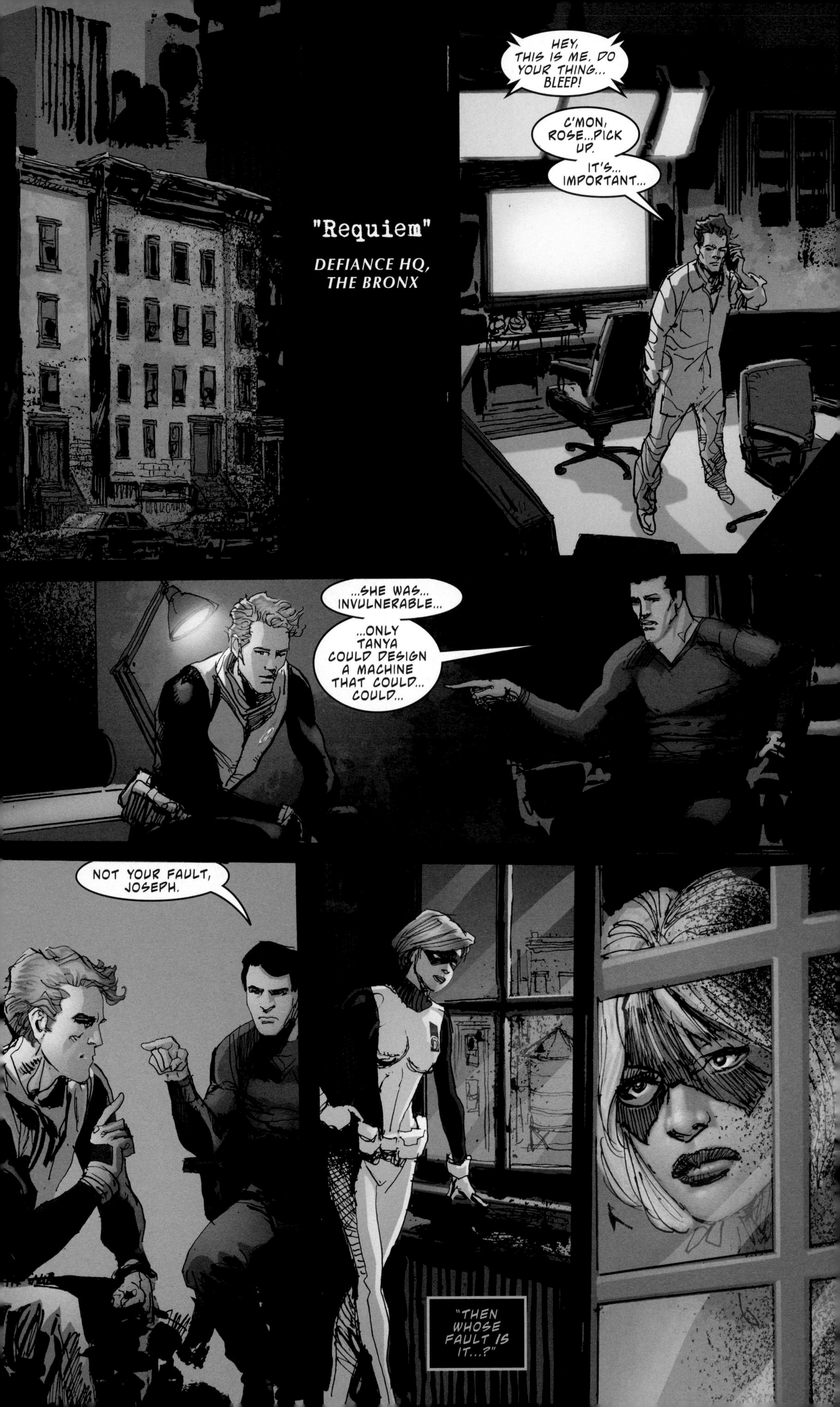
"Requiem"
DEFIANCE HQ, THE BRONX
HEY, THIS IS ME. DO YOUR THING... BLEEP!
C'MON, ROSE...PICK UP.
IT'S... IMPORTANT...
...SHE WAS... INVULNERABLE...
...ONLY TANYA COULD DESIGN A MACHINE THAT COULD... COULD...
NOT YOUR FAULT, JOSEPH.
"THEN WHOSE FAULT IS IT...?"

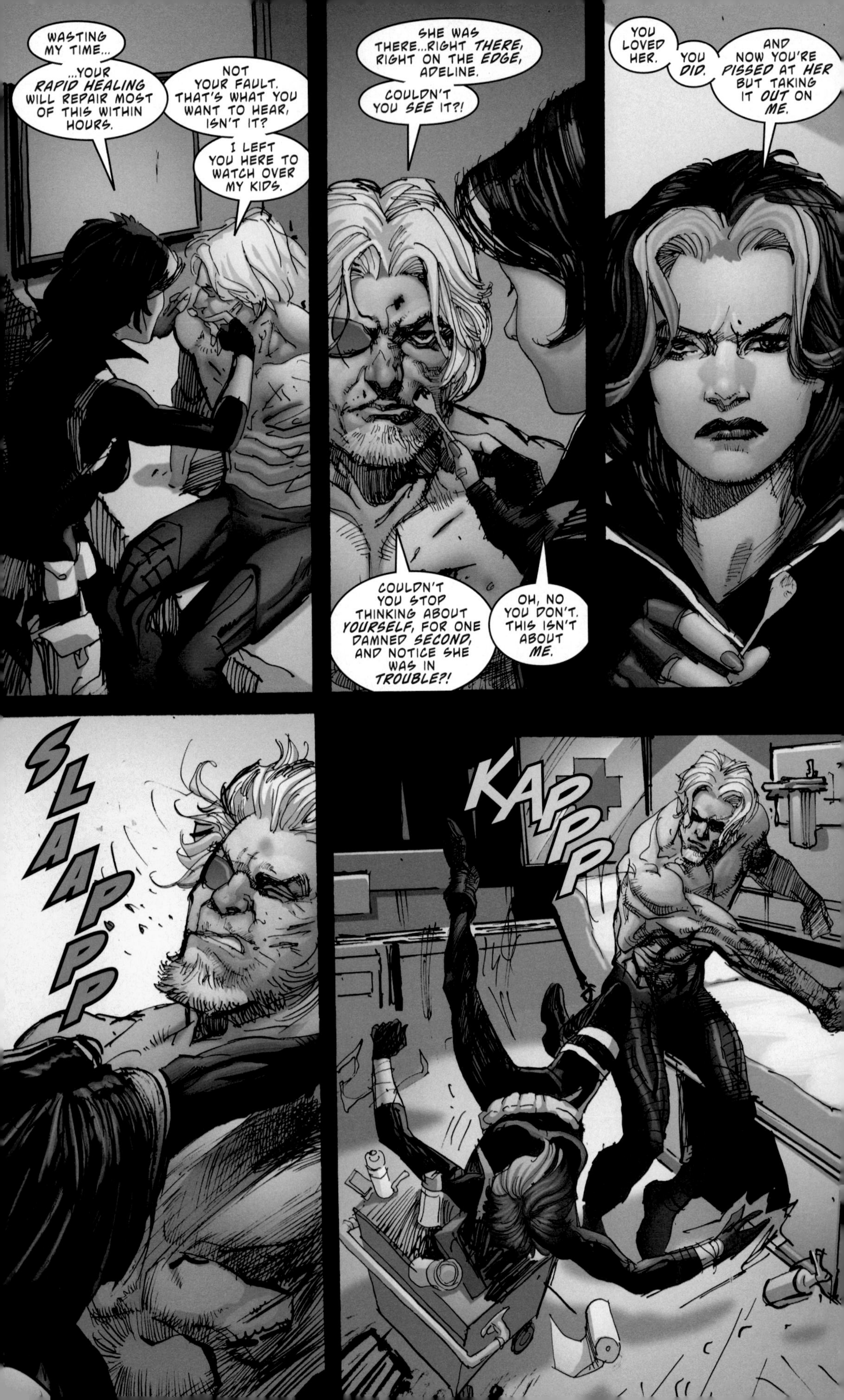

WASTING MY TIME...
...YOUR RAPID HEALING WILL REPAIR MOST OF THIS WITHIN HOURS.
NOT YOUR FAULT. THAT'S WHAT YOU WANT TO HEAR, ISN'T IT?
I LEFT YOU HERE TO WATCH OVER MY KIDS.
SHE WAS THERE...RIGHT THERE, RIGHT ON THE EDGE, ADELINE.
COULDN'T YOU SEE IT?!
COULDN'T YOU STOP THINKING ABOUT YOURSELF, FOR ONE DAMNED SECOND, AND NOTICE SHE WAS IN TROUBLE?!
OH, NO YOU DON'T. THIS ISN'T ABOUT ME.
YOU LOVED HER.
YOU DID.
AND NOW YOU'RE PISSED AT HER BUT TAKING IT OUT ON ME.
SLAAAPPP
KAPPP

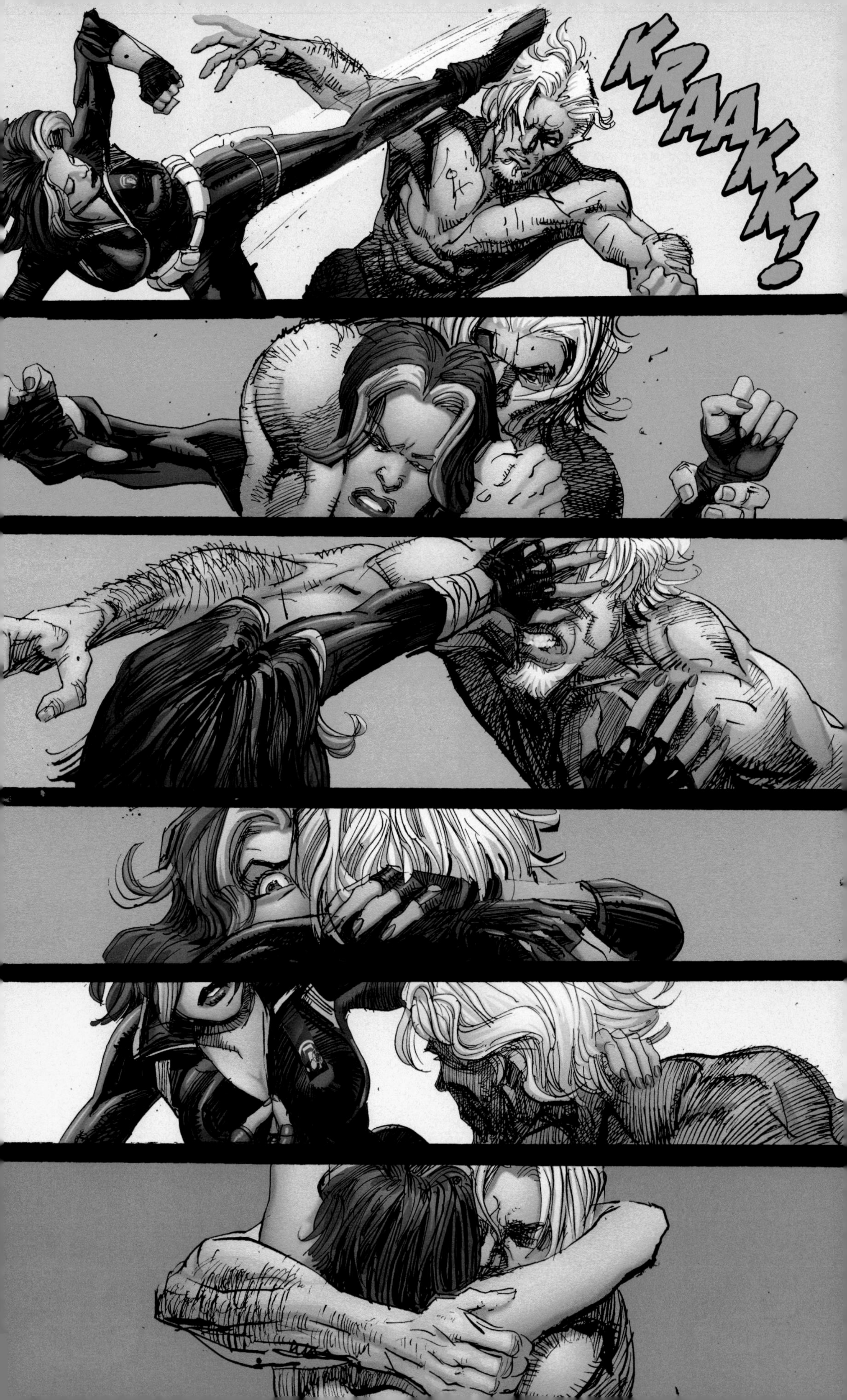
KRAAKK!

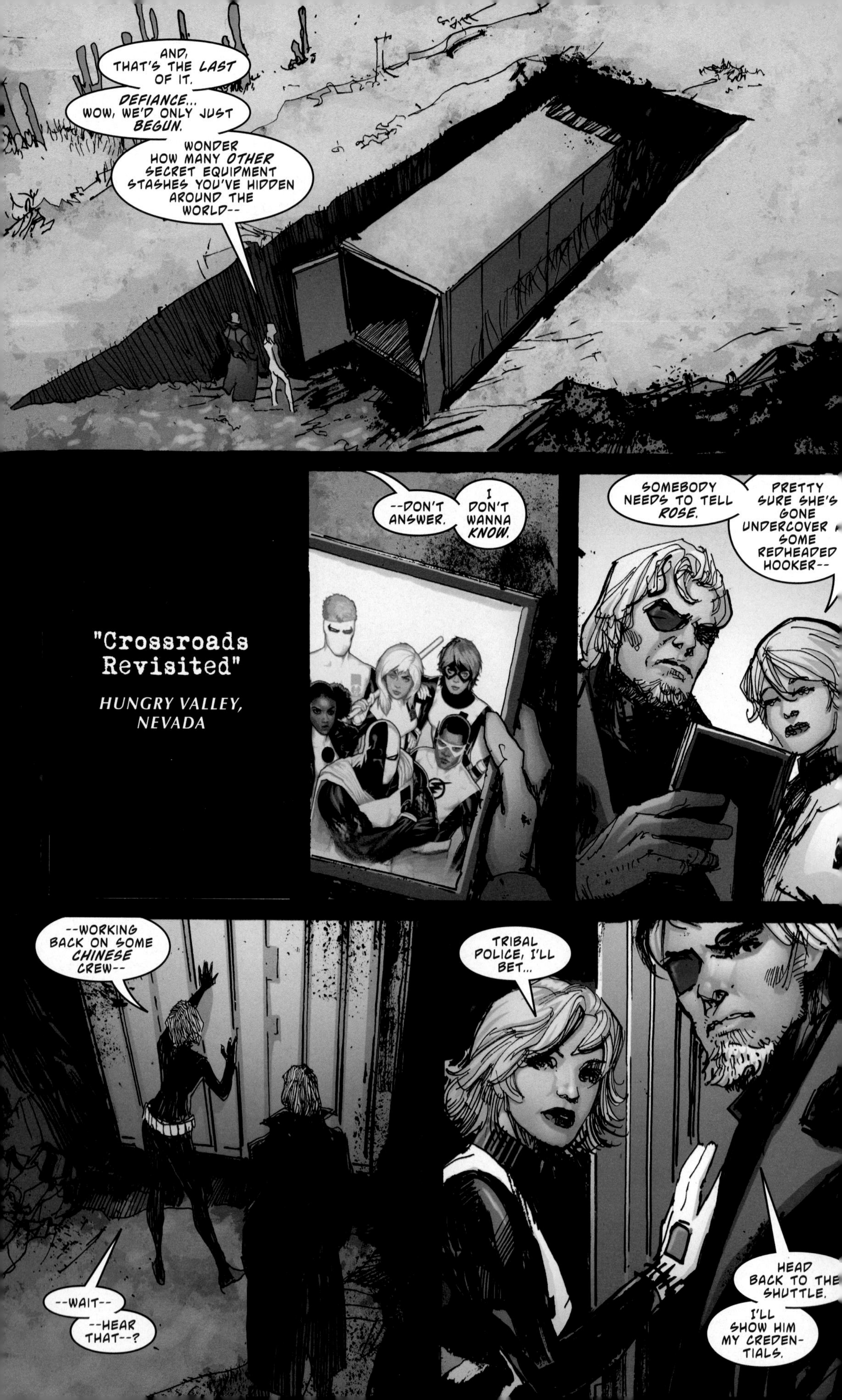
AND, THAT'S THE LAST OF IT.
DEFIANCE... WOW, WE'D ONLY JUST BEGUN.
WONDER HOW MANY OTHER SECRET EQUIPMENT STASHES YOU'VE HIDDEN AROUND THE WORLD--
"Crossroads Revisited"
HUNGRY VALLEY, NEVADA
--DON'T ANSWER.
I DON'T WANNA KNOW.
SOMEBODY NEEDS TO TELL ROSE.
PRETTY SURE SHE'S GONE UNDERCOVER SOME REDHEADED HOOKER--
--WORKING BACK ON SOME CHINESE CREW--
--WAIT--
--HEAR THAT--?
TRIBAL POLICE, I'LL BET...
HEAD BACK TO THE SHUTTLE.
I'LL SHOW HIM MY CREDEN-TIALS.

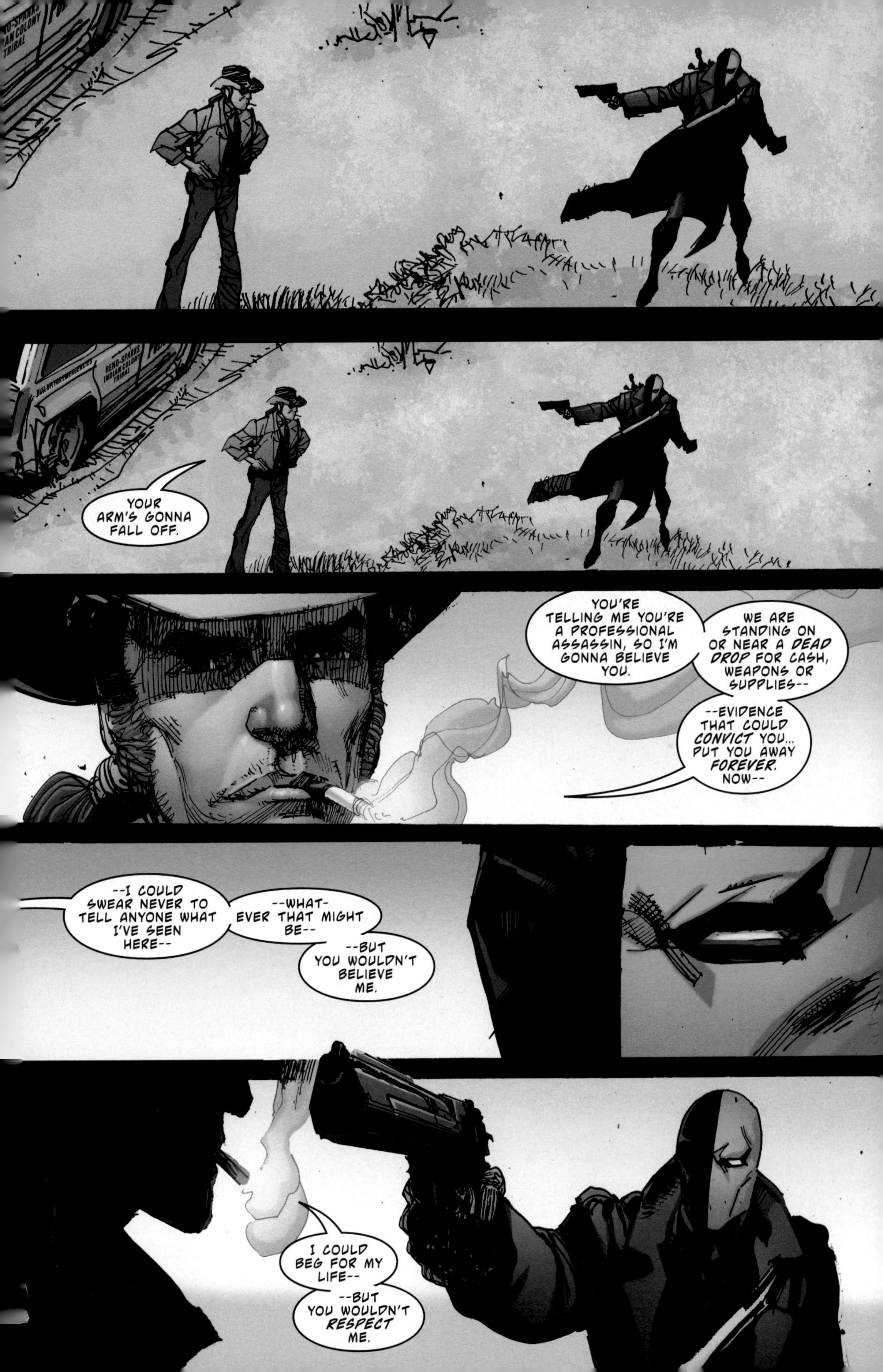
YOUR ARM'S GONNA FALL OFF.
YOU'RE TELLING ME YOU'RE A PROFESSIONAL ASSASSIN, SO I'M GONNA BELIEVE YOU.
WE ARE STANDING ON OR NEAR A *DEAD DROP* FOR CASH, WEAPONS OR SUPPLIES--
--EVIDENCE THAT COULD *CONVICT* YOU... PUT YOU AWAY *FOREVER.* NOW--
--I COULD SWEAR NEVER TO TELL ANYONE WHAT I'VE SEEN HERE--
--WHAT-EVER THAT MIGHT BE--
--BUT YOU WOULDN'T BELIEVE ME.
I COULD BEG FOR MY LIFE--
--BUT YOU WOULDN'T *RESPECT* ME.

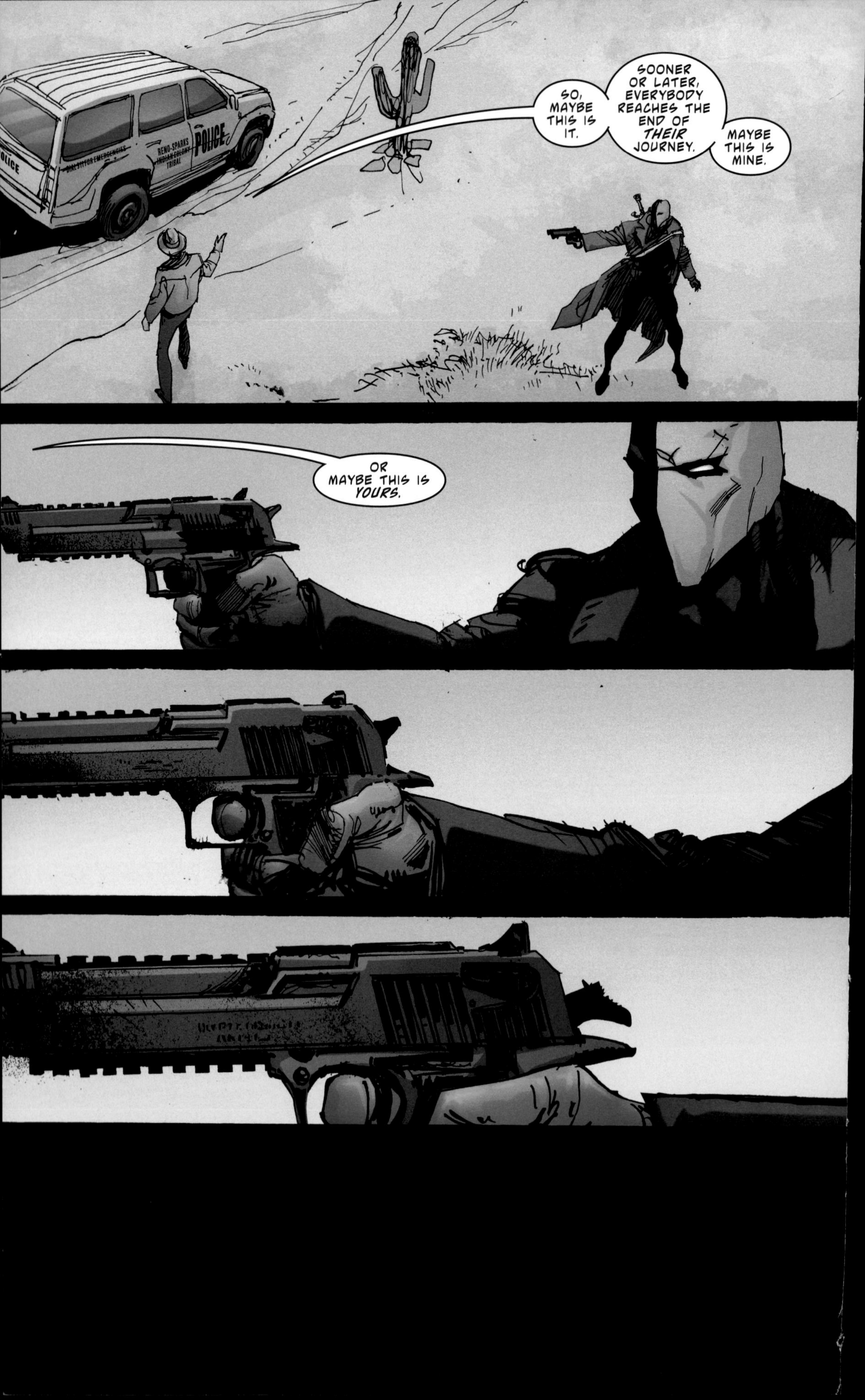
POLICE
SO, MAYBE THIS IS IT.
SOONER OR LATER, EVERYBODY REACHES THE END OF *THEIR* JOURNEY.
MAYBE THIS IS MINE.
OR MAYBE THIS IS *YOURS*.

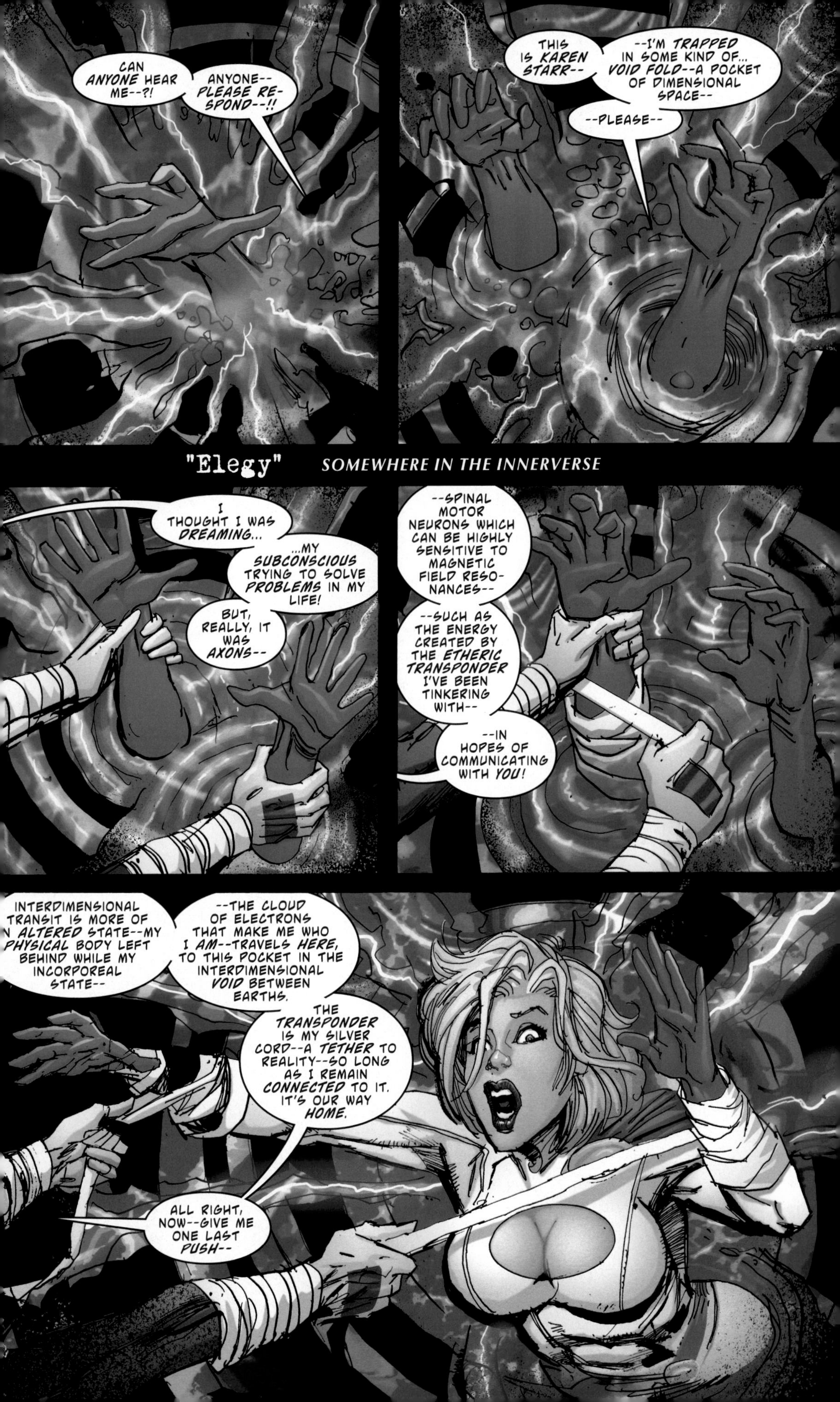
CAN ANYONE HEAR ME--?!
ANYONE-- PLEASE RESPOND--!!
THIS IS KAREN STARR--
--I'M TRAPPED IN SOME KIND OF... VOID FOLD--A POCKET OF DIMENSIONAL SPACE--
--PLEASE--
"Elegy" SOMEWHERE IN THE INNERVERSE
I THOUGHT I WAS DREAMING...
...MY SUBCONSCIOUS TRYING TO SOLVE PROBLEMS IN MY LIFE!
BUT, REALLY, IT WAS AXONS--
--SPINAL MOTOR NEURONS WHICH CAN BE HIGHLY SENSITIVE TO MAGNETIC FIELD RESONANCES--
--SUCH AS THE ENERGY CREATED BY THE ETHERIC TRANSPONDER I'VE BEEN TINKERING WITH--
--IN HOPES OF COMMUNICATING WITH YOU!
INTERDIMENSIONAL TRANSIT IS MORE OF AN ALTERED STATE--MY PHYSICAL BODY LEFT BEHIND WHILE MY INCORPOREAL STATE--
--THE CLOUD OF ELECTRONS THAT MAKE ME WHO I AM--TRAVELS HERE, TO THIS POCKET IN THE INTERDIMENSIONAL VOID BETWEEN EARTHS.
THE TRANSPONDER IS MY SILVER CORD--A TETHER TO REALITY--SO LONG AS I REMAIN CONNECTED TO IT. IT'S OUR WAY HOME.
ALL RIGHT, NOW--GIVE ME ONE LAST PUSH--

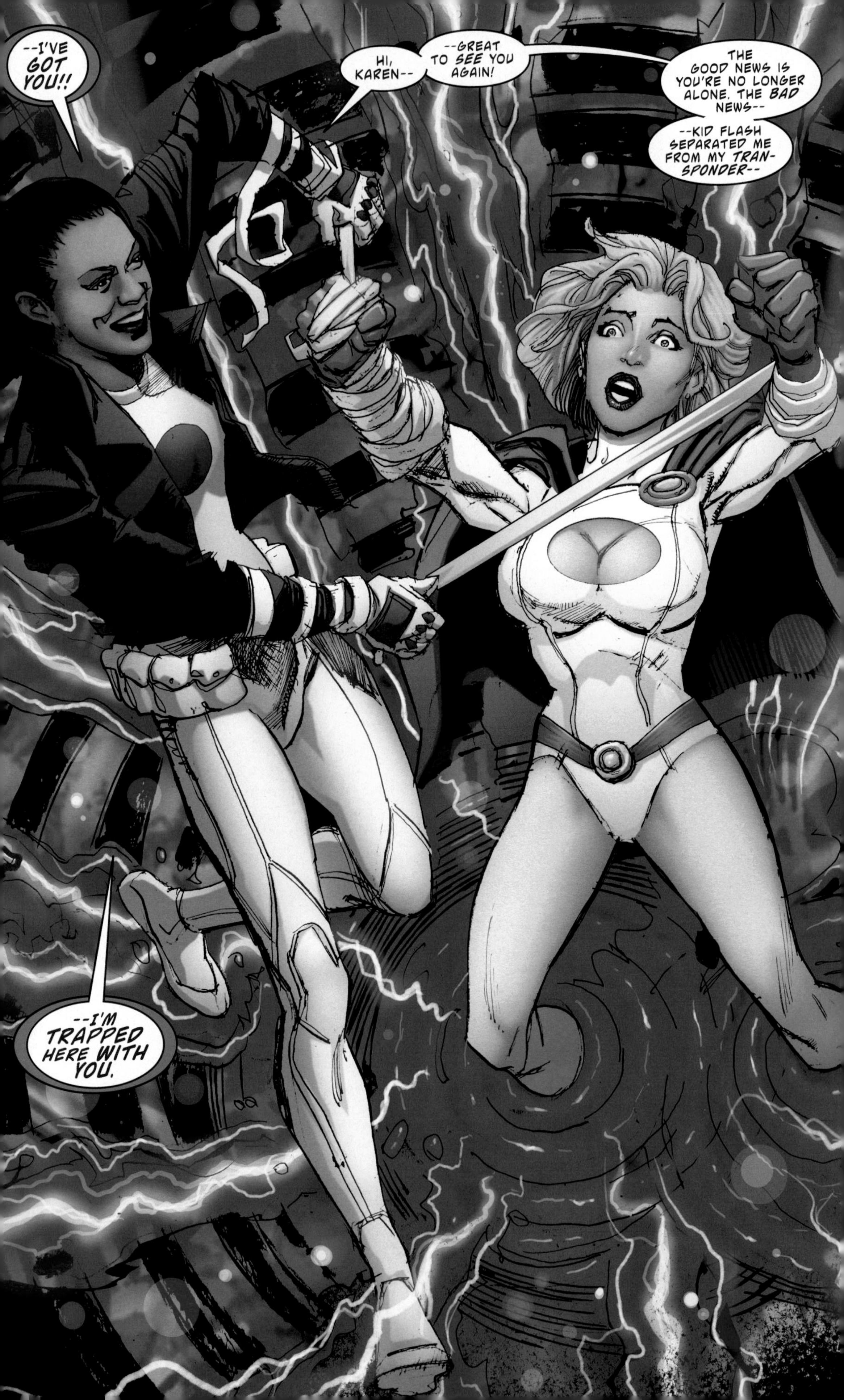
--I'VE GOT YOU!!
HI, KAREN--
--GREAT TO SEE YOU AGAIN!
THE GOOD NEWS IS YOU'RE NO LONGER ALONE. THE BAD NEWS--
--KID FLASH SEPARATED ME FROM MY TRANS-PONDER--
--I'M TRAPPED HERE WITH YOU.

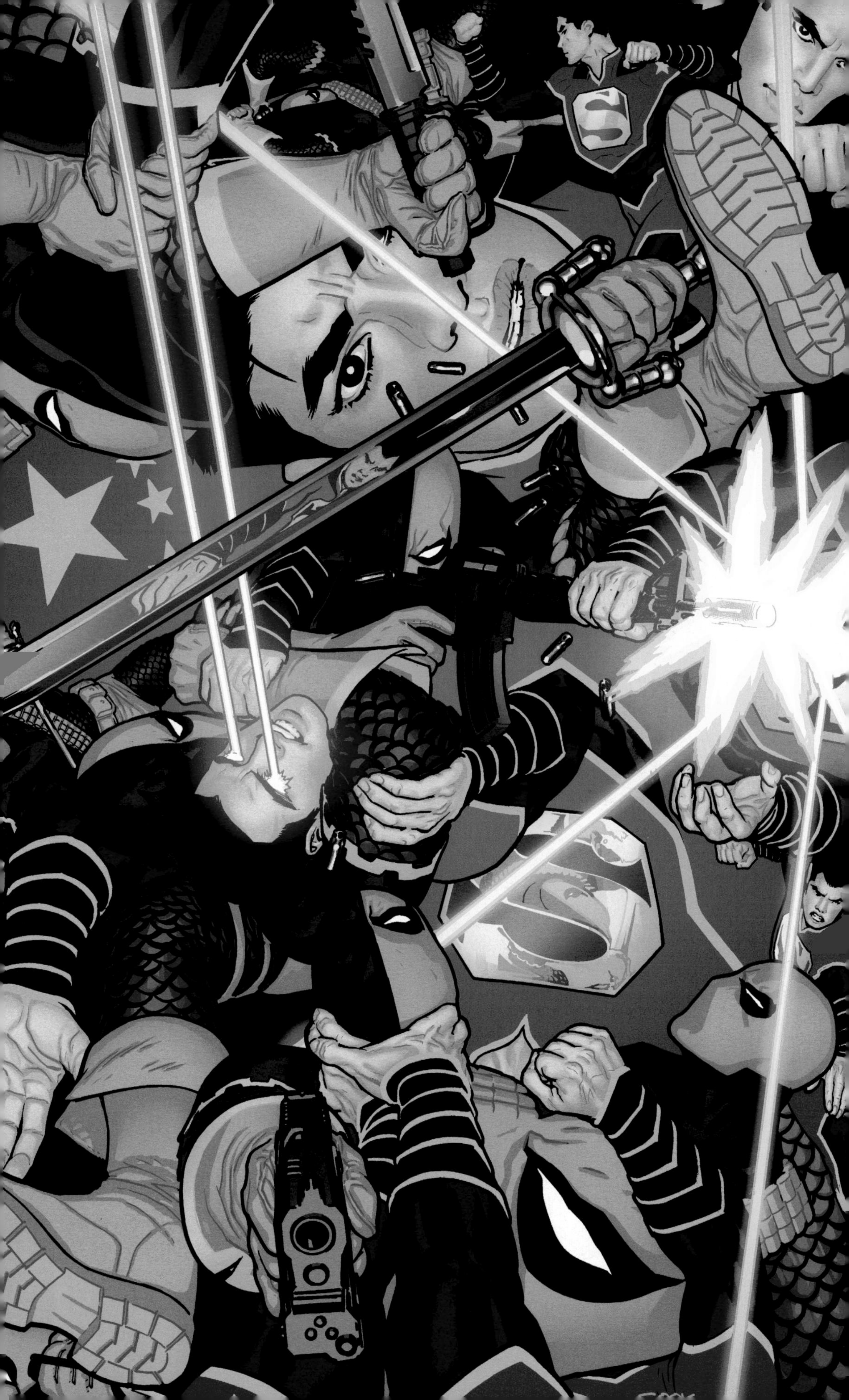

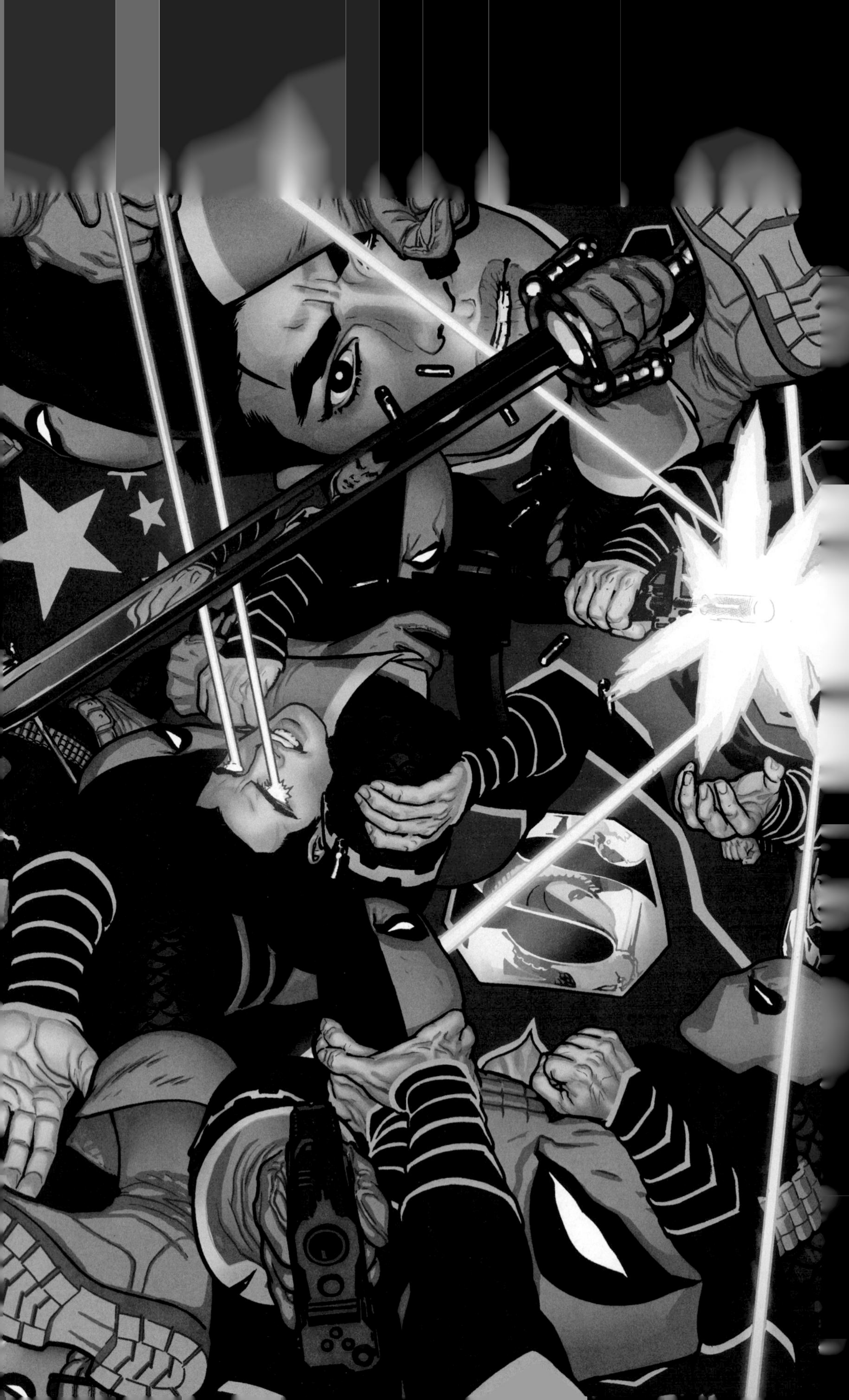

...THE SWORD DATES FROM THE ZHOU DYNASTY OF CHINA, ABOUT 232 BC. IT BELONGED TO NKAUJ NTXUAM--

--A HMONG WARRIOR PRINCESS, A KIND OF JOAN OF ARC, WHO WAS TORTURED AND KILLED.

"Failsafe"

MINNEAPOLIS
955 YEARS FROM NOW

TO PRESERVE THE HEIRLOOM, WE'VE PLATED IT OVER WITH *INERTRON*--

--WHICH REFLECTS 100 PERCENT OF HEAT AND LIGHT.

IT ALSO MAKES AN EFFECTIVE *ANTIGRAVITY* AGENT, AND IS USED IN THIS TRANSPORT...

"Priceless"

MINNEAPOLIS
ONE YEAR AGO

GIVE YA TEN BUCKS FOR IT.

BUT IT'S A FAMILY HEIRLOOM-- HISTORICAL-- PRICELESS--

IT'S GOT A PRICE HERE, PALLY. TEN BUCKS.

DONE.

WHOOOOSH!

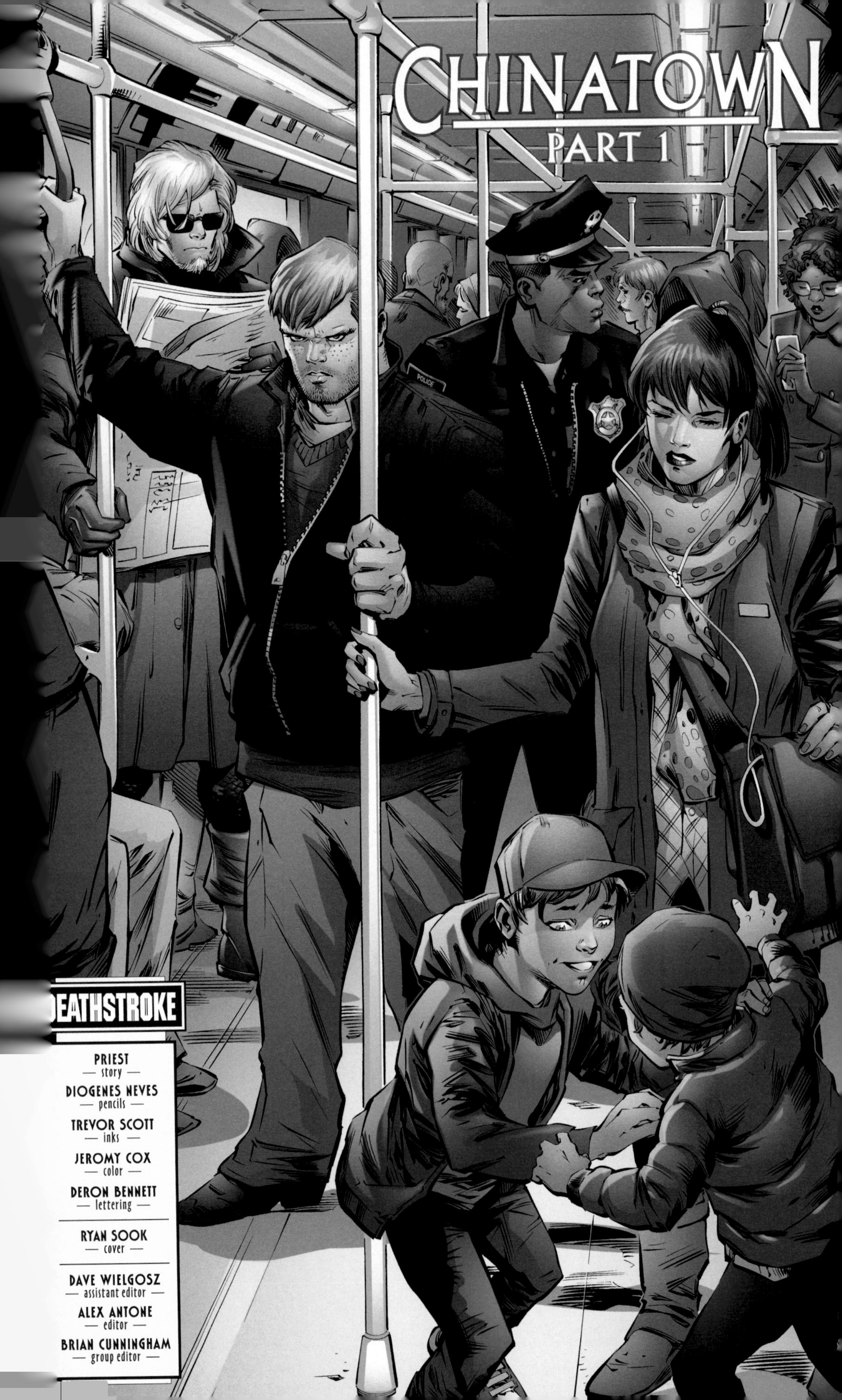

CHINATOWN
PART 1
POLICE
DEATHSTROKE
PRIEST
— story —
DIOGENES NEVES
— pencils —
TREVOR SCOTT
— inks —
JEROMY COX
— color —
DERON BENNETT
— lettering —
RYAN SOOK
— cover —
DAVE WIELGOSZ
— assistant editor —
ALEX ANTONE
— editor —
BRIAN CUNNINGHAM
— group editor —

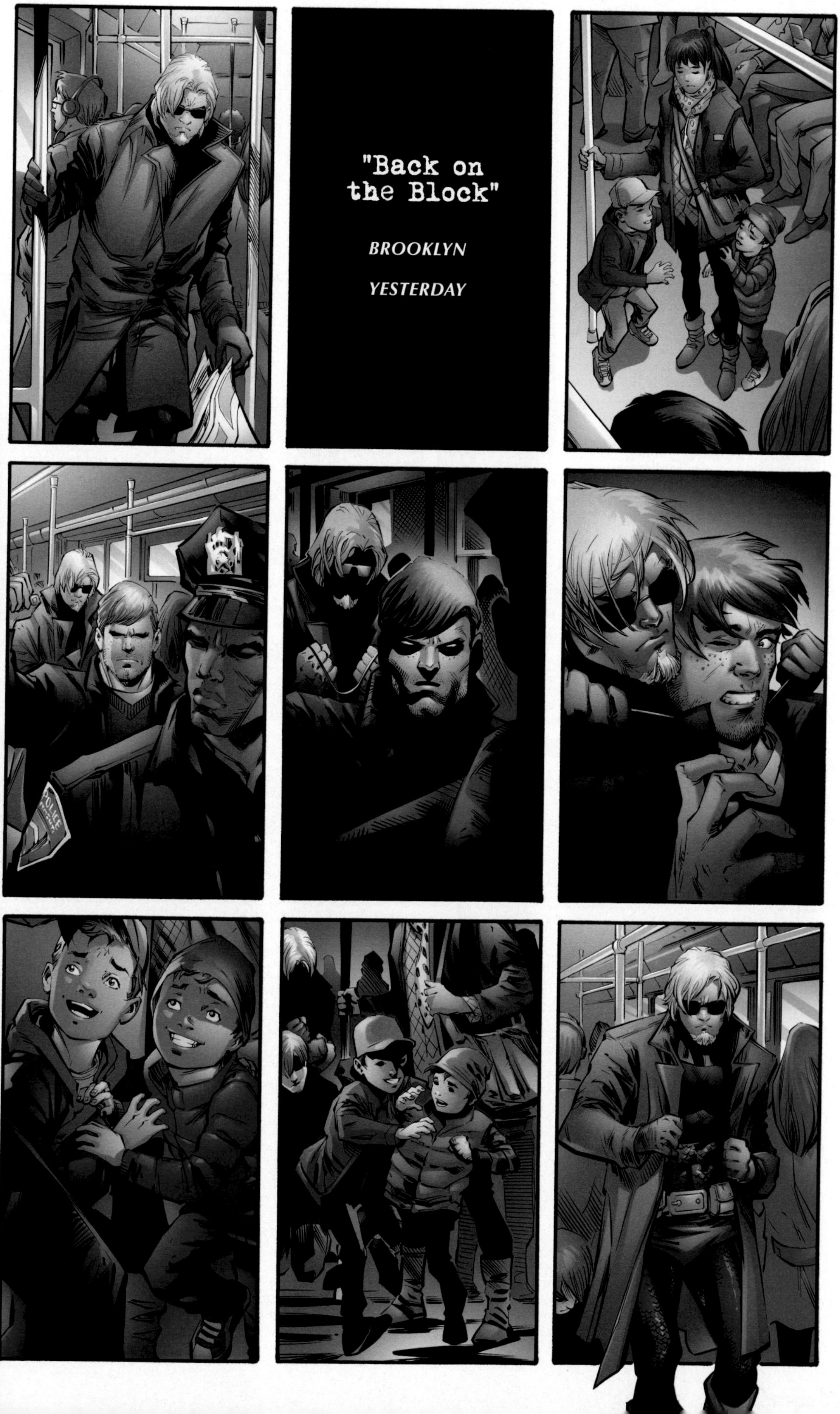
"Back on the Block"
BROOKLYN
YESTERDAY
POLICE

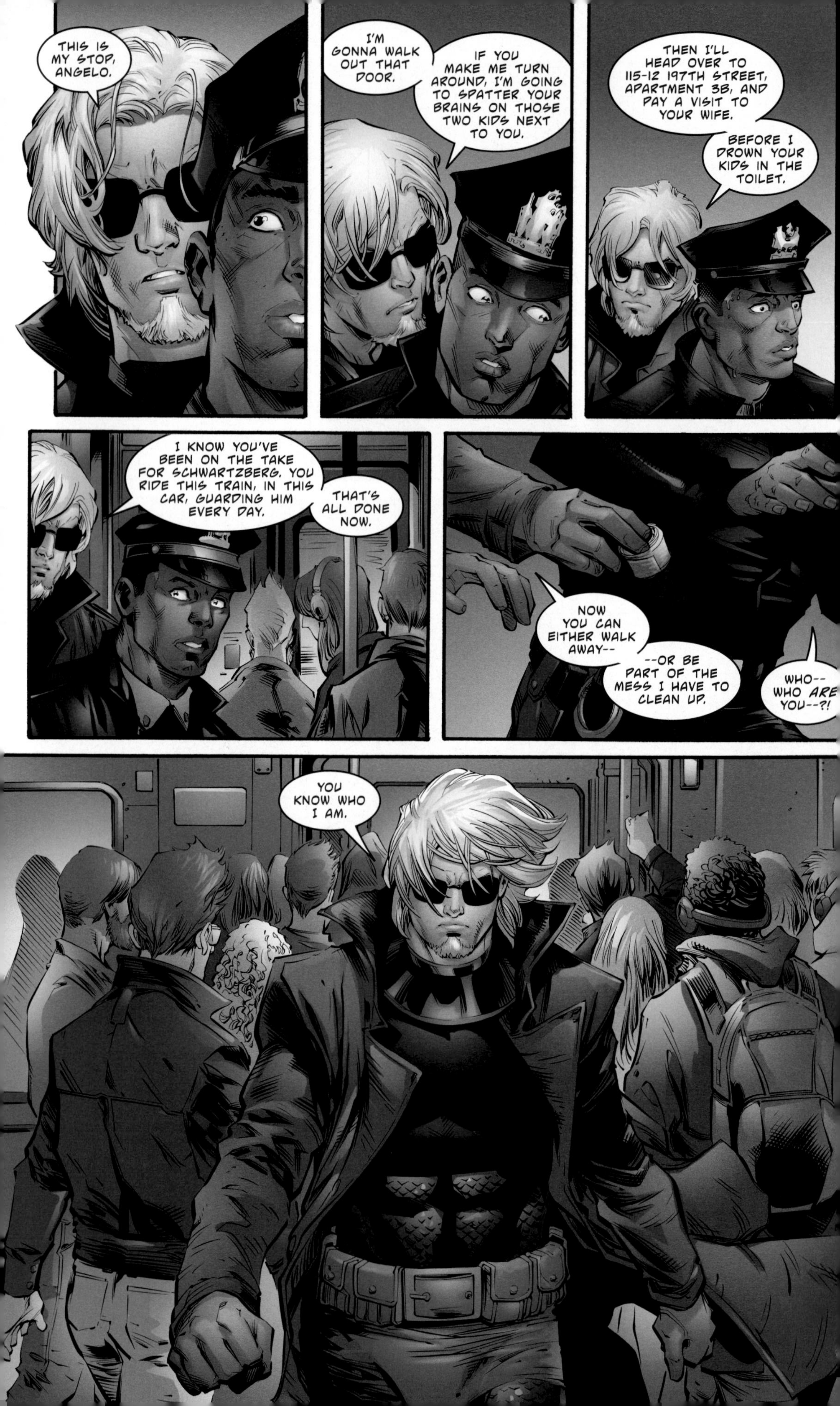

THIS IS MY STOP, ANGELO.
I'M GONNA WALK OUT THAT DOOR.
IF YOU MAKE ME TURN AROUND, I'M GOING TO SPATTER YOUR BRAINS ON THOSE TWO KIDS NEXT TO YOU.
THEN I'LL HEAD OVER TO 115-12 197TH STREET, APARTMENT 3B, AND PAY A VISIT TO YOUR WIFE.
BEFORE I DROWN YOUR KIDS IN THE TOILET.
I KNOW YOU'VE BEEN ON THE TAKE FOR SCHWARTZBERG. YOU RIDE THIS TRAIN, IN THIS CAR, GUARDING HIM EVERY DAY.
THAT'S ALL DONE NOW.
NOW YOU CAN EITHER WALK AWAY--
--OR BE PART OF THE MESS I HAVE TO CLEAN UP.
WHO-- WHO *ARE* YOU--?!
YOU KNOW WHO I AM.

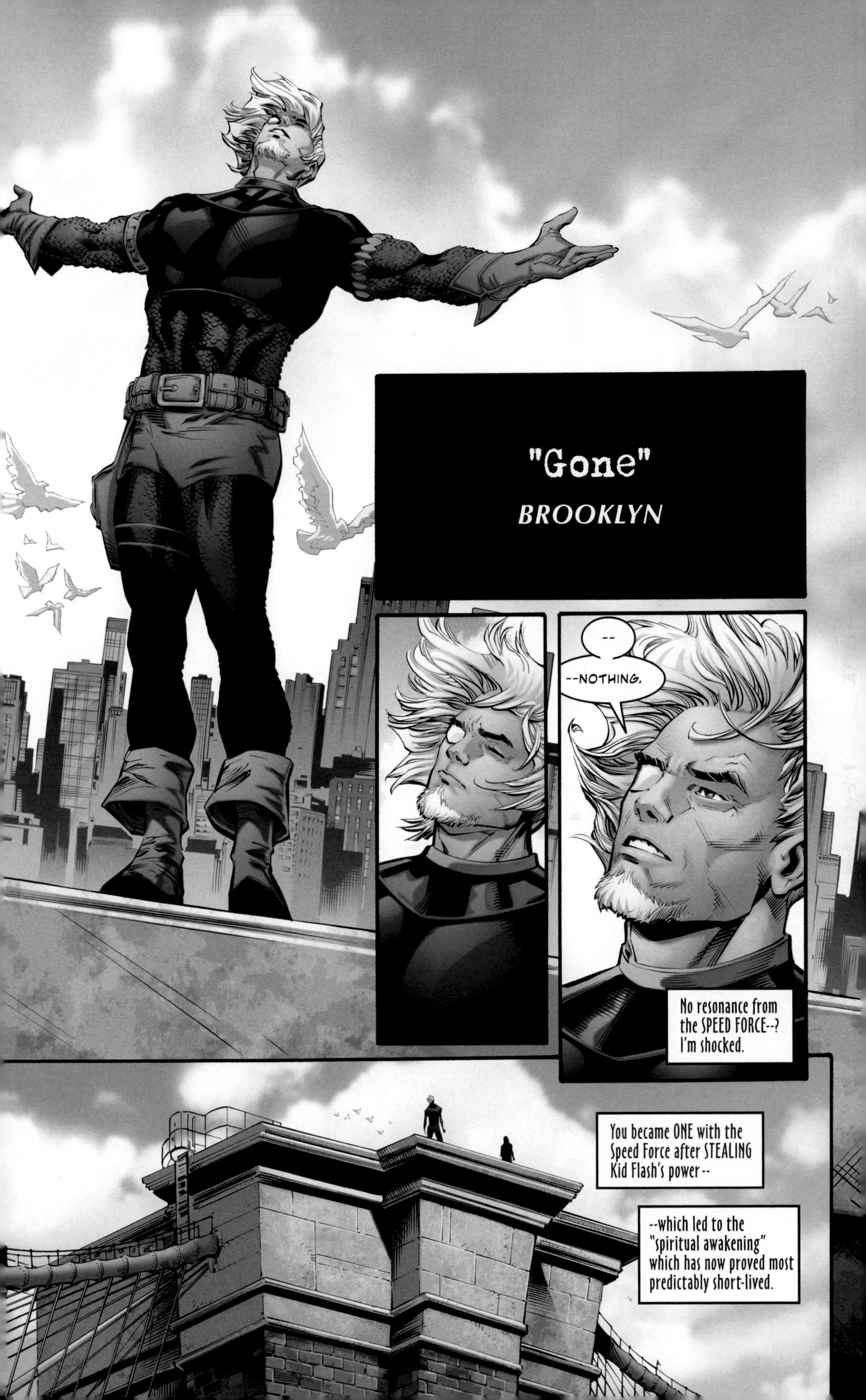
"Gone"
BROOKLYN
--
--NOTHING.
No resonance from the SPEED FORCE--? I'm shocked.
You became ONE with the Speed Force after STEALING Kid Flash's power--
--which led to the "spiritual awakening" which has now proved most predictably short-lived.

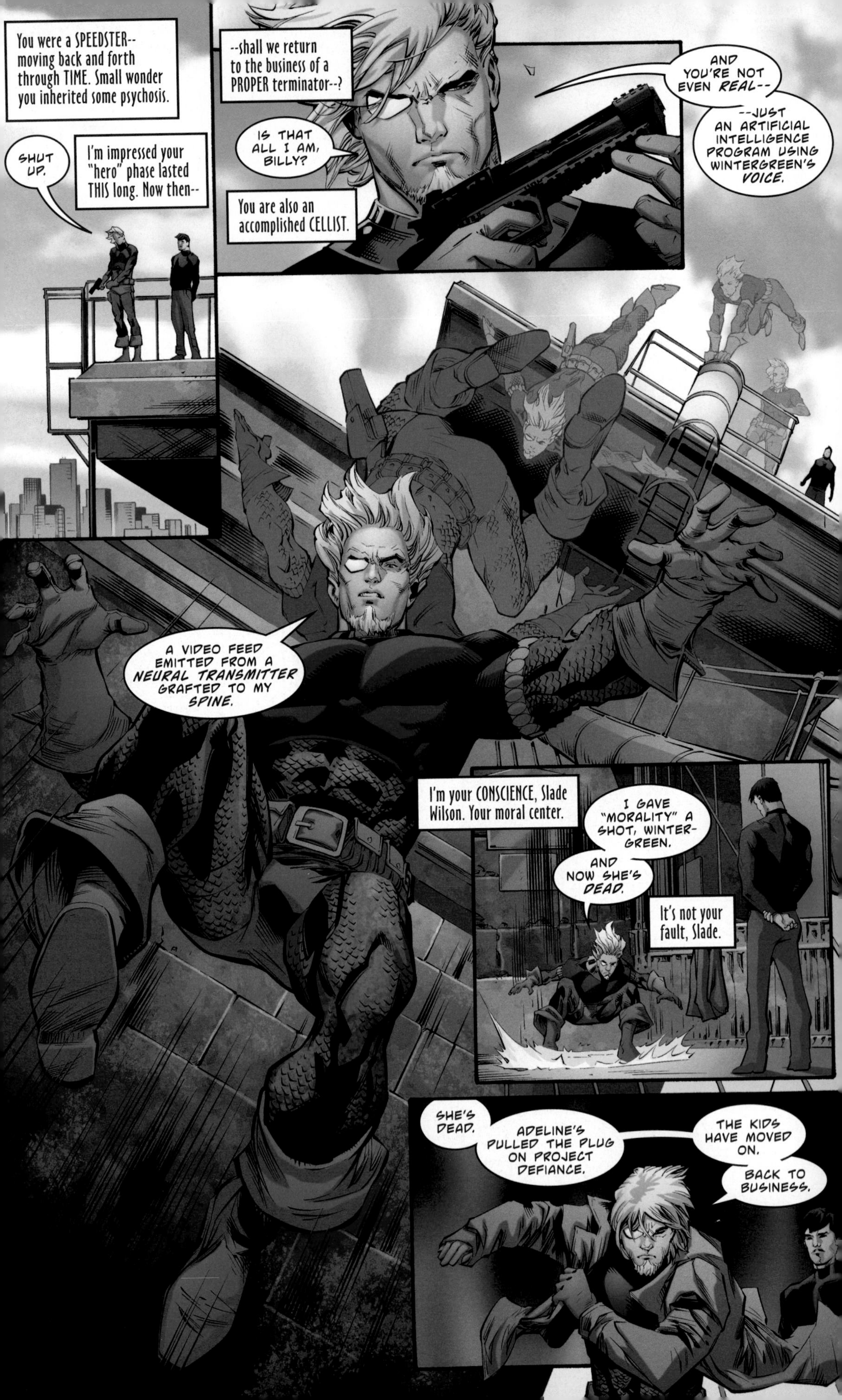
You were a SPEEDSTER--moving back and forth through TIME. Small wonder you inherited some psychosis.
SHUT UP.
I'm impressed your "hero" phase lasted THIS long. Now then--
--shall we return to the business of a PROPER terminator--?
IS THAT ALL I AM, BILLY?
You are also an accomplished CELLIST.
AND YOU'RE NOT EVEN REAL--
--JUST AN ARTIFICIAL INTELLIGENCE PROGRAM USING WINTERGREEN'S VOICE.
A VIDEO FEED EMITTED FROM A NEURAL TRANSMITTER GRAFTED TO MY SPINE.
I'm your CONSCIENCE, Slade Wilson. Your moral center.
I GAVE "MORALITY" A SHOT, WINTER-GREEN.
AND NOW SHE'S DEAD.
It's not your fault, Slade.
SHE'S DEAD.
ADELINE'S PULLED THE PLUG ON PROJECT DEFIANCE.
THE KIDS HAVE MOVED ON.
BACK TO BUSINESS.

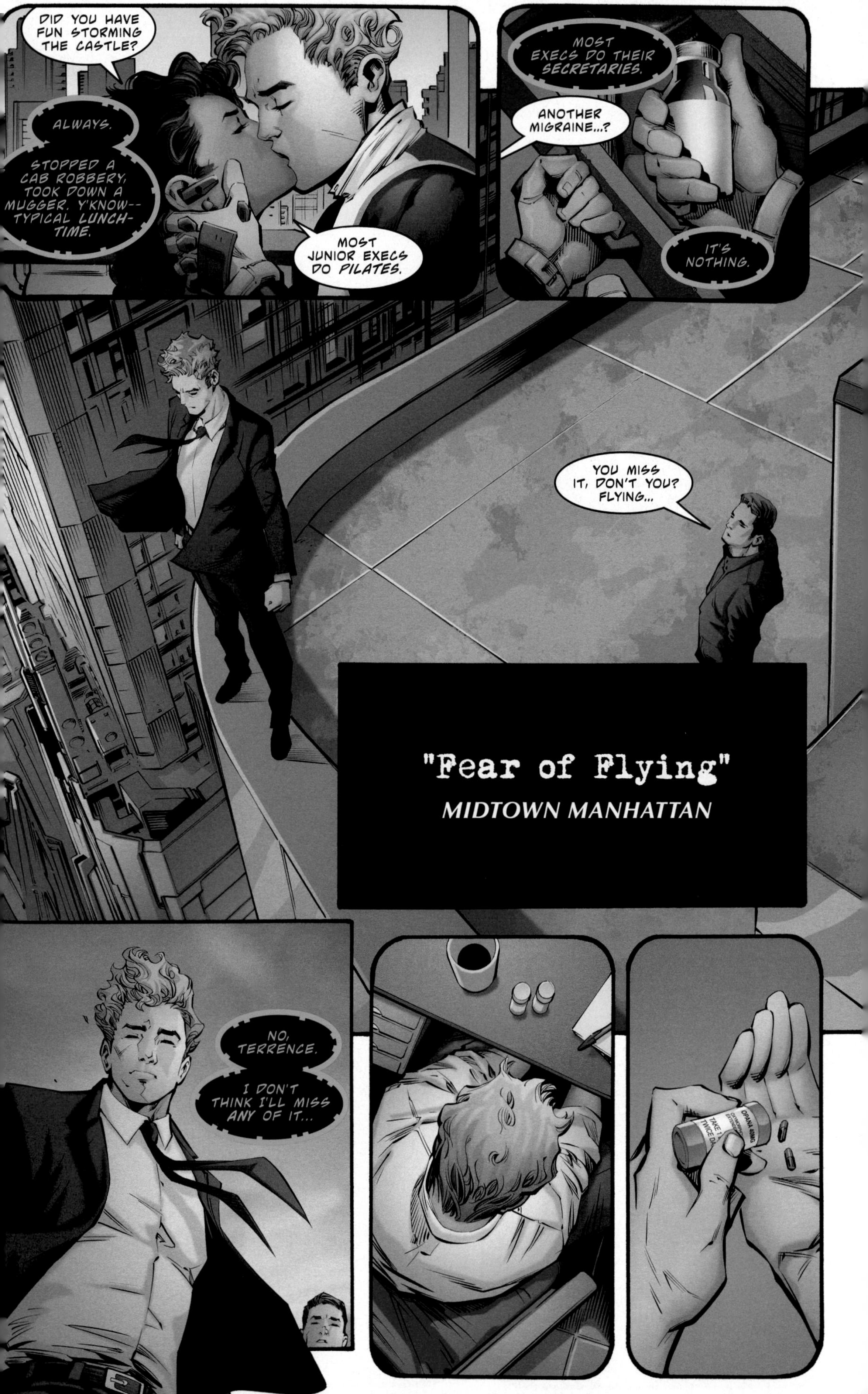
DID YOU HAVE FUN STORMING THE CASTLE?
ALWAYS.
STOPPED A CAB ROBBERY, TOOK DOWN A MUGGER. Y'KNOW--TYPICAL LUNCH-TIME.
MOST JUNIOR EXECS DO PILATES.
MOST EXECS DO THEIR SECRETARIES.
ANOTHER MIGRAINE...?
IT'S NOTHING.
YOU MISS IT, DON'T YOU? FLYING...
"Fear of Flying"
MIDTOWN MANHATTAN
NO, TERRENCE.
I DON'T THINK I'LL MISS ANY OF IT...

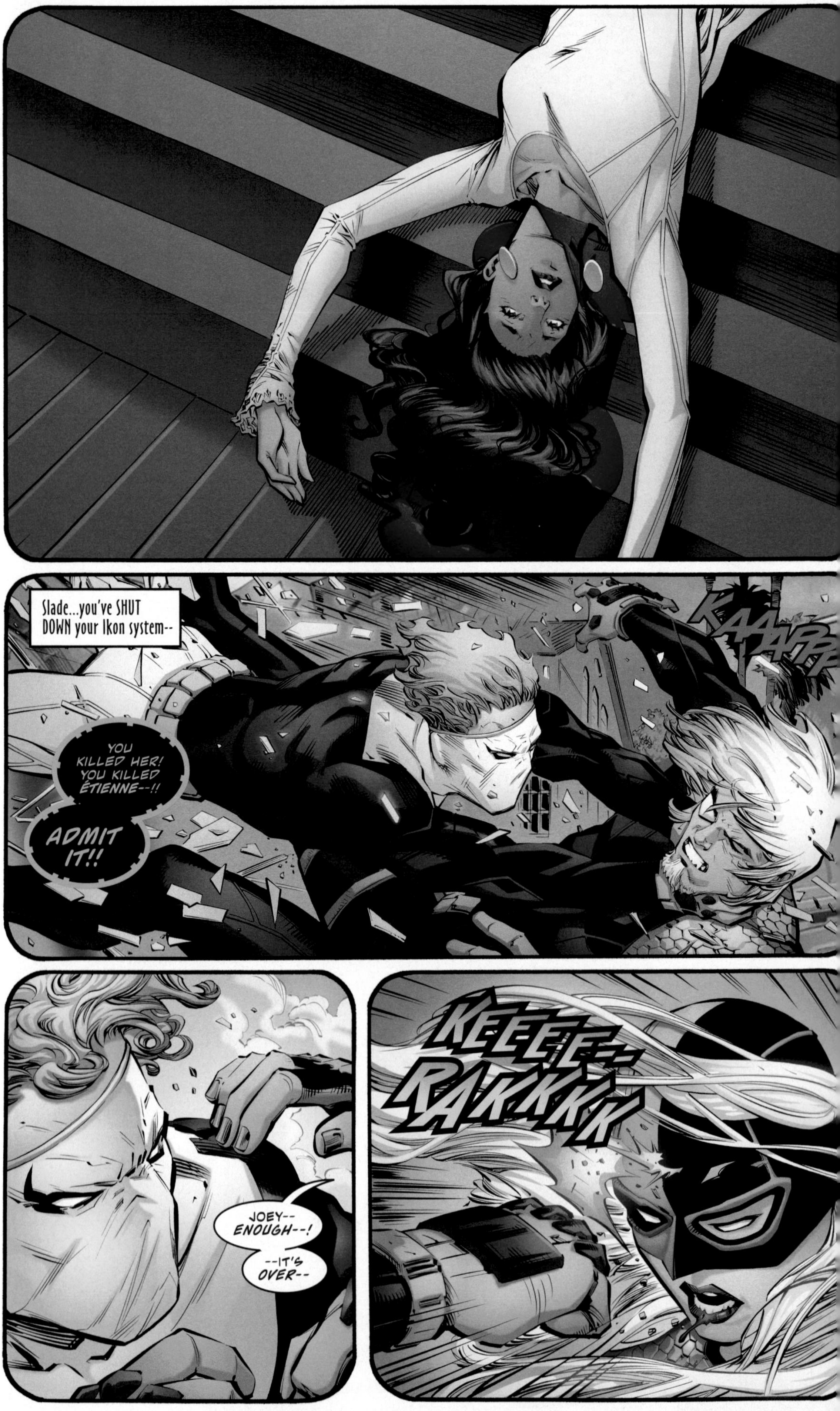
Slade...you've SHUT DOWN your Ikon system--
YOU KILLED HER! YOU KILLED ÉTIENNE--!!
ADMIT IT!!
JOEY-- ENOUGH--!
--IT'S OVER--
KEEEEE-- RAKKKKK

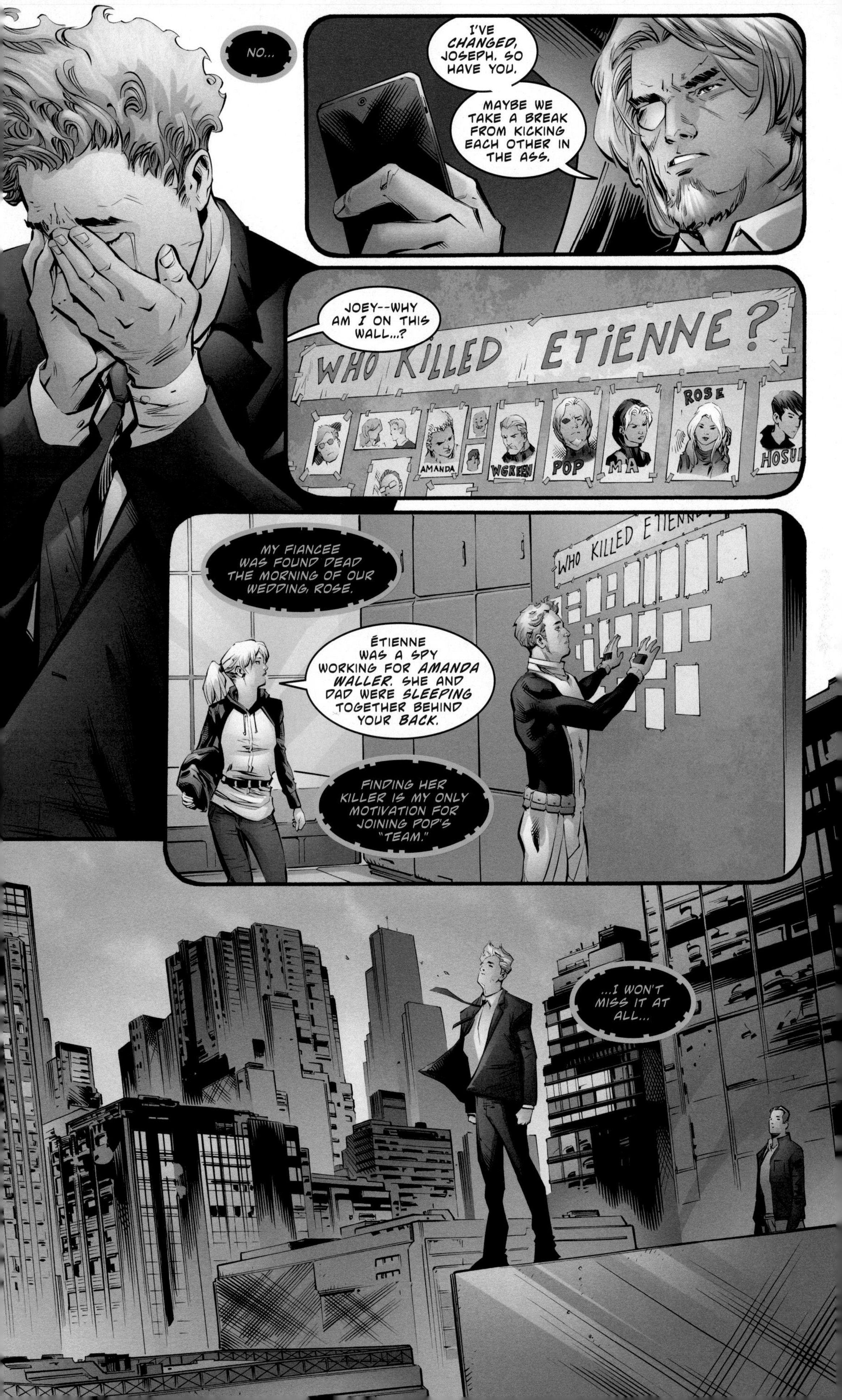
NO...
I'VE CHANGED, JOSEPH. SO HAVE YOU.
MAYBE WE TAKE A BREAK FROM KICKING EACH OTHER IN THE ASS.
JOEY--WHY AM I ON THIS WALL...?
WHO KILLED ETIENNE?
AMANDA
WGREEN
POP
MA
ROSE
MY FIANCEE WAS FOUND DEAD THE MORNING OF OUR WEDDING, ROSE.
WHO KILLED ETIENNE
ÉTIENNE WAS A SPY WORKING FOR AMANDA WALLER. SHE AND DAD WERE SLEEPING TOGETHER BEHIND YOUR BACK.
FINDING HER KILLER IS MY ONLY MOTIVATION FOR JOINING POP'S "TEAM."
...I WON'T MISS IT AT ALL...

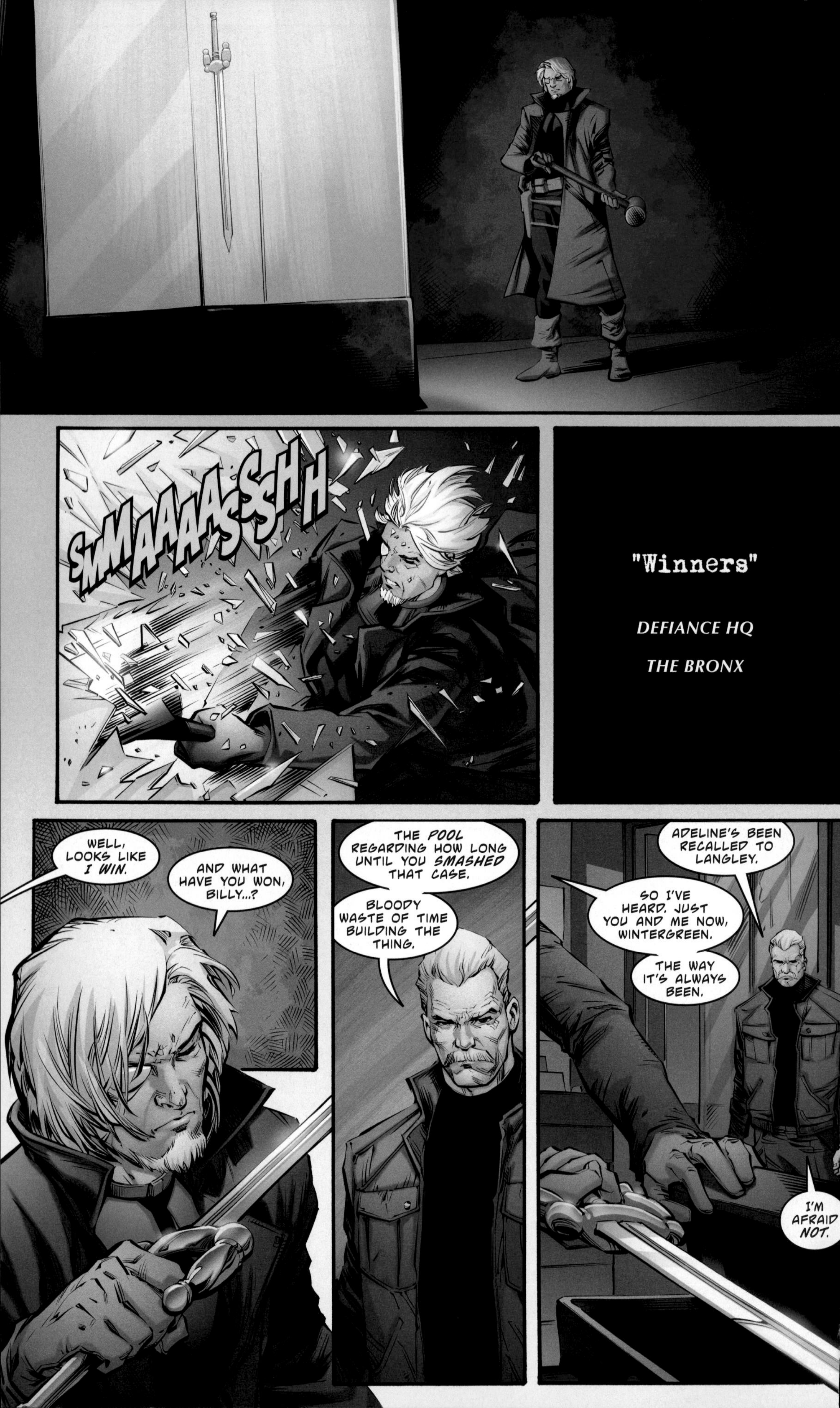
SMMAAAASSHH
"Winners"
DEFIANCE HQ
THE BRONX
WELL, LOOKS LIKE I *WIN*.
AND WHAT HAVE YOU WON, BILLY...?
THE *POOL* REGARDING HOW LONG UNTIL YOU *SMASHED* THAT CASE.
BLOODY WASTE OF TIME BUILDING THE THING.
ADELINE'S BEEN RECALLED TO LANGLEY.
SO I'VE HEARD. JUST YOU AND ME NOW, WINTERGREEN.
THE WAY IT'S ALWAYS BEEN.
I'M AFRAID *NOT*.

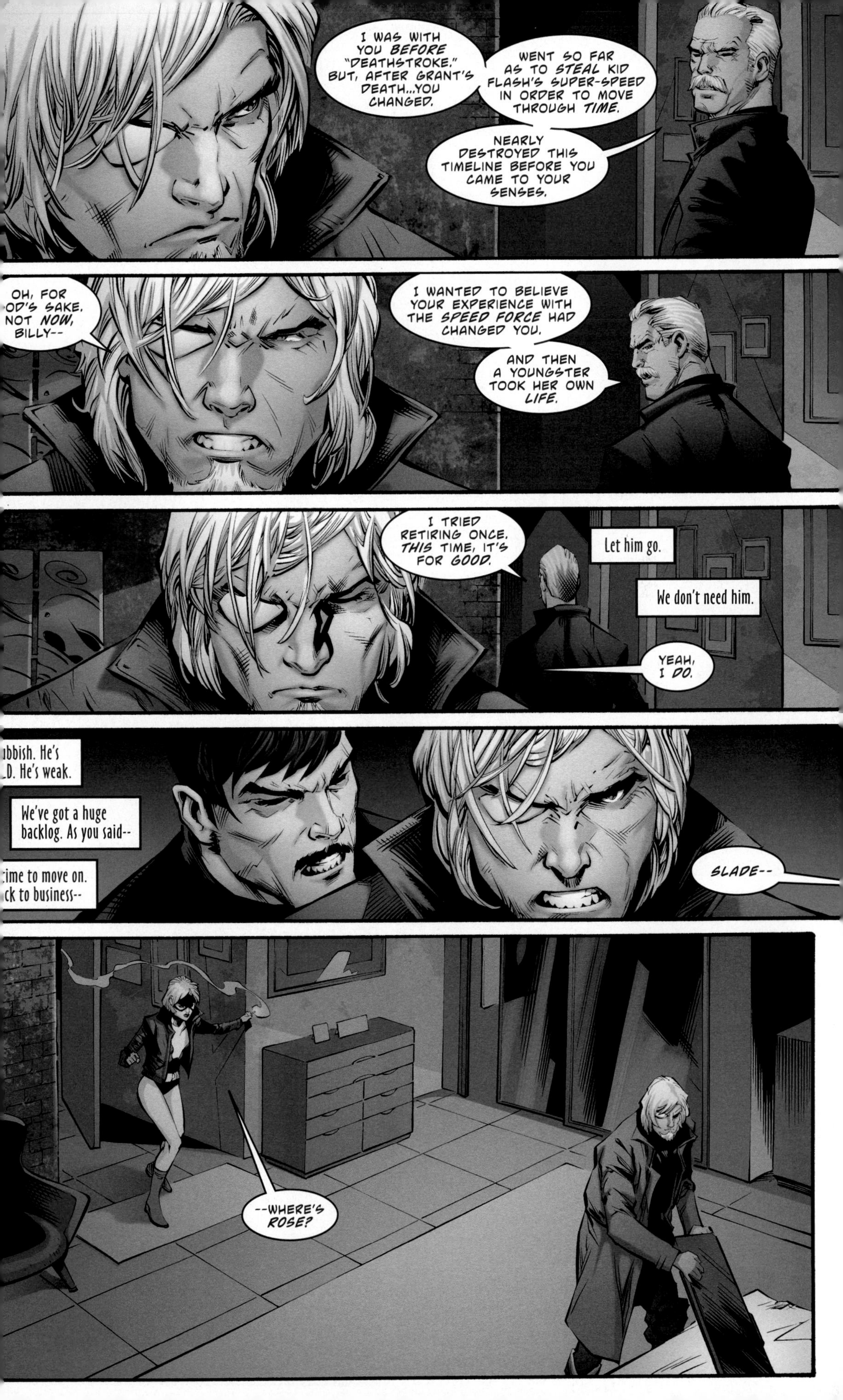
I WAS WITH YOU BEFORE "DEATHSTROKE." BUT, AFTER GRANT'S DEATH...YOU CHANGED.
WENT SO FAR AS TO STEAL KID FLASH'S SUPER-SPEED IN ORDER TO MOVE THROUGH TIME.
NEARLY DESTROYED THIS TIMELINE BEFORE YOU CAME TO YOUR SENSES.
OH, FOR OD'S SAKE, NOT NOW, BILLY--
I WANTED TO BELIEVE YOUR EXPERIENCE WITH THE SPEED FORCE HAD CHANGED YOU.
AND THEN A YOUNGSTER TOOK HER OWN LIFE.
I TRIED RETIRING ONCE. THIS TIME, IT'S FOR GOOD.
Let him go.
We don't need him.
YEAH, I DO.
ubbish. He's
.D. He's weak.
We've got a huge backlog. As you said--
ime to move on.
ck to business--
SLADE--
--WHERE'S ROSE?

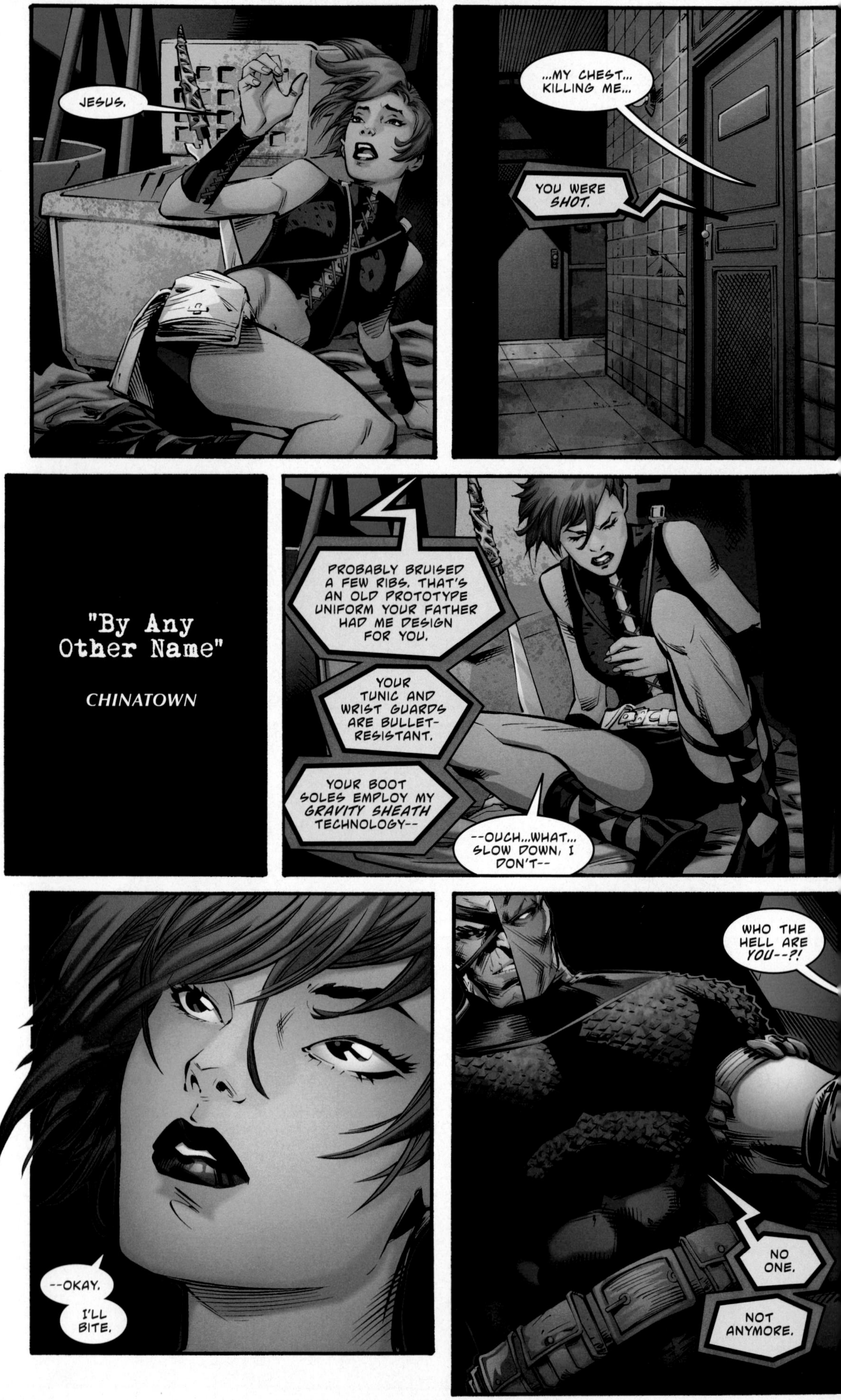
JESUS.
...MY CHEST... KILLING ME...
YOU WERE SHOT.
"By Any Other Name"
CHINATOWN
PROBABLY BRUISED A FEW RIBS. THAT'S AN OLD PROTOTYPE UNIFORM YOUR FATHER HAD ME DESIGN FOR YOU.
YOUR TUNIC AND WRIST GUARDS ARE BULLET-RESISTANT.
YOUR BOOT SOLES EMPLOY MY GRAVITY SHEATH TECHNOLOGY--
--OUCH...WHAT... SLOW DOWN, I DON'T--
--OKAY.
I'LL BITE.
WHO THE HELL ARE YOU--?!
NO ONE.
NOT ANYMORE.

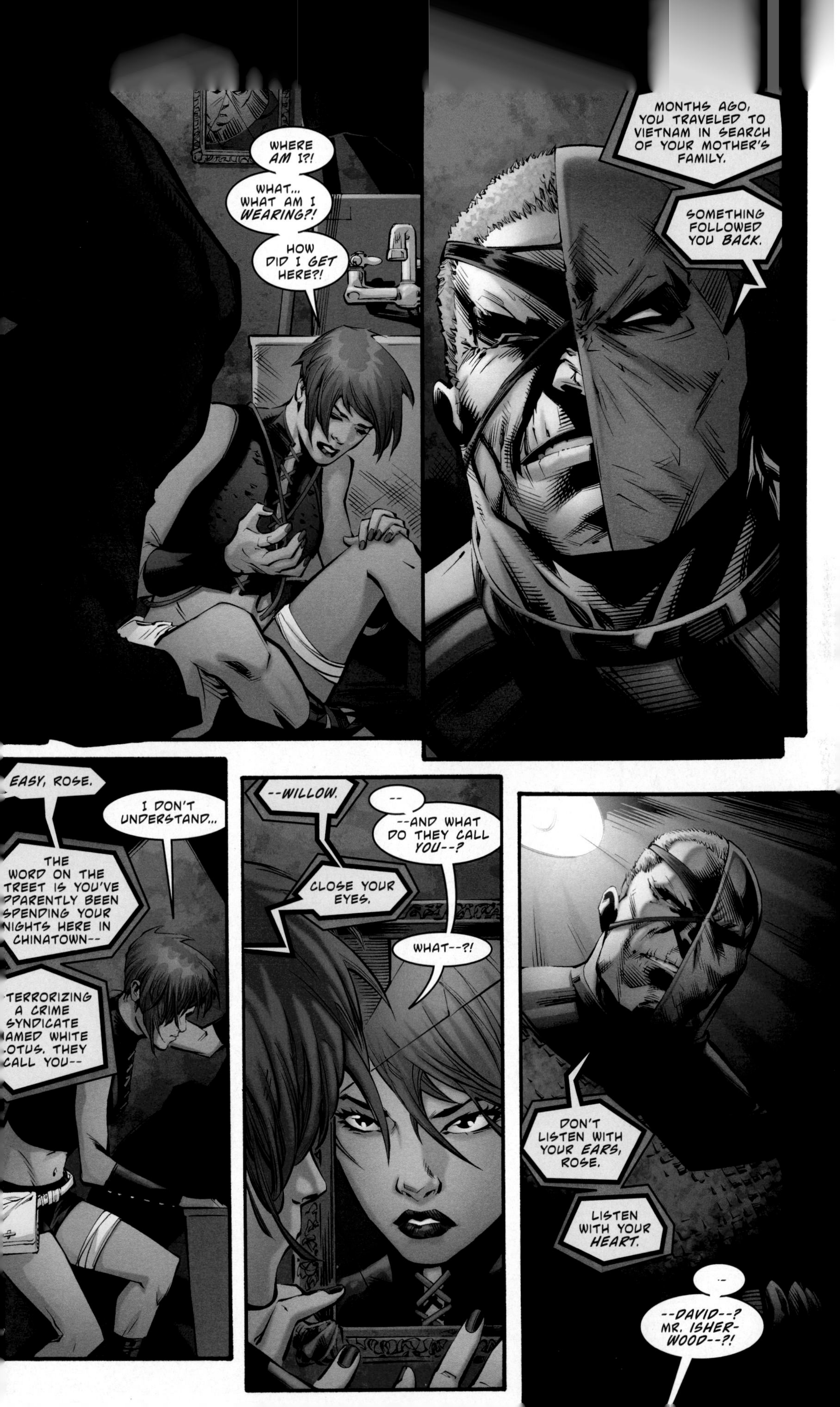
WHERE AM I?!
WHAT... WHAT AM I WEARING?!
HOW DID I GET HERE?!
MONTHS AGO, YOU TRAVELED TO VIETNAM IN SEARCH OF YOUR MOTHER'S FAMILY.
SOMETHING FOLLOWED YOU BACK.
EASY, ROSE.
I DON'T UNDERSTAND...
THE WORD ON THE TREET IS YOU'VE PPARENTLY BEEN SPENDING YOUR NIGHTS HERE IN CHINATOWN--
TERRORIZING A CRIME SYNDICATE AMED WHITE OTUS. THEY CALL YOU--
--WILLOW.
--
--AND WHAT DO THEY CALL YOU--?
CLOSE YOUR EYES.
WHAT--?!
DON'T LISTEN WITH YOUR EARS, ROSE.
LISTEN WITH YOUR HEART.
--
--DAVID--? MR. ISHERWOOD--?!

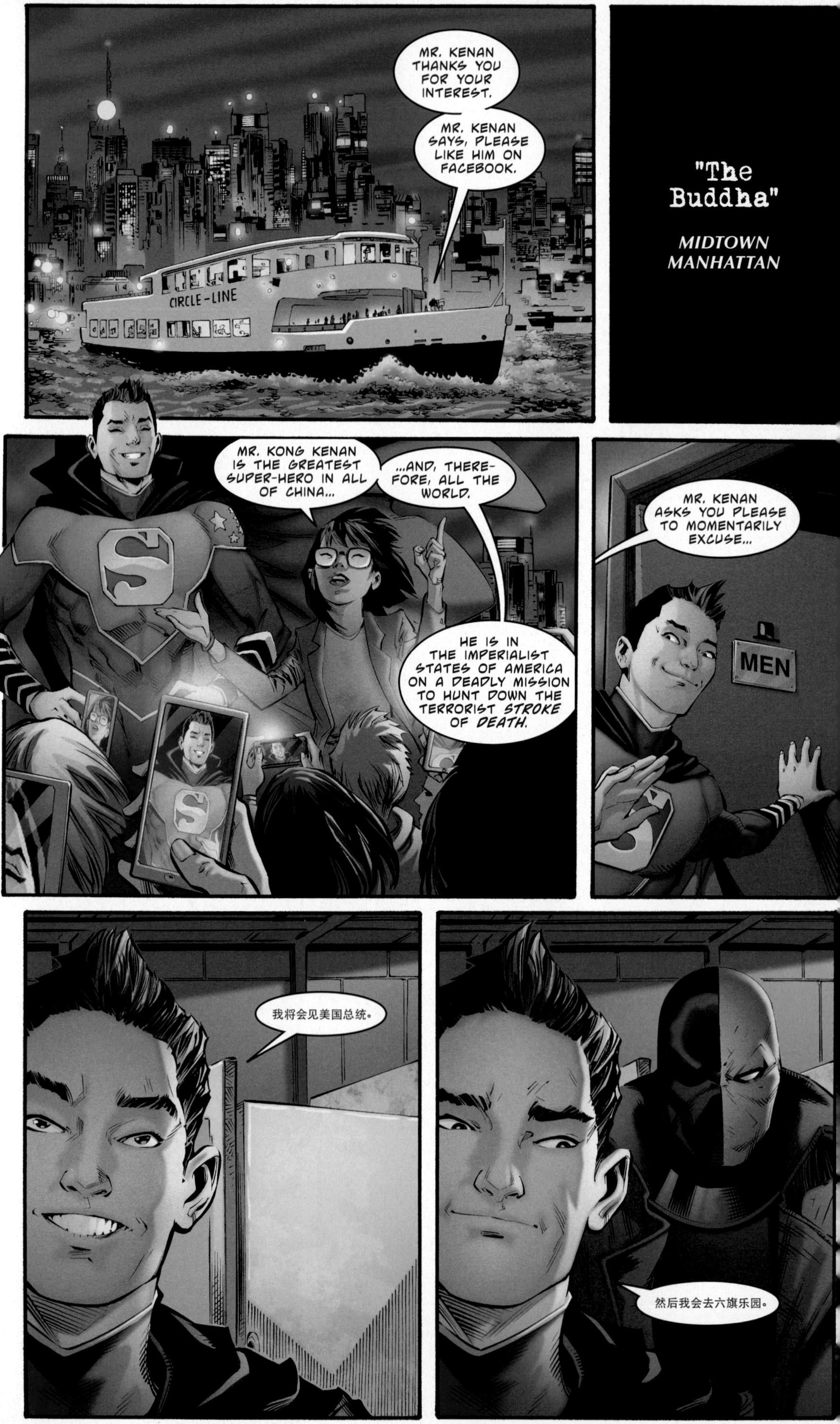

MR. KENAN THANKS YOU FOR YOUR INTEREST.
MR. KENAN SAYS, PLEASE LIKE HIM ON FACEBOOK.
CIRCLE-LINE
"The Buddha"
MIDTOWN MANHATTAN
MR. KONG KENAN IS THE GREATEST SUPER-HERO IN ALL OF CHINA...
...AND, THEREFORE, ALL THE WORLD.
HE IS IN THE IMPERIALIST STATES OF AMERICA ON A DEADLY MISSION TO HUNT DOWN THE TERRORIST STROKE OF DEATH.
MR. KENAN ASKS YOU PLEASE TO MOMENTARILY EXCUSE...
MEN
我将会见美国总统。
然后我会去六旗乐园。

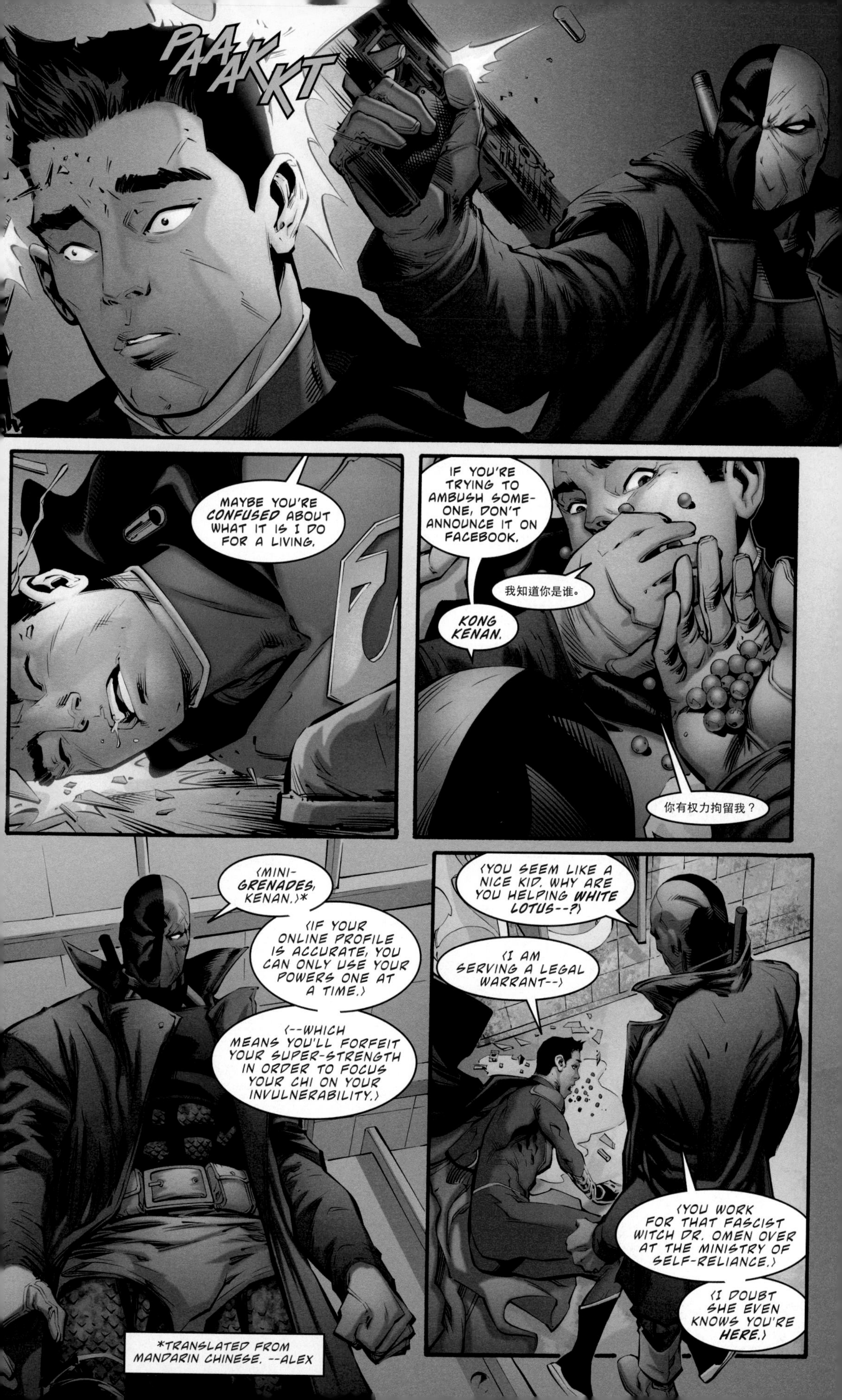
PAAAKKT
MAYBE YOU'RE CONFUSED ABOUT WHAT IT IS I DO FOR A LIVING.
IF YOU'RE TRYING TO AMBUSH SOME-ONE, DON'T ANNOUNCE IT ON FACEBOOK.
我知道你是谁。
KONG KENAN.
你有权力拘留我？
‹MINI-GRENADES, KENAN.›*
‹IF YOUR ONLINE PROFILE IS ACCURATE, YOU CAN ONLY USE YOUR POWERS ONE AT A TIME.›
‹--WHICH MEANS YOU'LL FORFEIT YOUR SUPER-STRENGTH IN ORDER TO FOCUS YOUR CHI ON YOUR INVULNERABILITY.›
*TRANSLATED FROM MANDARIN CHINESE. --ALEX
‹YOU SEEM LIKE A NICE KID. WHY ARE YOU HELPING WHITE LOTUS--?›
‹I AM SERVING A LEGAL WARRANT--›
‹YOU WORK FOR THAT FASCIST WITCH DR. OMEN OVER AT THE MINISTRY OF SELF-RELIANCE.›
‹I DOUBT SHE EVEN KNOWS YOU'RE HERE.›

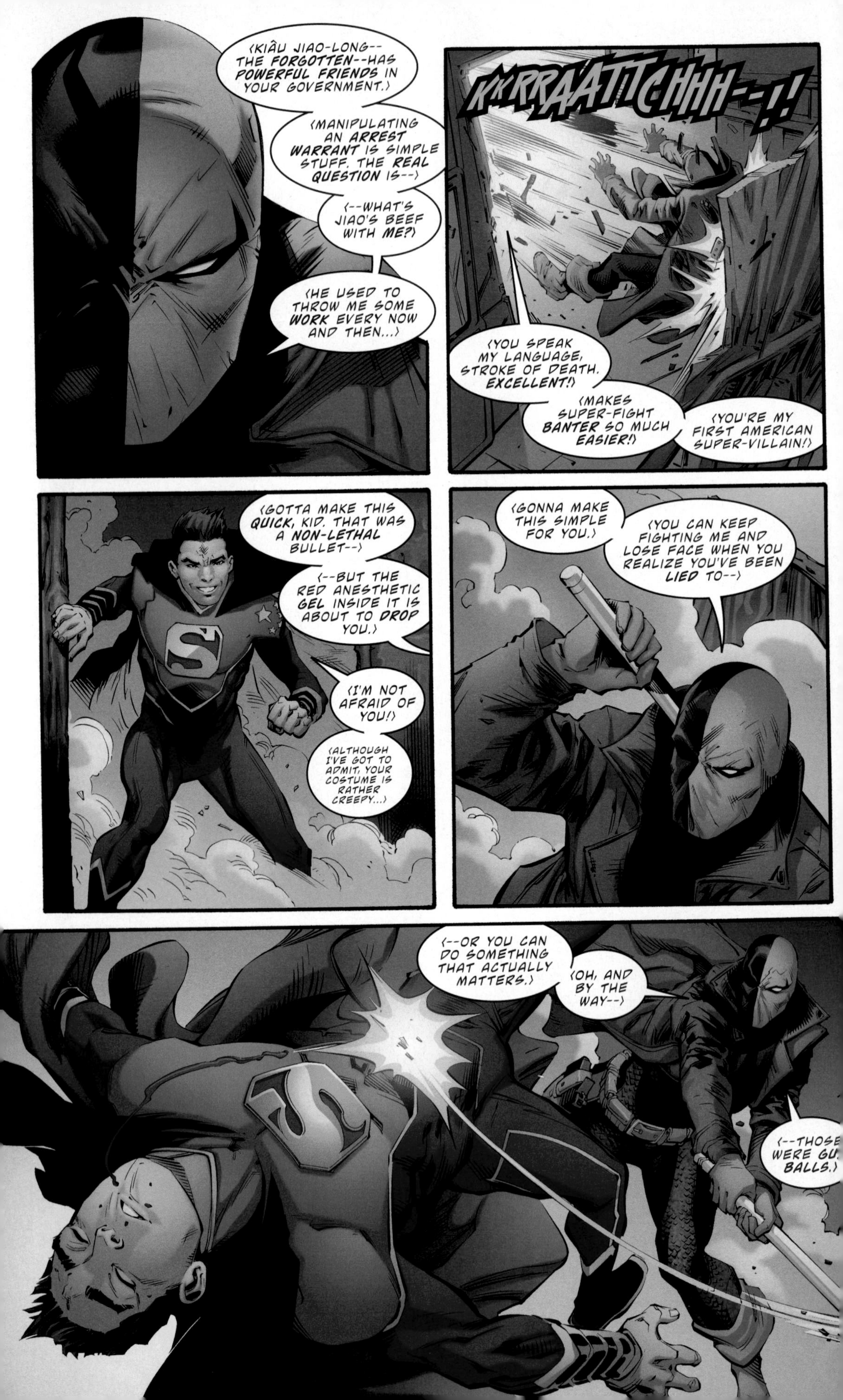

⟨KIÂU JIAO-LONG--THE FORGOTTEN--HAS POWERFUL FRIENDS IN YOUR GOVERNMENT.⟩
⟨MANIPULATING AN ARREST WARRANT IS SIMPLE STUFF. THE REAL QUESTION IS--⟩
⟨--WHAT'S JIAO'S BEEF WITH ME?⟩
⟨HE USED TO THROW ME SOME WORK EVERY NOW AND THEN...⟩
KKRRAATTCHHH--!!
⟨YOU SPEAK MY LANGUAGE, STROKE OF DEATH. EXCELLENT!⟩
⟨MAKES SUPER-FIGHT BANTER SO MUCH EASIER!⟩
⟨YOU'RE MY FIRST AMERICAN SUPER-VILLAIN!⟩
⟨GOTTA MAKE THIS QUICK, KID. THAT WAS A NON-LETHAL BULLET--⟩
⟨--BUT THE RED ANESTHETIC GEL INSIDE IT IS ABOUT TO DROP YOU.⟩
⟨I'M NOT AFRAID OF YOU!⟩
⟨ALTHOUGH I'VE GOT TO ADMIT, YOUR COSTUME IS RATHER CREEPY...⟩
⟨GONNA MAKE THIS SIMPLE FOR YOU.⟩
⟨YOU CAN KEEP FIGHTING ME AND LOSE FACE WHEN YOU REALIZE YOU'VE BEEN LIED TO--⟩
⟨--OR YOU CAN DO SOMETHING THAT ACTUALLY MATTERS.⟩
⟨OH, AND BY THE WAY--⟩

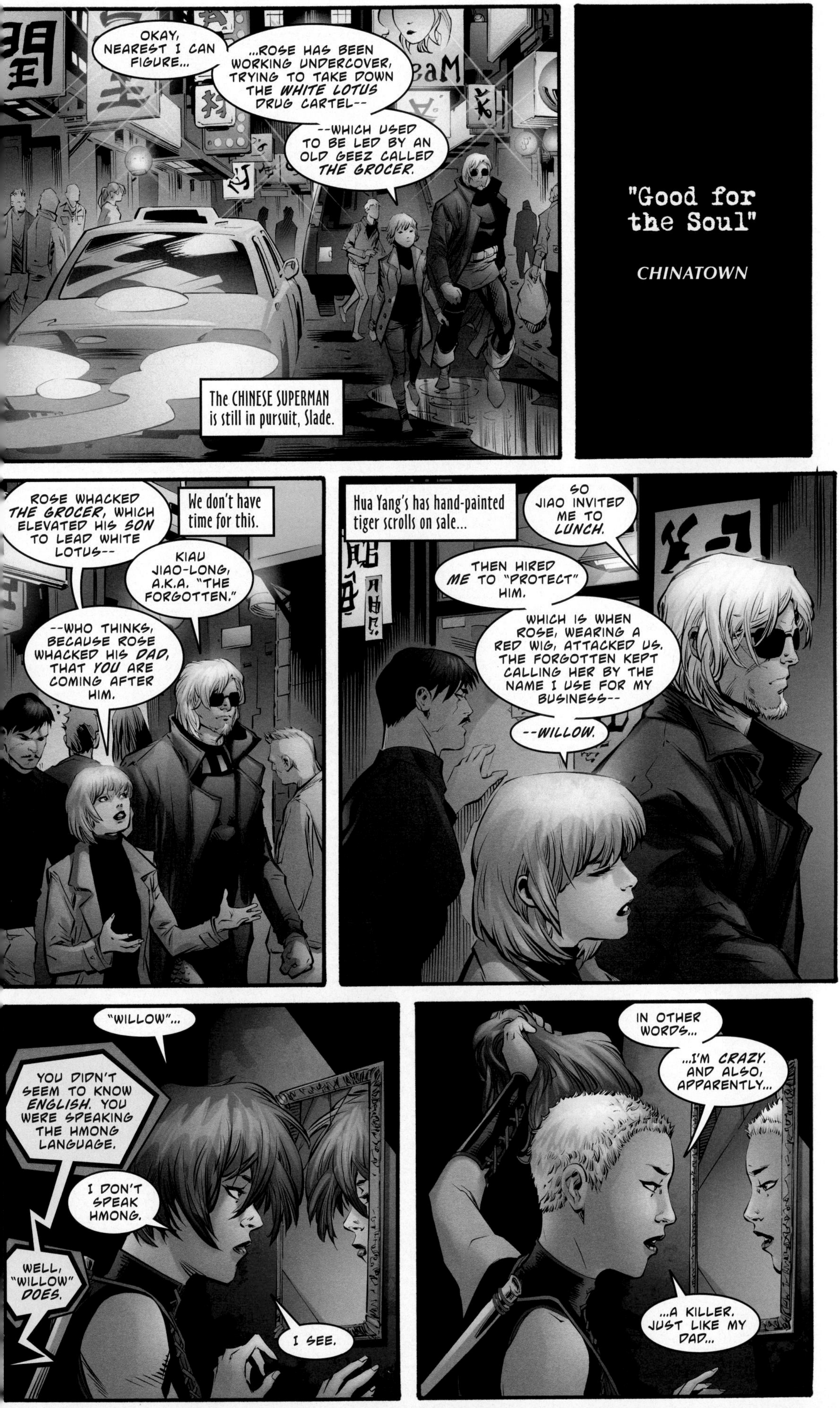
OKAY, NEAREST I CAN FIGURE...
...ROSE HAS BEEN WORKING UNDERCOVER, TRYING TO TAKE DOWN THE WHITE LOTUS DRUG CARTEL--
--WHICH USED TO BE LED BY AN OLD GEEZ CALLED THE GROCER.
The CHINESE SUPERMAN is still in pursuit, Slade.
"Good for the Soul"
CHINATOWN
ROSE WHACKED THE GROCER, WHICH ELEVATED HIS SON TO LEAD WHITE LOTUS--
We don't have time for this.
KIAU JIAO-LONG, A.K.A. "THE FORGOTTEN."
--WHO THINKS, BECAUSE ROSE WHACKED HIS DAD, THAT YOU ARE COMING AFTER HIM.
Hua Yang's has hand-painted tiger scrolls on sale...
SO JIAO INVITED ME TO LUNCH.
THEN HIRED ME TO "PROTECT" HIM.
WHICH IS WHEN ROSE, WEARING A RED WIG, ATTACKED US. THE FORGOTTEN KEPT CALLING HER BY THE NAME I USE FOR MY BUSINESS--
--WILLOW.
"WILLOW"...
YOU DIDN'T SEEM TO KNOW ENGLISH. YOU WERE SPEAKING THE HMONG LANGUAGE.
I DON'T SPEAK HMONG.
WELL, "WILLOW" DOES.
I SEE.
IN OTHER WORDS...
...I'M CRAZY. AND ALSO, APPARENTLY...
...A KILLER. JUST LIKE MY DAD...

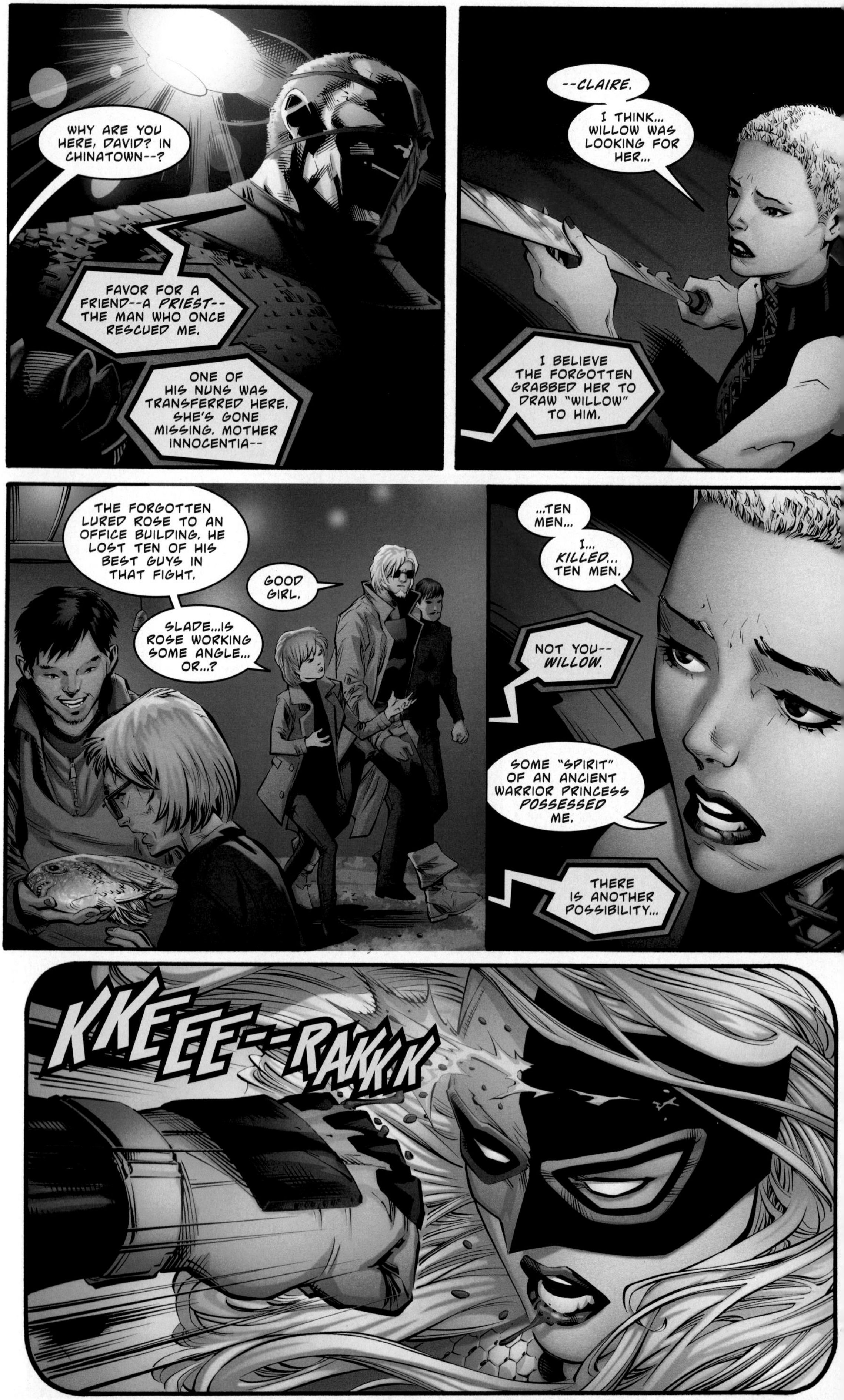

WHY ARE YOU HERE, DAVID? IN CHINATOWN--?
FAVOR FOR A FRIEND--A PRIEST--THE MAN WHO ONCE RESCUED ME.
ONE OF HIS NUNS WAS TRANSFERRED HERE. SHE'S GONE MISSING. MOTHER INNOCENTIA--
--CLAIRE.
I THINK... WILLOW WAS LOOKING FOR HER...
I BELIEVE THE FORGOTTEN GRABBED HER TO DRAW "WILLOW" TO HIM.
THE FORGOTTEN LURED ROSE TO AN OFFICE BUILDING. HE LOST TEN OF HIS BEST GUYS IN THAT FIGHT.
GOOD GIRL.
SLADE...IS ROSE WORKING SOME ANGLE... OR...?
...TEN MEN...
I... KILLED... TEN MEN.
NOT YOU--WILLOW.
SOME "SPIRIT" OF AN ANCIENT WARRIOR PRINCESS POSSESSED ME.
THERE IS ANOTHER POSSIBILITY...
KKEEE--RAKKK

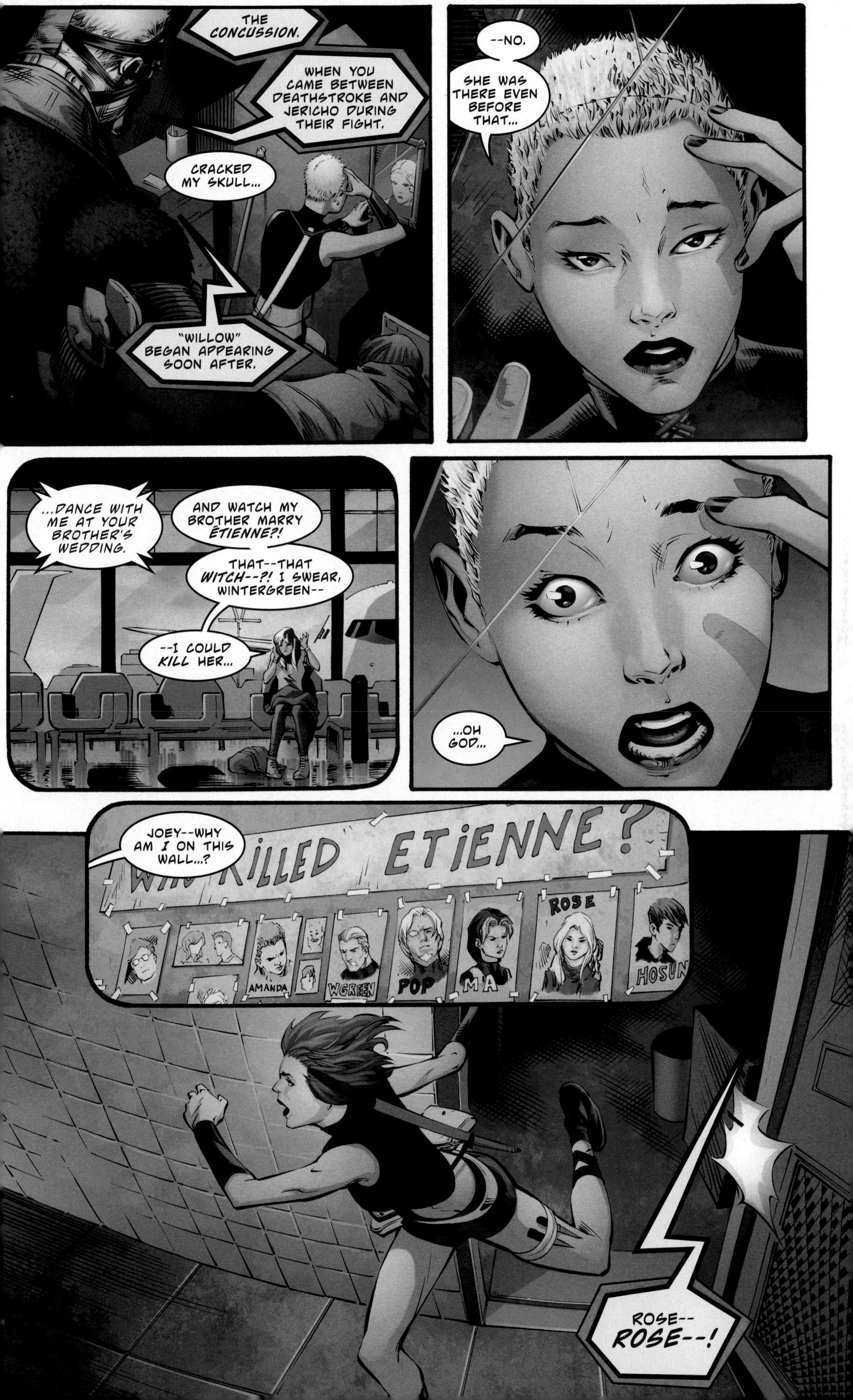
THE CONCUSSION.
WHEN YOU CAME BETWEEN DEATHSTROKE AND JERICHO DURING THEIR FIGHT.
CRACKED MY SKULL...
"WILLOW" BEGAN APPEARING SOON AFTER.
--NO.
SHE WAS THERE EVEN BEFORE THAT...
...DANCE WITH ME AT YOUR BROTHER'S WEDDING.
AND WATCH MY BROTHER MARRY ÉTIENNE?!
THAT--THAT WITCH--?! I SWEAR, WINTERGREEN--
--I COULD KILL HER...
...OH GOD...
JOEY--WHY AM I ON THIS WALL...?
ETiENNE?
ROSE
AMANDA
WGREEN
POP
MA
HOSUN
ROSE-- ROSE--!

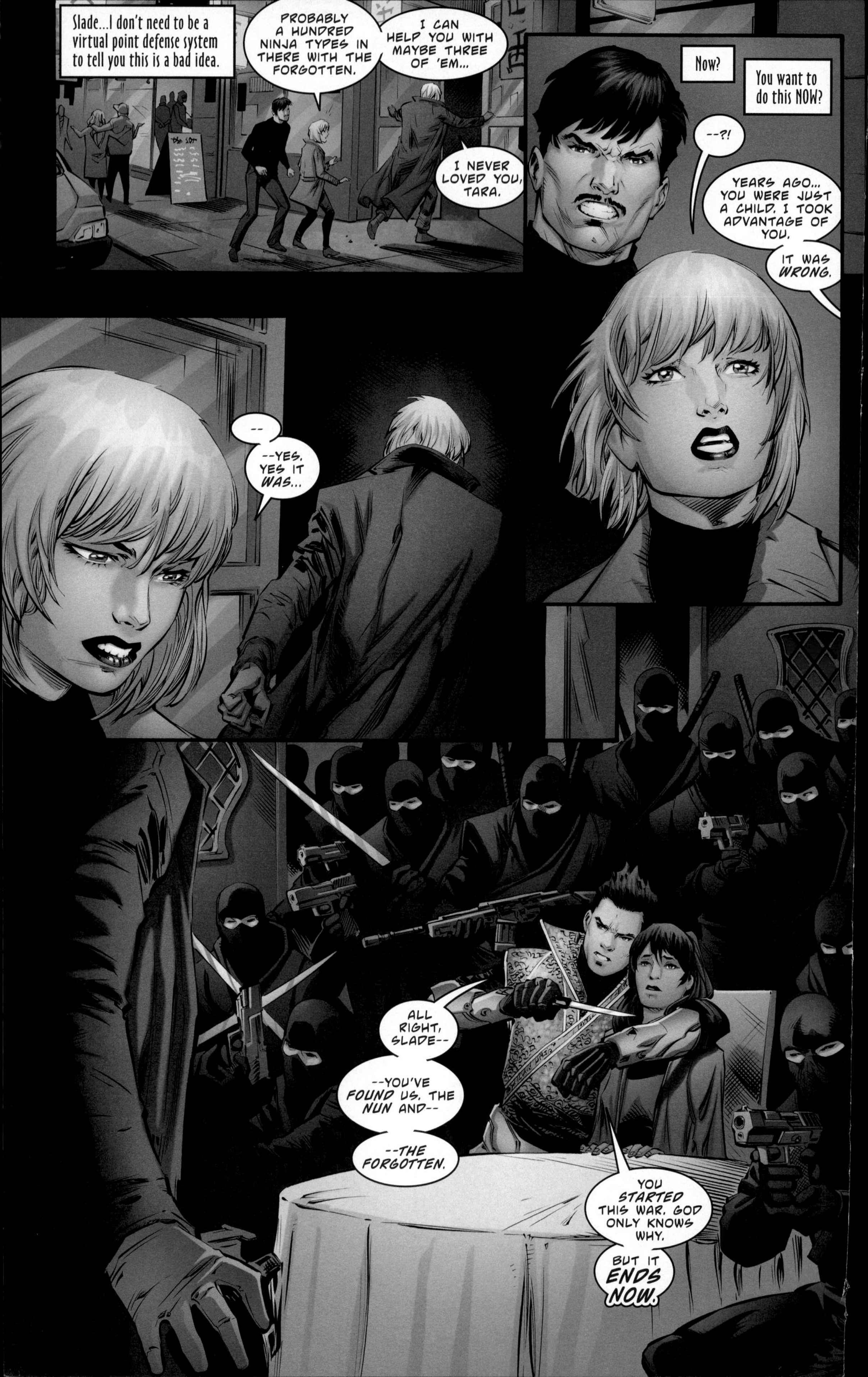
Slade...I don't need to be a virtual point defense system to tell you this is a bad idea.
PROBABLY A HUNDRED NINJA TYPES IN THERE WITH THE FORGOTTEN.
I CAN HELP YOU WITH MAYBE THREE OF 'EM...
I NEVER LOVED YOU, TARA.
Now?
You want to do this NOW?
--?!
YEARS AGO... YOU WERE JUST A CHILD. I TOOK ADVANTAGE OF YOU.
IT WAS WRONG.
--
--YES. YES IT WAS...
ALL RIGHT, SLADE--
--YOU'VE FOUND US. THE NUN AND--
--THE FORGOTTEN.
YOU STARTED THIS WAR. GOD ONLY KNOWS WHY.
BUT IT ENDS NOW.

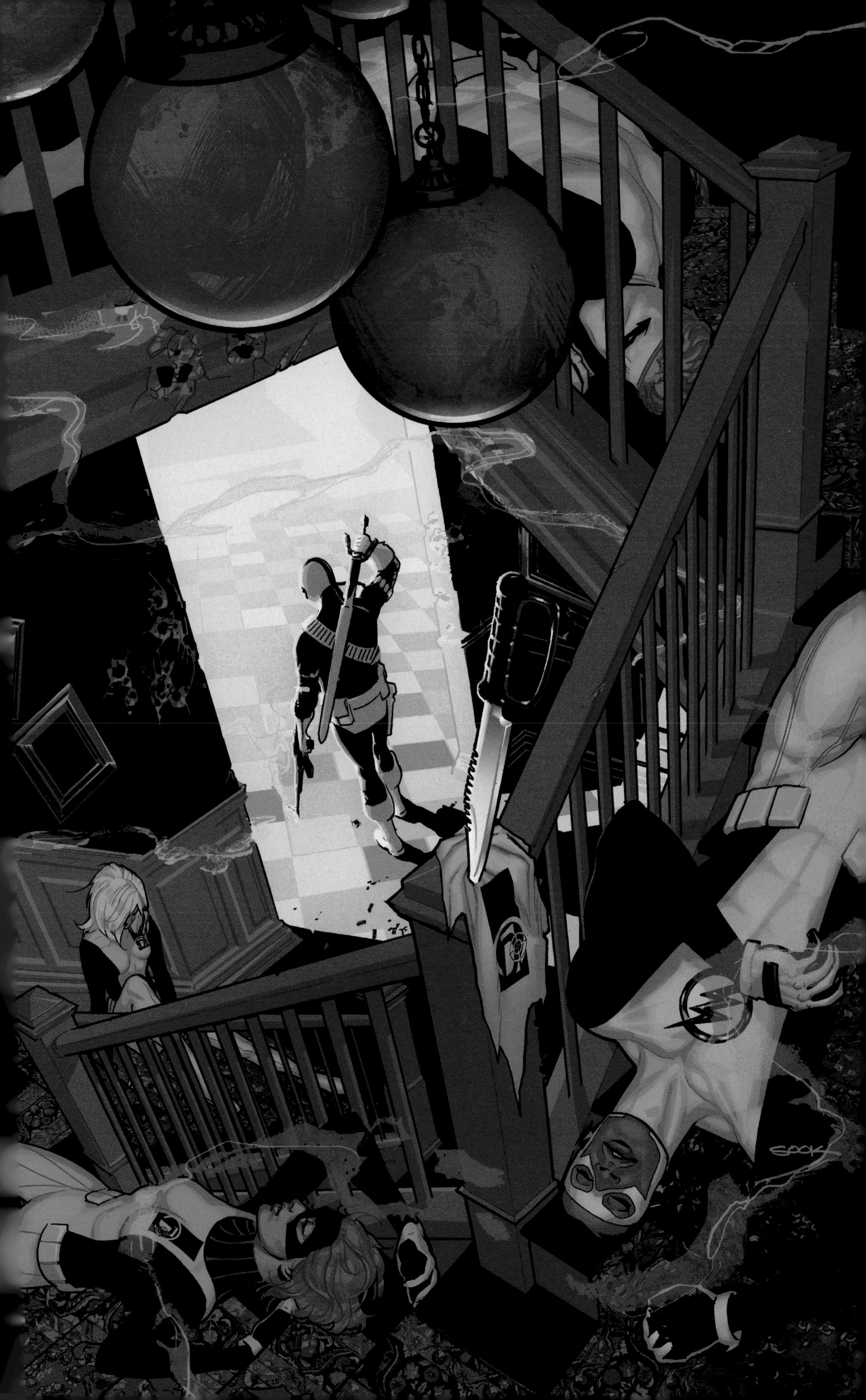
SOOK

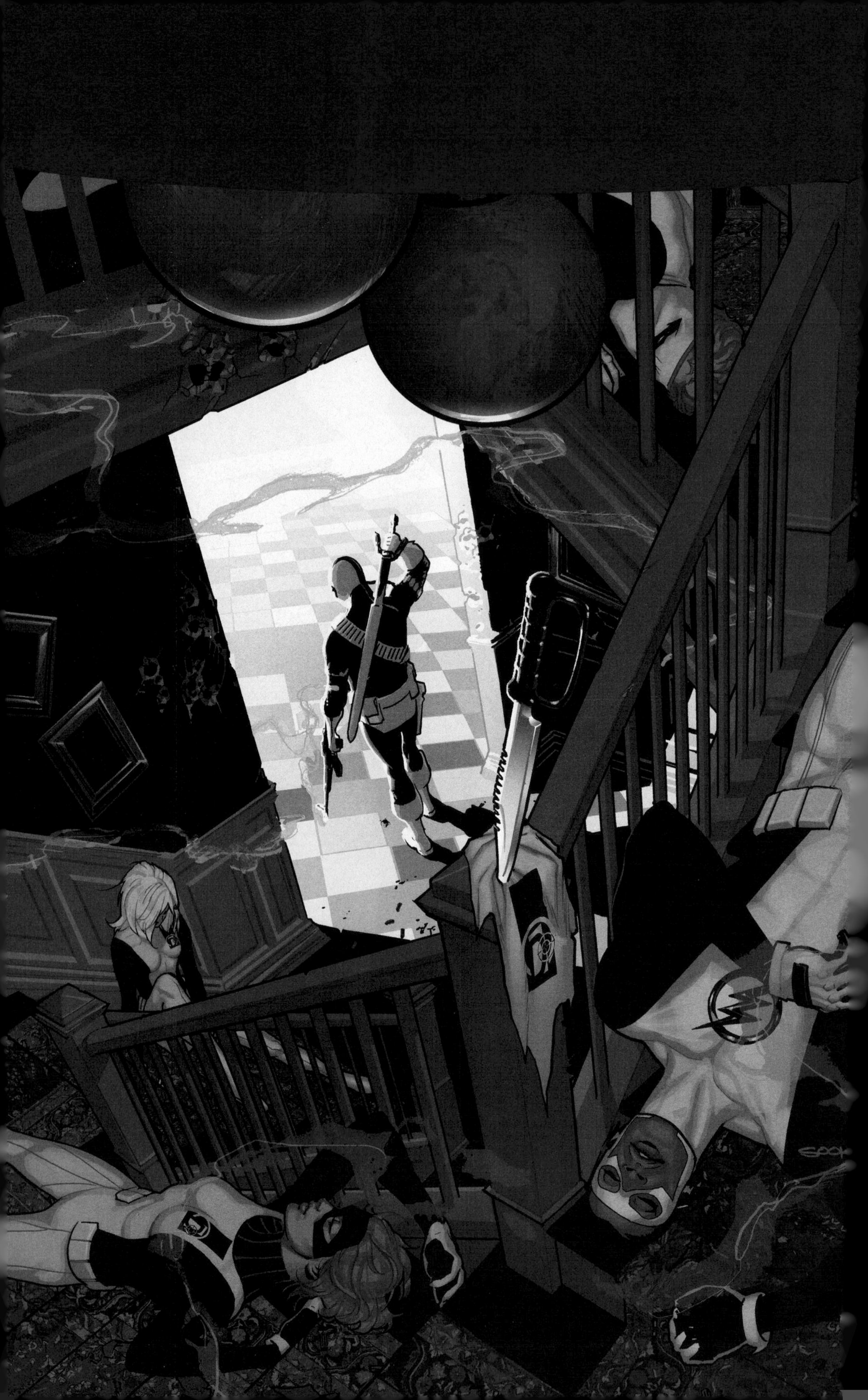

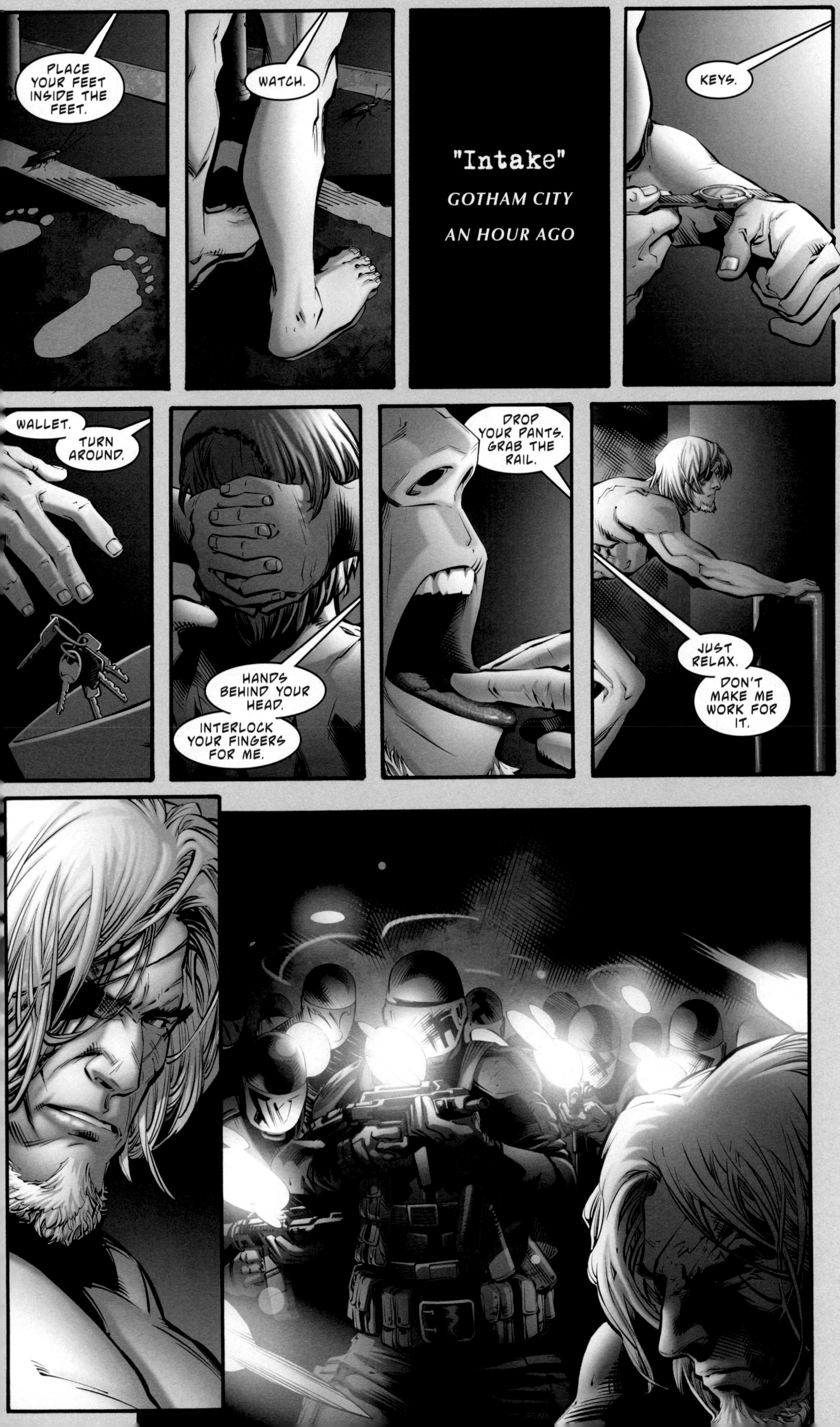
PLACE YOUR FEET INSIDE THE FEET.
WATCH.
"Intake"
GOTHAM CITY
AN HOUR AGO
KEYS.
WALLET.
TURN AROUND.
HANDS BEHIND YOUR HEAD.
INTERLOCK YOUR FINGERS FOR ME.
DROP YOUR PANTS. GRAB THE RAIL.
JUST RELAX.
DON'T MAKE ME WORK FOR IT.

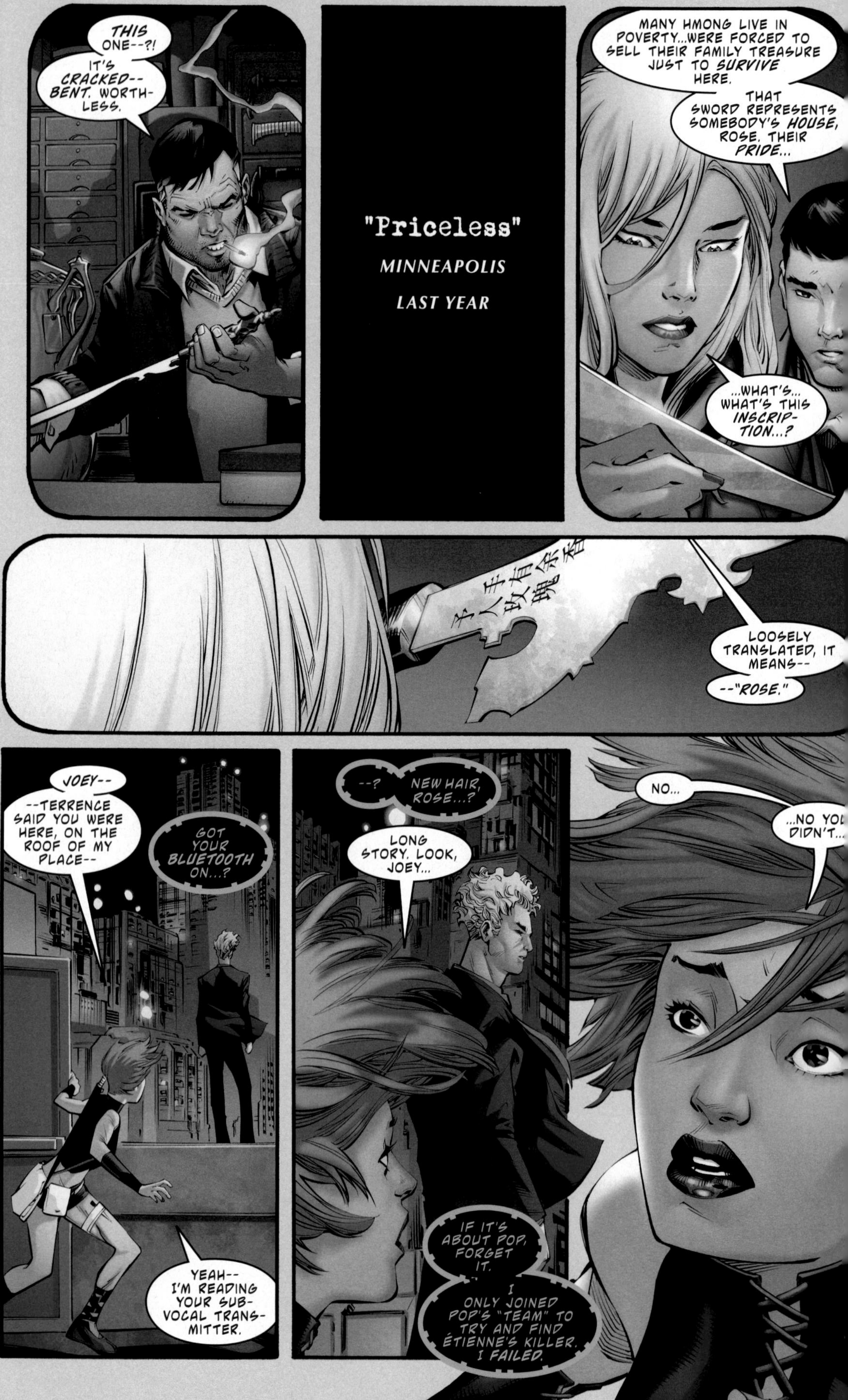
THIS ONE--?!
IT'S CRACKED--BENT. WORTHLESS.
"Priceless"
MINNEAPOLIS
LAST YEAR
MANY HMONG LIVE IN POVERTY...WERE FORCED TO SELL THEIR FAMILY TREASURE JUST TO SURVIVE HERE.
THAT SWORD REPRESENTS SOMEBODY'S HOUSE, ROSE. THEIR PRIDE...
...WHAT'S... WHAT'S THIS INSCRIPTION...?
予人玫瑰
手有余香
LOOSELY TRANSLATED, IT MEANS--
--"ROSE."
JOEY--
--TERRENCE SAID YOU WERE HERE, ON THE ROOF OF MY PLACE--
GOT YOUR BLUETOOTH ON...?
YEAH--I'M READING YOUR SUB-VOCAL TRANSMITTER.
--?
NEW HAIR, ROSE...?
LONG STORY. LOOK, JOEY...
IF IT'S ABOUT POP, FORGET IT.
I ONLY JOINED POP'S "TEAM" TO TRY AND FIND ÉTIENNE'S KILLER. I FAILED.
NO...
...NO YOU DIDN'T...

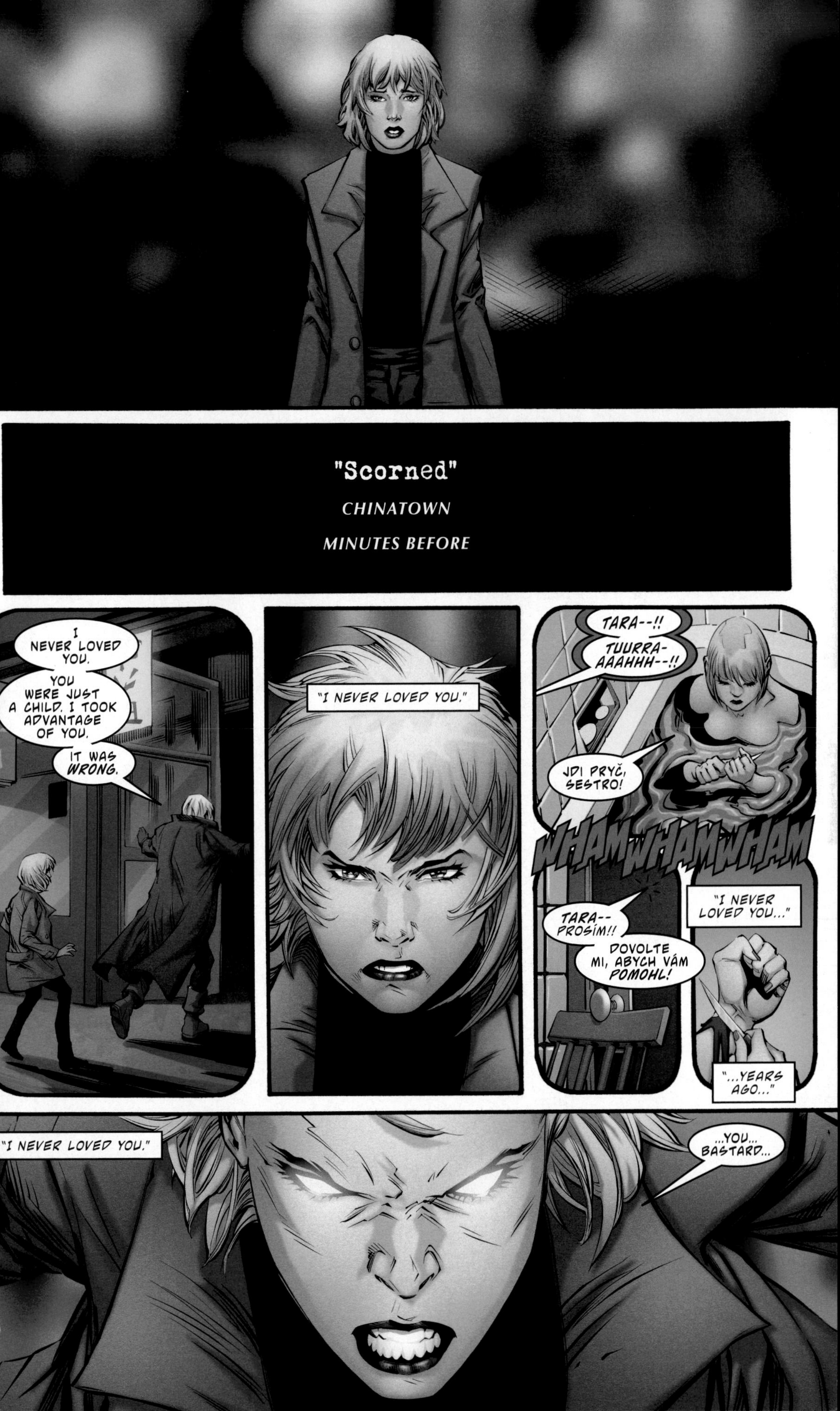
"Scorned"
CHINATOWN
MINUTES BEFORE
I NEVER LOVED YOU.
YOU WERE JUST A CHILD. I TOOK ADVANTAGE OF YOU.
IT WAS WRONG.
"I NEVER LOVED YOU."
TARA--!!
TUURRA-AAAHHH--!!
JDI PRYČ, SESTRO!
WHAMWHAMWHAM
TARA-- PROSÍM!!
DOVOLTE MI, ABYCH VÁM POMOHL!
"I NEVER LOVED YOU..."
"...YEARS AGO..."
"I NEVER LOVED YOU."
...YOU... BASTARD...

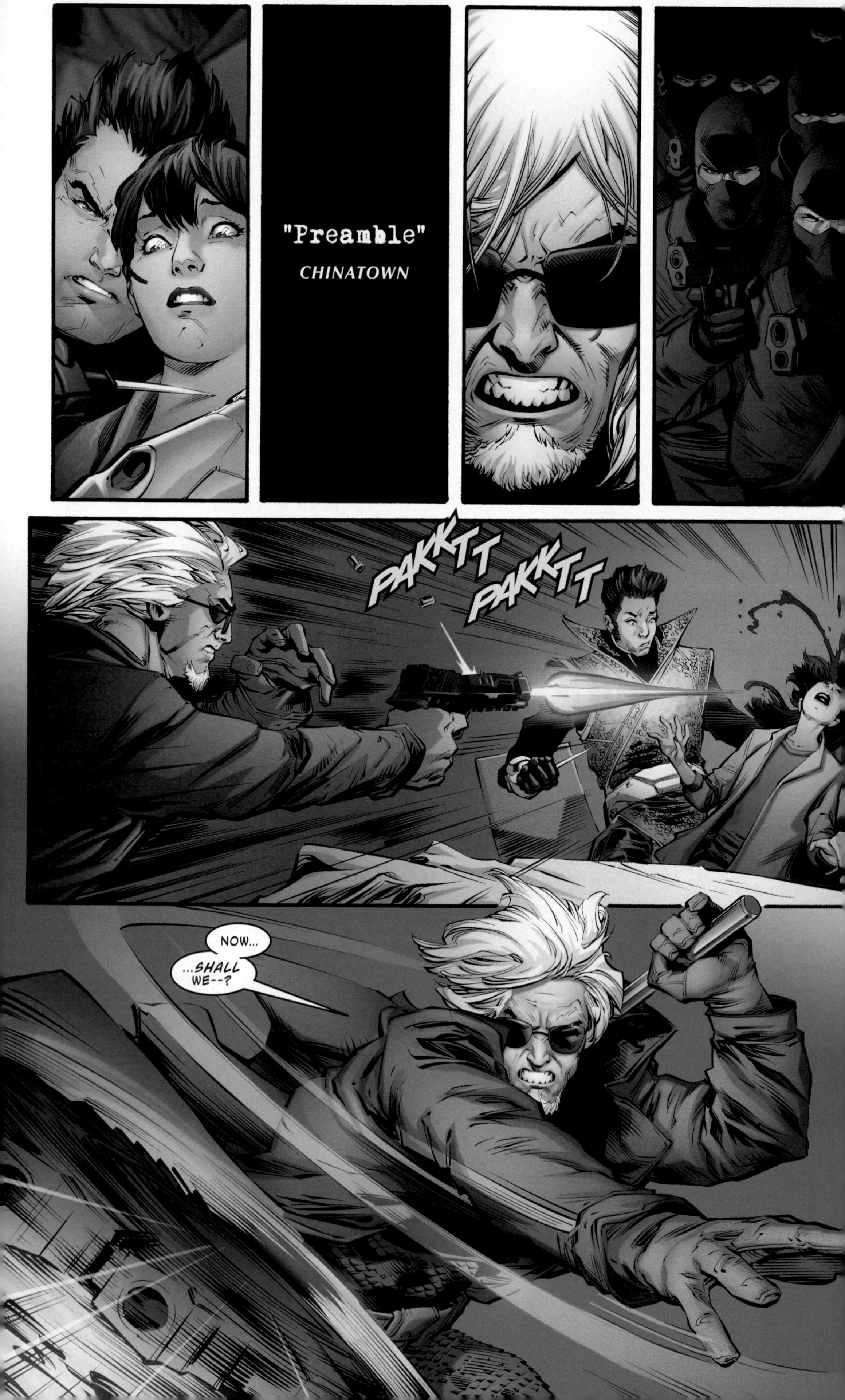
"Preamble"
CHINATOWN
PAKKTT
PAKKTT
NOW...
...SHALL WE--?

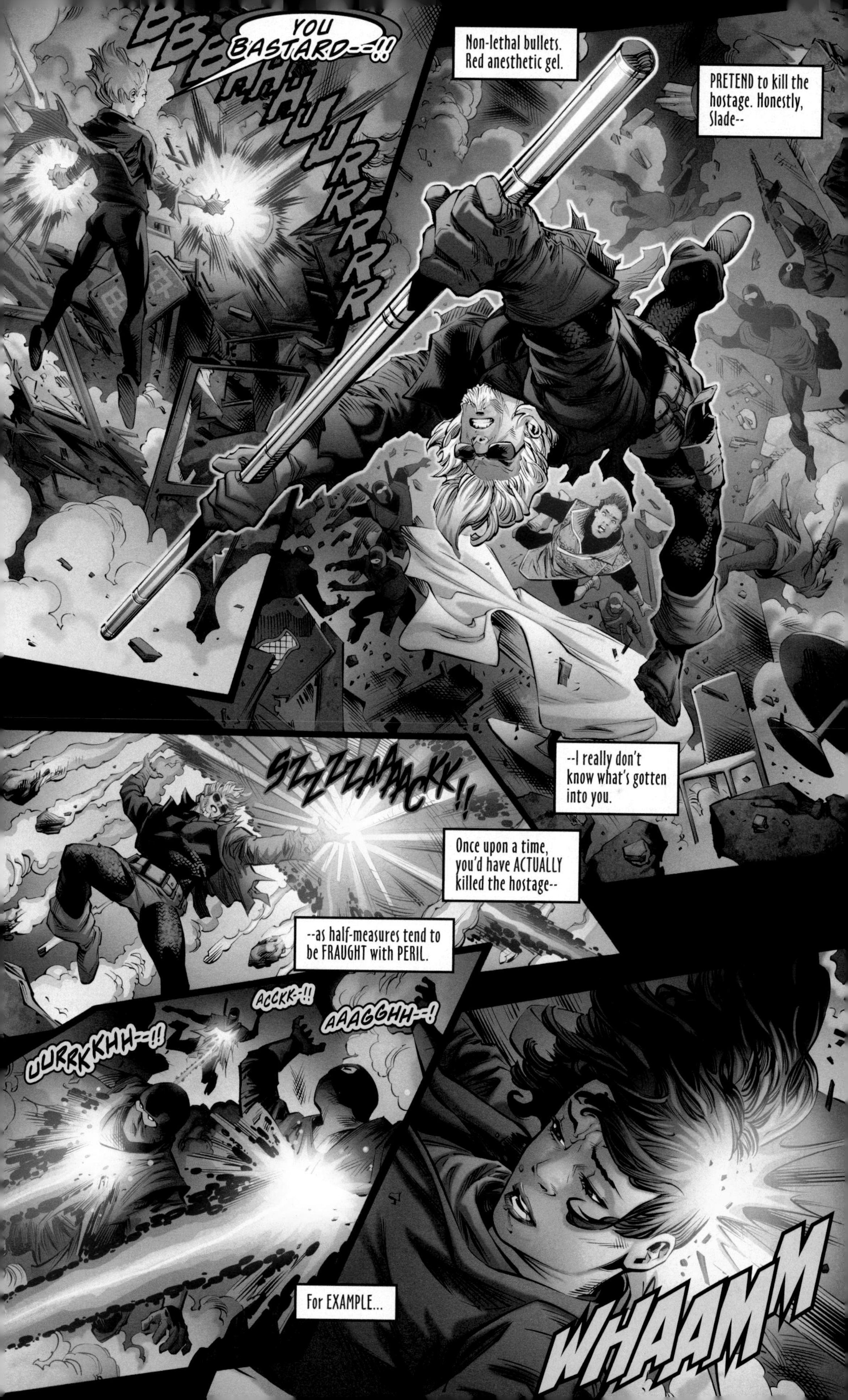
YOU BASTARD--!!
BBBRRRRHURRRRRRR
Non-lethal bullets. Red anesthetic gel.
PRETEND to kill the hostage. Honestly, Slade--
SZZZZZAAAACKK!!
--I really don't know what's gotten into you.
Once upon a time, you'd have ACTUALLY killed the hostage--
--as half-measures tend to be FRAUGHT with PERIL.
ACCKK-!!
AAAGGHH--!
UURRKKHH--!!
For EXAMPLE...
WHAAMM

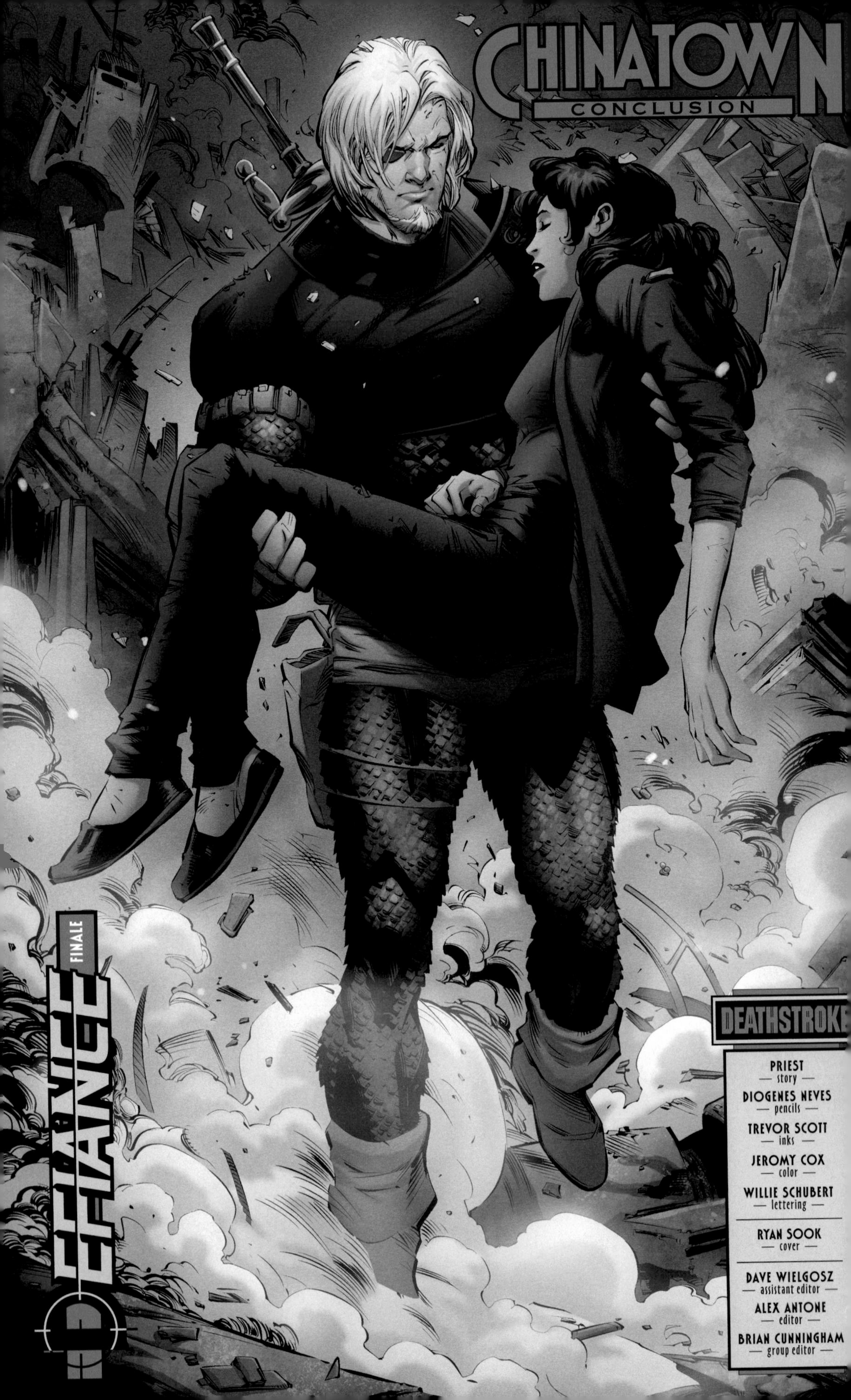
CHINATOWN
CONCLUSION
DEFIANCE
FINALE
DEATHSTROKE
PRIEST
— story —
DIOGENES NEVES
— pencils —
TREVOR SCOTT
— inks —
JEROMY COX
— color —
WILLIE SCHUBERT
— lettering —
RYAN SOOK
— cover —
DAVE WIELGOSZ
— assistant editor —
ALEX ANTONE
— editor —
BRIAN CUNNINGHAM
— group editor —

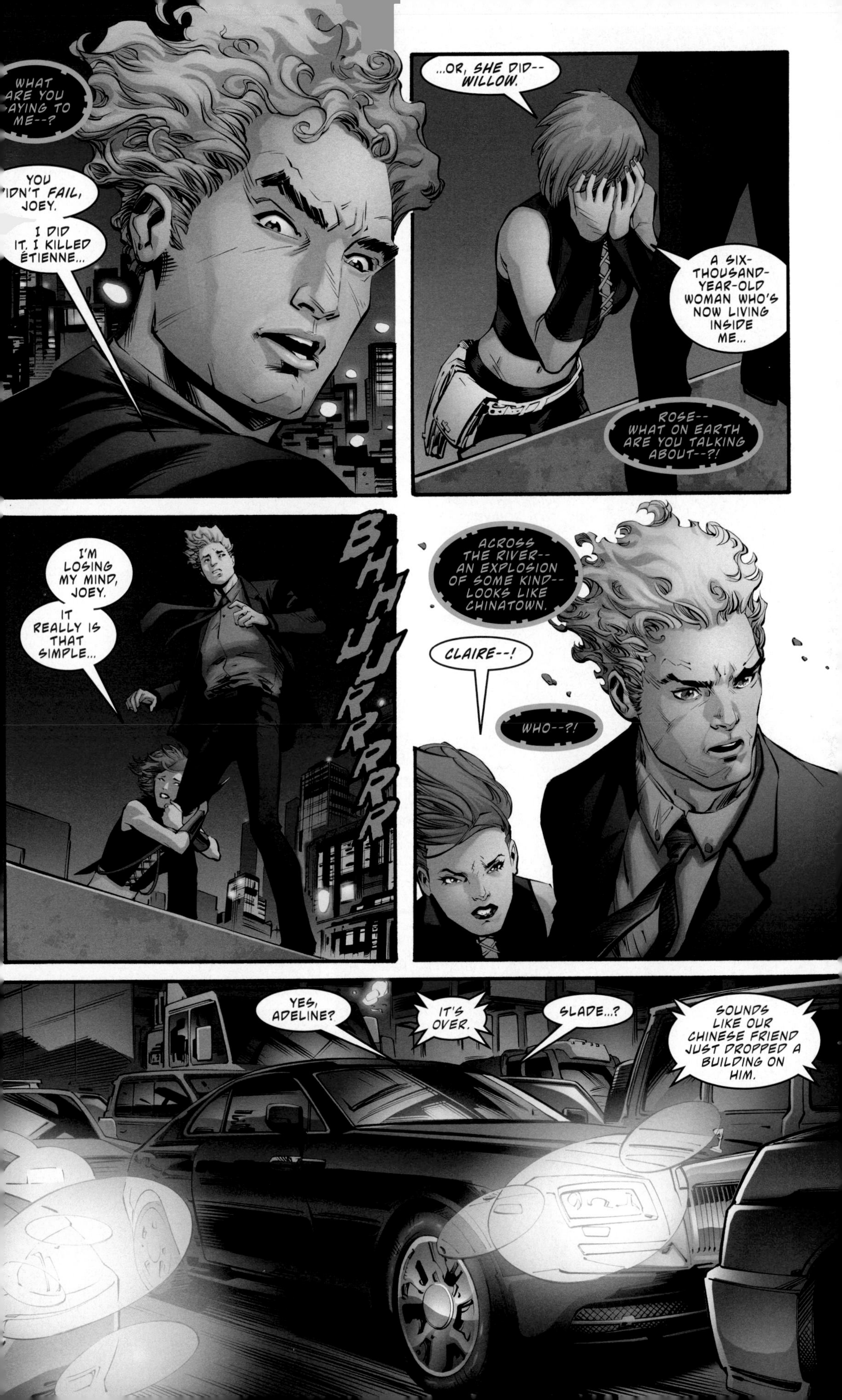
WHAT ARE YOU AYING TO ME--?
YOU IDN'T FAIL, JOEY.
I DID IT. I KILLED ÉTIENNE...
...OR, SHE DID-- WILLOW.
A SIX-THOUSAND-YEAR-OLD WOMAN WHO'S NOW LIVING INSIDE ME...
ROSE-- WHAT ON EARTH ARE YOU TALKING ABOUT--?!
I'M LOSING MY MIND, JOEY.
IT REALLY IS THAT SIMPLE...
BHHUURRRRR
ACROSS THE RIVER-- AN EXPLOSION OF SOME KIND-- LOOKS LIKE CHINATOWN.
CLAIRE--!
WHO--?!
YES, ADELINE?
IT'S OVER.
SLADE...?
SOUNDS LIKE OUR CHINESE FRIEND JUST DROPPED A BUILDING ON HIM.

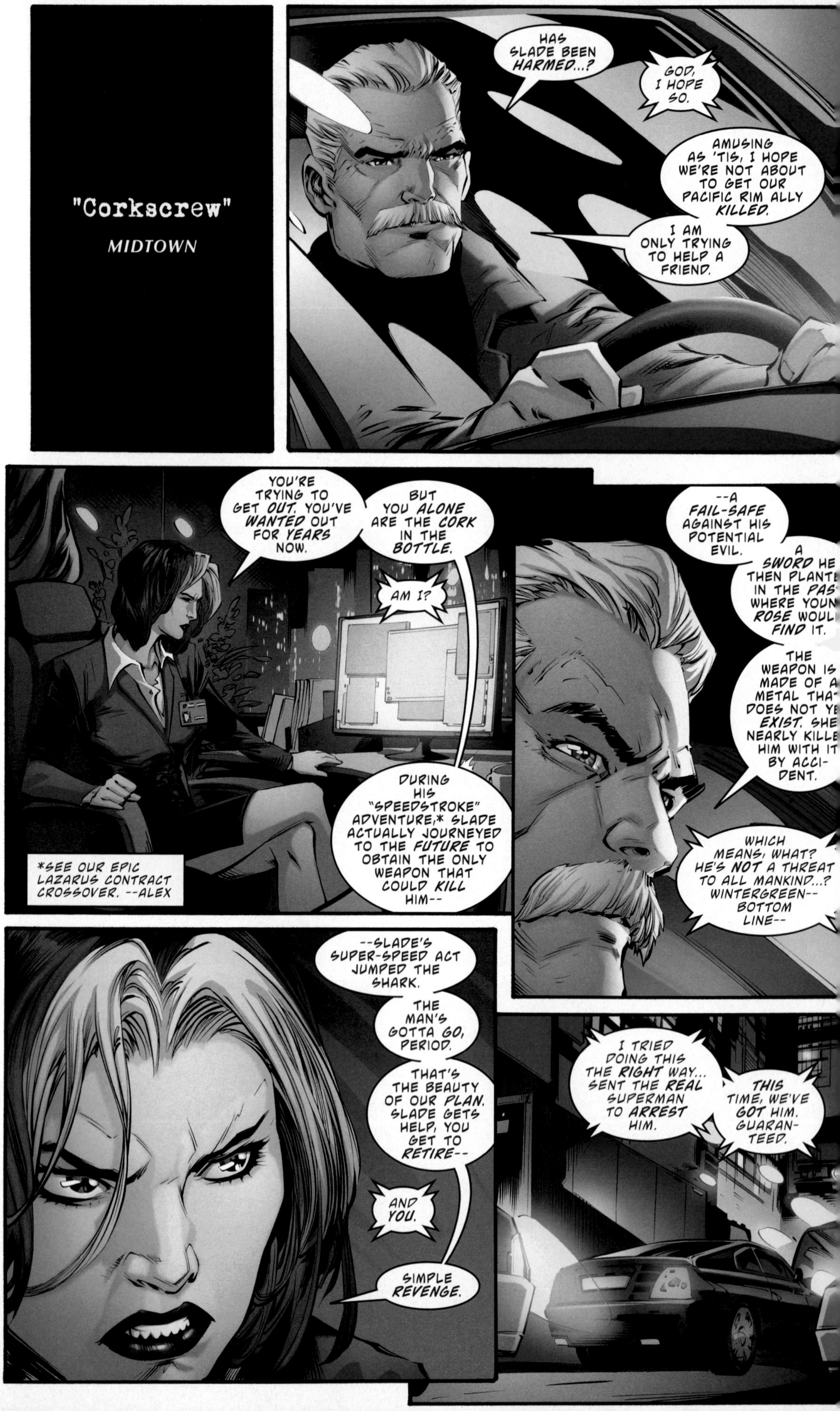
"Corkscrew"
MIDTOWN
HAS SLADE BEEN HARMED...?
GOD, I HOPE SO.
AMUSING AS 'TIS, I HOPE WE'RE NOT ABOUT TO GET OUR PACIFIC RIM ALLY KILLED.
I AM ONLY TRYING TO HELP A FRIEND.
YOU'RE TRYING TO GET OUT. YOU'VE WANTED OUT FOR YEARS NOW.
BUT YOU ALONE ARE THE CORK IN THE BOTTLE.
AM I?
DURING HIS "SPEEDSTROKE" ADVENTURE,* SLADE ACTUALLY JOURNEYED TO THE FUTURE TO OBTAIN THE ONLY WEAPON THAT COULD KILL HIM--
*SEE OUR EPIC LAZARUS CONTRACT CROSSOVER. --ALEX
--A FAIL-SAFE AGAINST HIS POTENTIAL EVIL.
A SWORD HE THEN PLANTE IN THE PAS WHERE YOUN ROSE WOUL FIND IT.
THE WEAPON IS MADE OF A METAL THA DOES NOT YE EXIST. SHE NEARLY KILLE HIM WITH IT BY ACCI-DENT.
WHICH MEANS, WHAT? HE'S NOT A THREAT TO ALL MANKIND...? WINTERGREEN-- BOTTOM LINE--
--SLADE'S SUPER-SPEED ACT JUMPED THE SHARK.
THE MAN'S GOTTA GO, PERIOD.
THAT'S THE BEAUTY OF OUR PLAN. SLADE GETS HELP, YOU GET TO RETIRE--
AND YOU.
SIMPLE REVENGE.
I TRIED DOING THIS THE RIGHT WAY... SENT THE REAL SUPERMAN TO ARREST HIM.
THIS TIME, WE'VE GOT HIM. GUARAN-TEED.

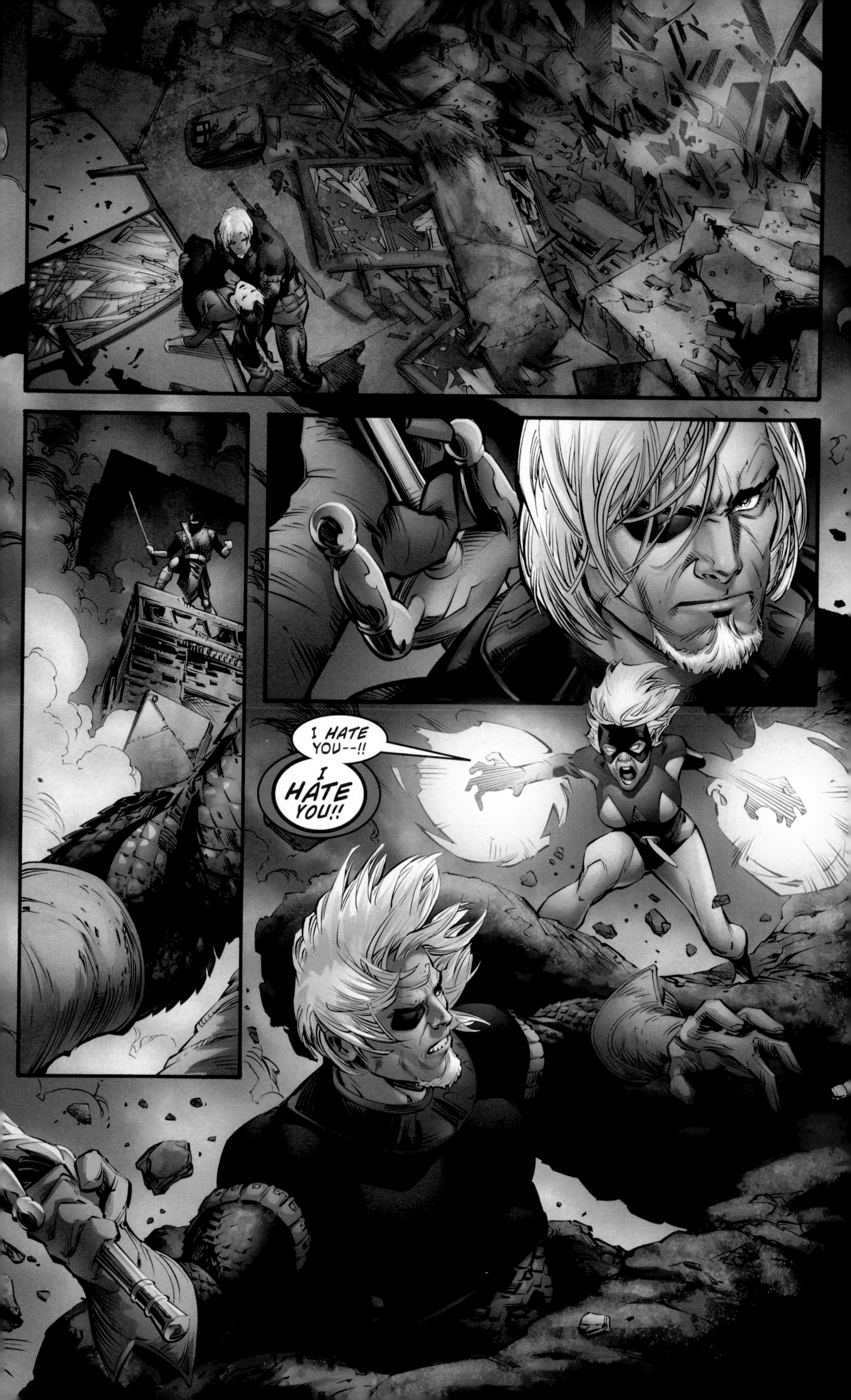
I HATE YOU--!!
I HATE YOU!!

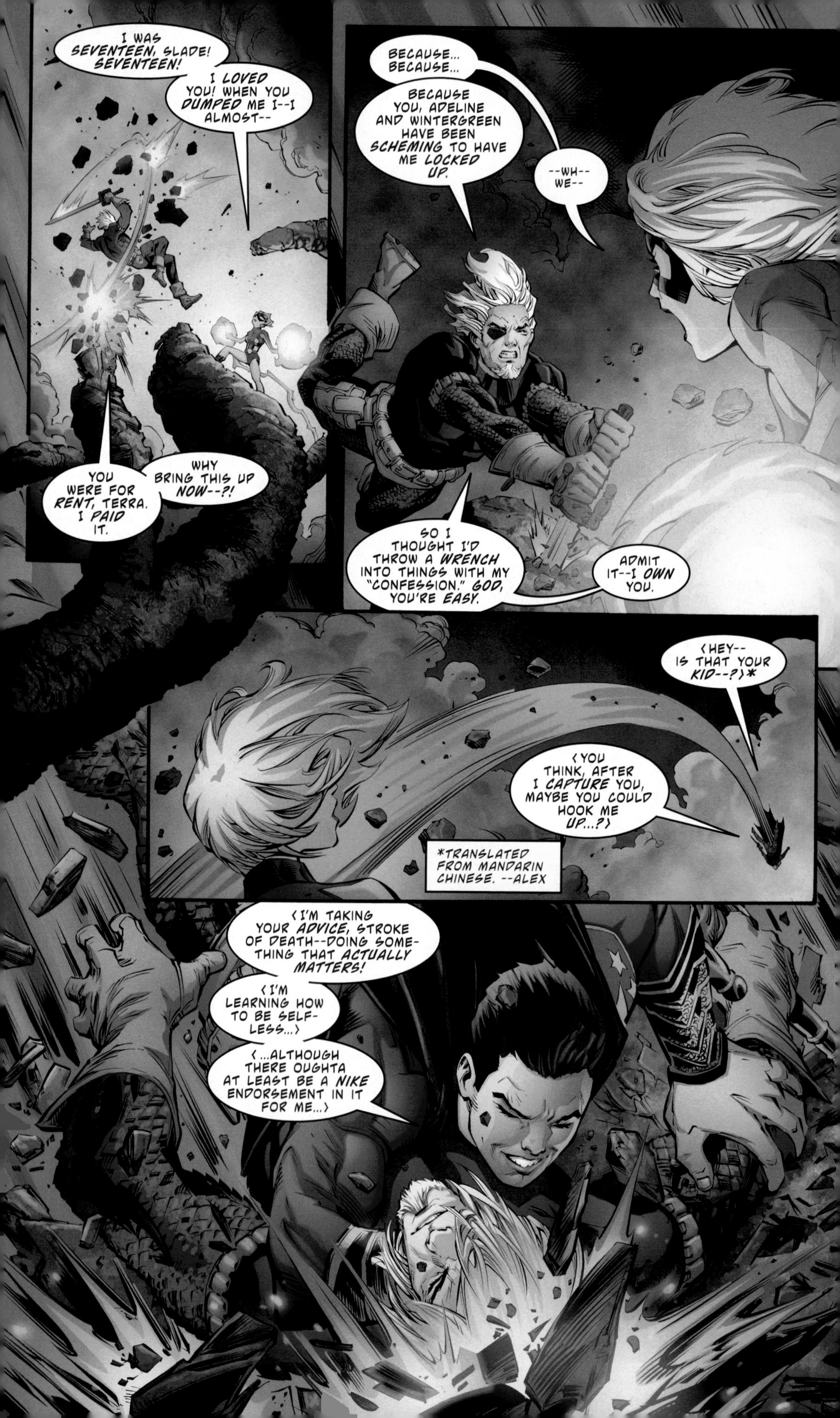
I WAS SEVENTEEN, SLADE! SEVENTEEN!
I LOVED YOU! WHEN YOU DUMPED ME I--I ALMOST--
WHY BRING THIS UP NOW--?!
YOU WERE FOR RENT, TERRA. I PAID IT.
BECAUSE... BECAUSE...
BECAUSE YOU, ADELINE AND WINTERGREEN HAVE BEEN SCHEMING TO HAVE ME LOCKED UP.
--WH-- WE--
SO I THOUGHT I'D THROW A WRENCH INTO THINGS WITH MY "CONFESSION." GOD, YOU'RE EASY.
ADMIT IT--I OWN YOU.
‹HEY-- IS THAT YOUR KID--?›*
‹YOU THINK, AFTER I CAPTURE YOU, MAYBE YOU COULD HOOK ME UP...?›
*TRANSLATED FROM MANDARIN CHINESE. --ALEX
‹I'M TAKING YOUR ADVICE, STROKE OF DEATH--DOING SOME-THING THAT ACTUALLY MATTERS!
‹I'M LEARNING HOW TO BE SELF-LESS...›
‹...ALTHOUGH THERE OUGHTA AT LEAST BE A NIKE ENDORSEMENT IN IT FOR ME...›

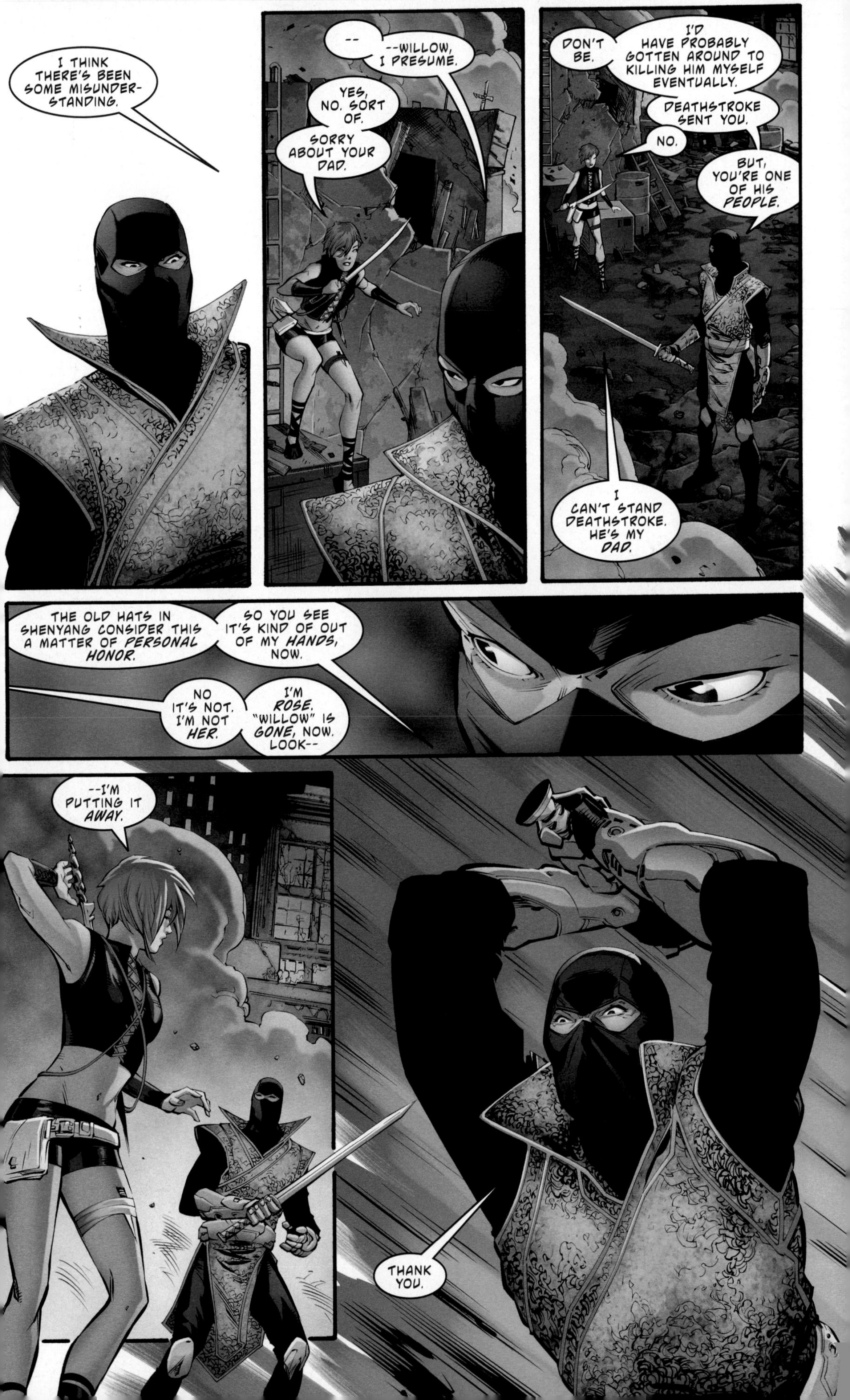
I THINK THERE'S BEEN SOME MISUNDER-STANDING.
--
--WILLOW, I PRESUME.
YES, NO. SORT OF.
SORRY ABOUT YOUR DAD.
DON'T BE.
I'D HAVE PROBABLY GOTTEN AROUND TO KILLING HIM MYSELF EVENTUALLY.
DEATHSTROKE SENT YOU.
NO.
BUT, YOU'RE ONE OF HIS PEOPLE.
I CAN'T STAND DEATHSTROKE. HE'S MY DAD.
THE OLD HATS IN SHENYANG CONSIDER THIS A MATTER OF PERSONAL HONOR.
SO YOU SEE IT'S KIND OF OUT OF MY HANDS, NOW.
NO IT'S NOT. I'M NOT HER.
I'M ROSE. "WILLOW" IS GONE, NOW. LOOK--
--I'M PUTTING IT AWAY.
THANK YOU.

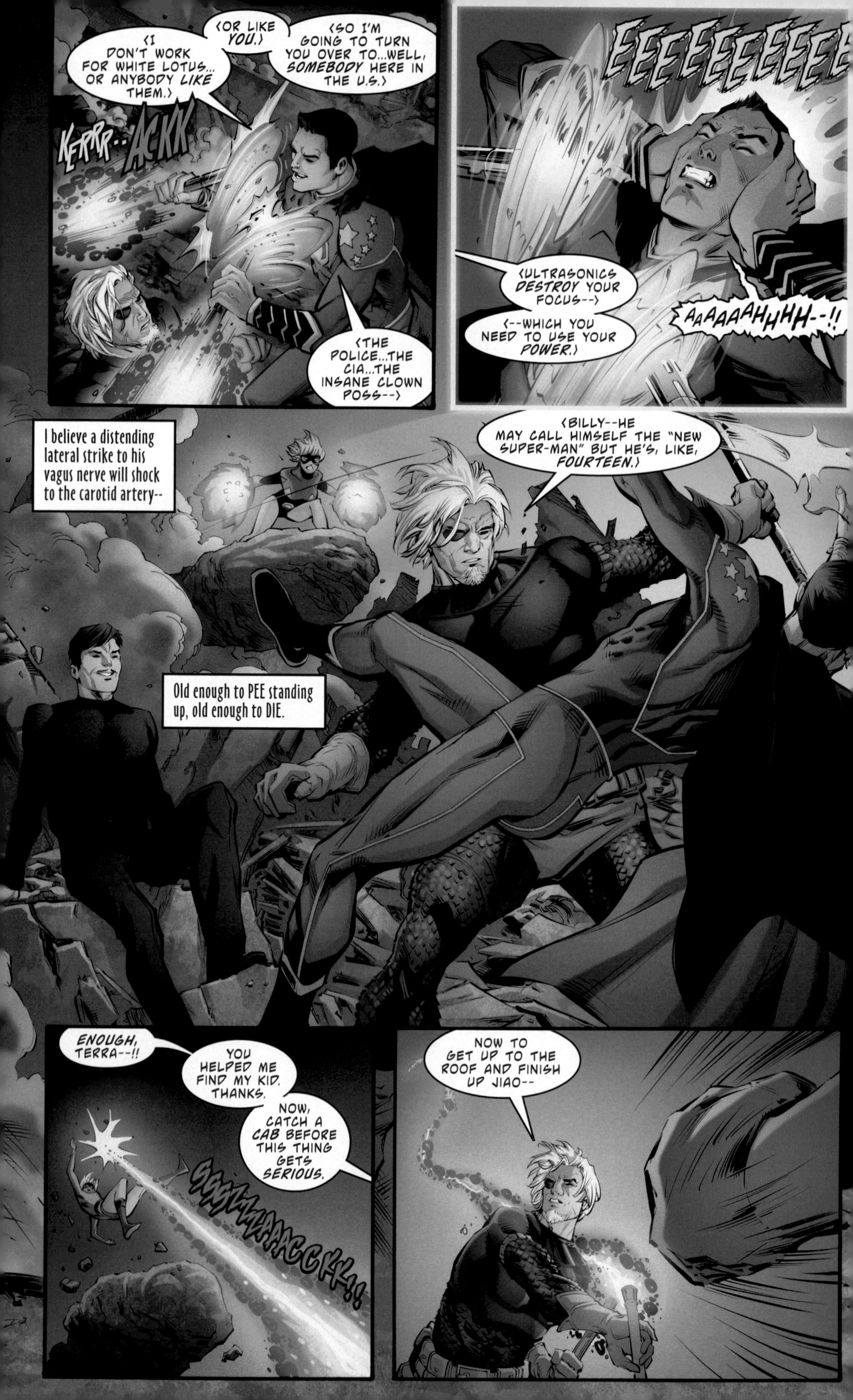
‹I DON'T WORK FOR WHITE LOTUS... OR ANYBODY LIKE THEM.›
‹OR LIKE YOU.›
‹SO I'M GOING TO TURN YOU OVER TO...WELL, SOMEBODY HERE IN THE U.S.›
KERRR--ACKK
‹THE POLICE...THE CIA...THE INSANE CLOWN POSS--›
EEEEEEEEEE
‹ULTRASONICS DESTROY YOUR FOCUS--›
‹--WHICH YOU NEED TO USE YOUR POWER.›
AAAAAAHHHH--!!
I believe a distending lateral strike to his vagus nerve will shock to the carotid artery--
‹BILLY--HE MAY CALL HIMSELF THE "NEW SUPER-MAN" BUT HE'S, LIKE, FOURTEEN.›
Old enough to PEE standing up, old enough to DIE.
ENOUGH, TERRA--!!
YOU HELPED ME FIND MY KID. THANKS.
NOW, CATCH A CAB BEFORE THIS THING GETS SERIOUS.
SSSMAAACCKK!!
NOW TO GET UP TO THE ROOF AND FINISH UP JIAO--

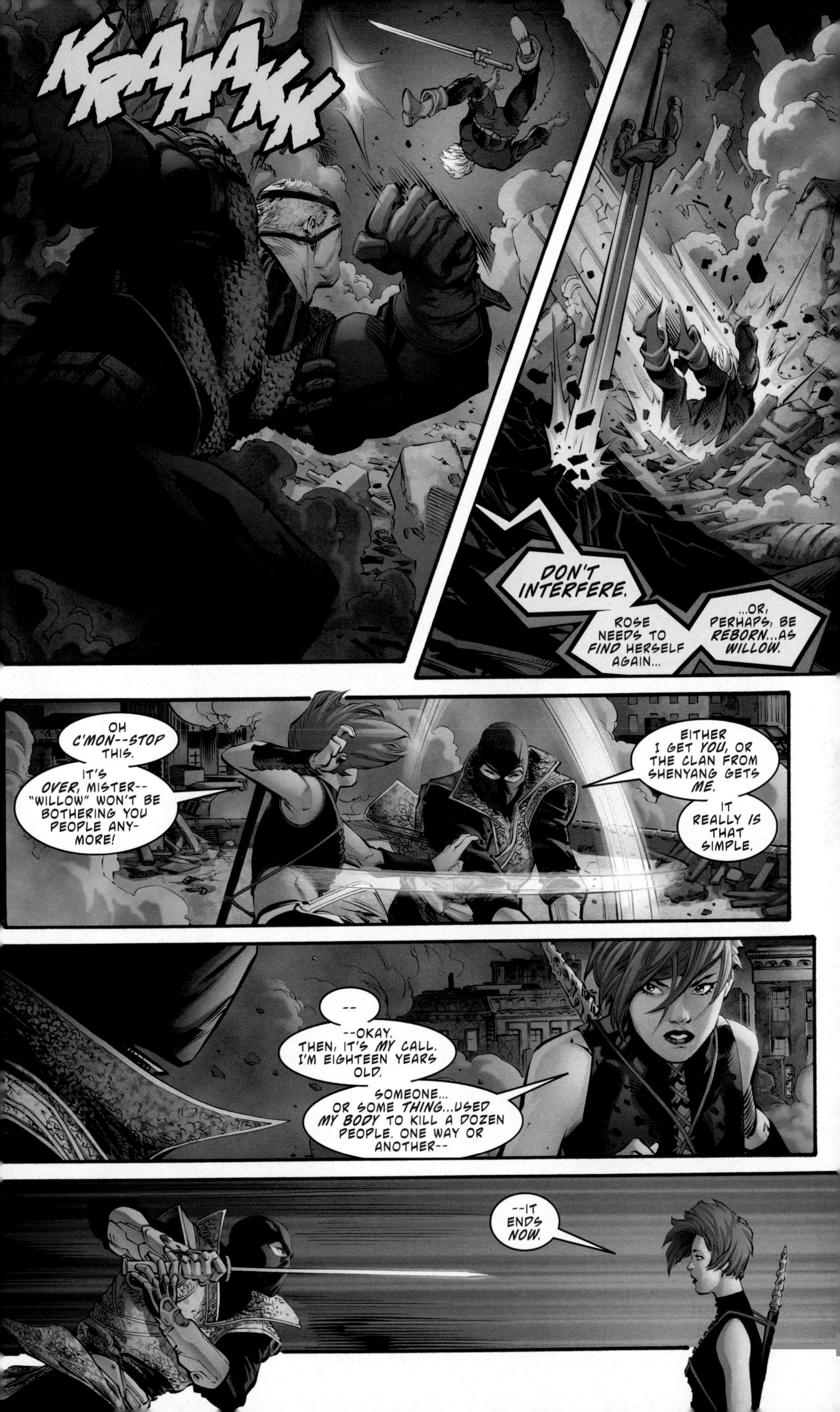
KRAAAKK
DON'T INTERFERE.
ROSE NEEDS TO FIND HERSELF AGAIN...
...OR, PERHAPS, BE REBORN...AS WILLOW.
OH C'MON--STOP THIS.
IT'S OVER, MISTER--"WILLOW" WON'T BE BOTHERING YOU PEOPLE ANY-MORE!
EITHER I GET YOU, OR THE CLAN FROM SHENYANG GETS ME.
IT REALLY IS THAT SIMPLE.
--
--OKAY. THEN, IT'S MY CALL. I'M EIGHTEEN YEARS OLD.
SOMEONE... OR SOME THING...USED MY BODY TO KILL A DOZEN PEOPLE. ONE WAY OR ANOTHER--
--IT ENDS NOW.

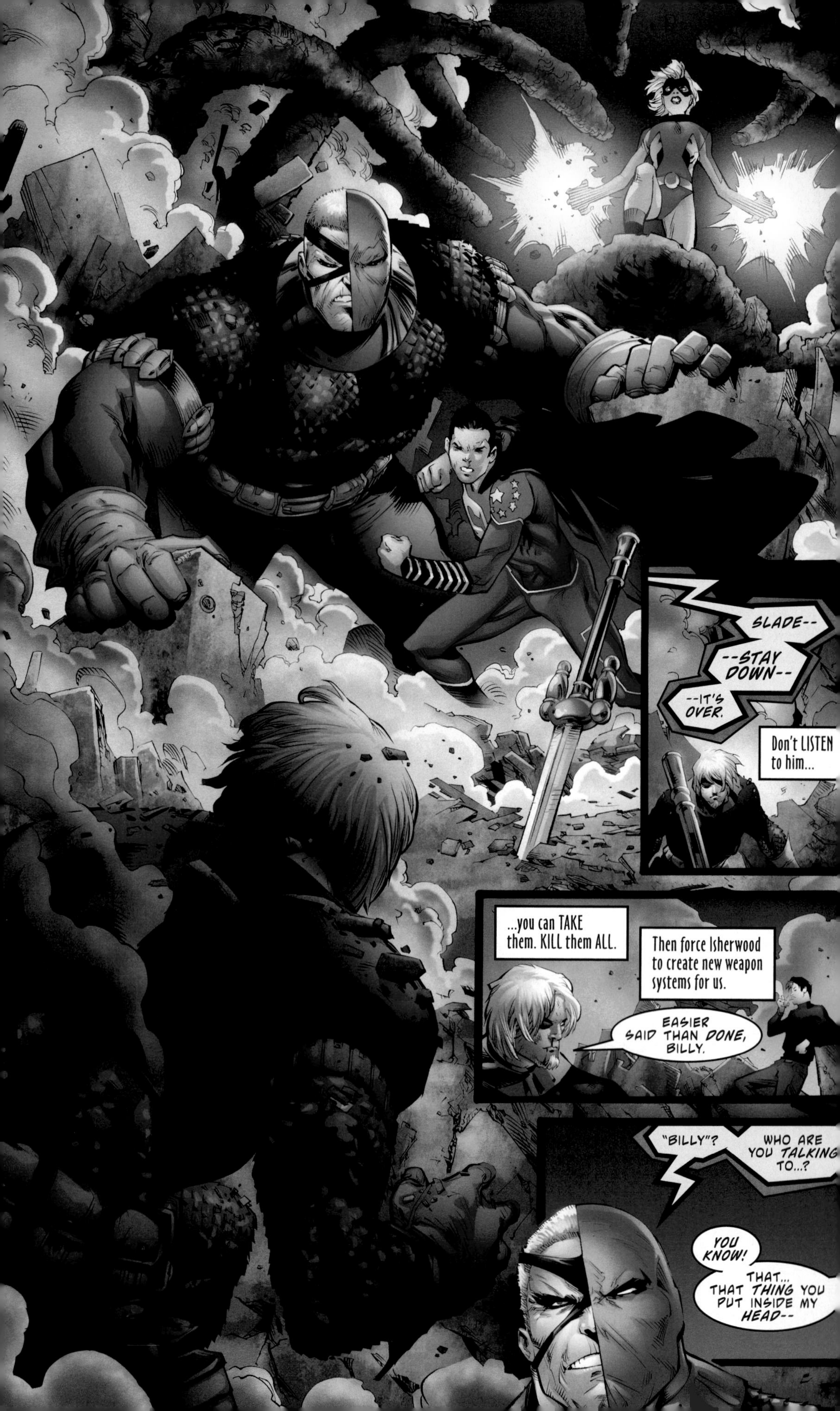
SLADE--
--STAY DOWN--
--IT'S OVER.
Don't LISTEN to him...
...you can TAKE them. KILL them ALL.
Then force Isherwood to create new weapon systems for us.
EASIER SAID THAN DONE, BILLY.
"BILLY"?
WHO ARE YOU TALKING TO...?
YOU KNOW!
THAT... THAT THING YOU PUT INSIDE MY HEAD--

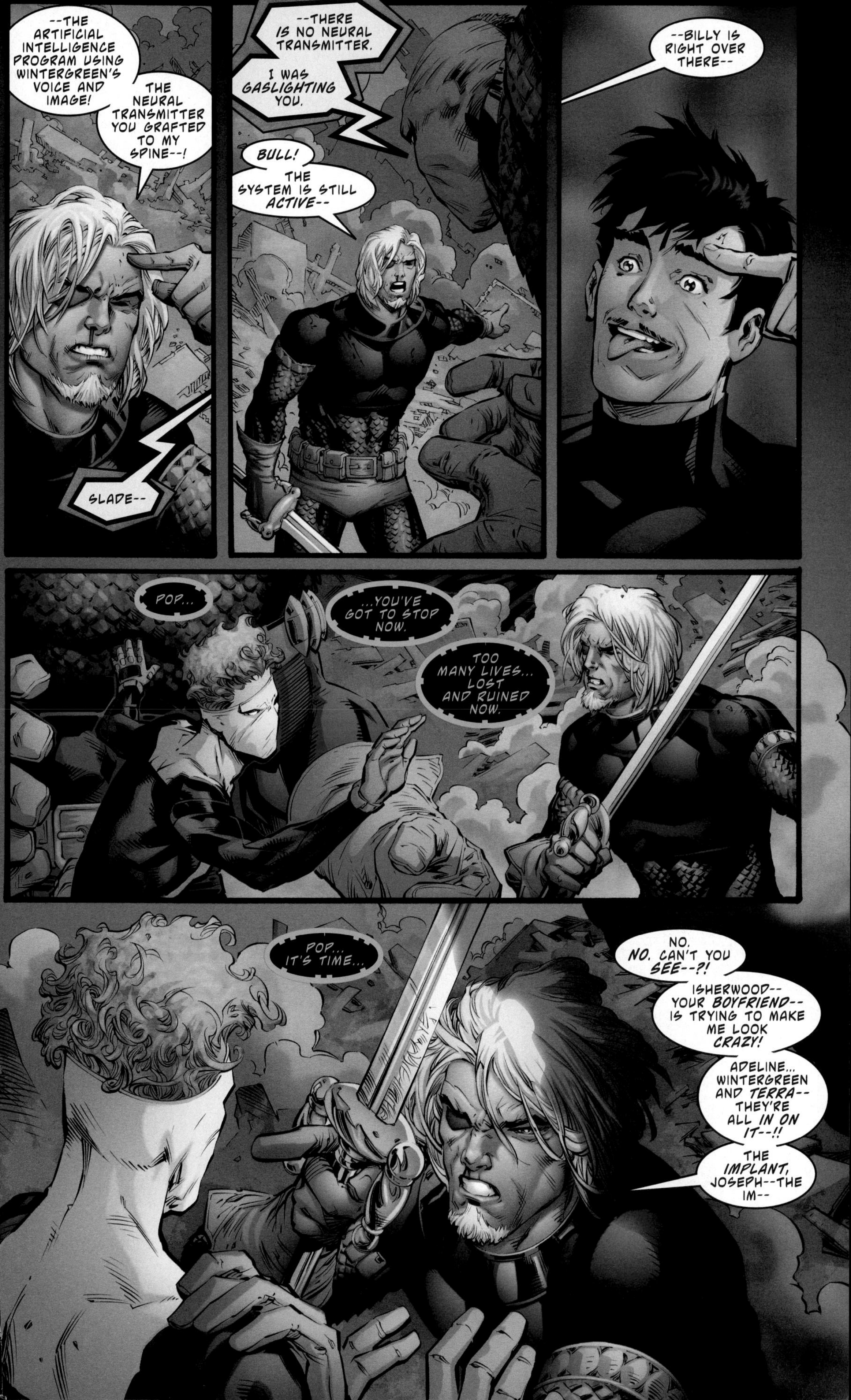
--THE ARTIFICIAL INTELLIGENCE PROGRAM USING WINTERGREEN'S VOICE AND IMAGE!
THE NEURAL TRANSMITTER YOU GRAFTED TO MY SPINE--!
SLADE--
--THERE IS NO NEURAL TRANSMITTER.
I WAS GASLIGHTING YOU.
BULL!
THE SYSTEM IS STILL ACTIVE--
--BILLY IS RIGHT OVER THERE--
POP...
...YOU'VE GOT TO STOP NOW.
TOO MANY LIVES... LOST AND RUINED NOW.
POP... IT'S TIME...
NO. NO. CAN'T YOU SEE--?!
ISHERWOOD-- YOUR BOYFRIEND-- IS TRYING TO MAKE ME LOOK CRAZY!
ADELINE... WINTERGREEN AND TERRA-- THEY'RE ALL IN ON IT--!!
THE IMPLANT, JOSEPH--THE IM--

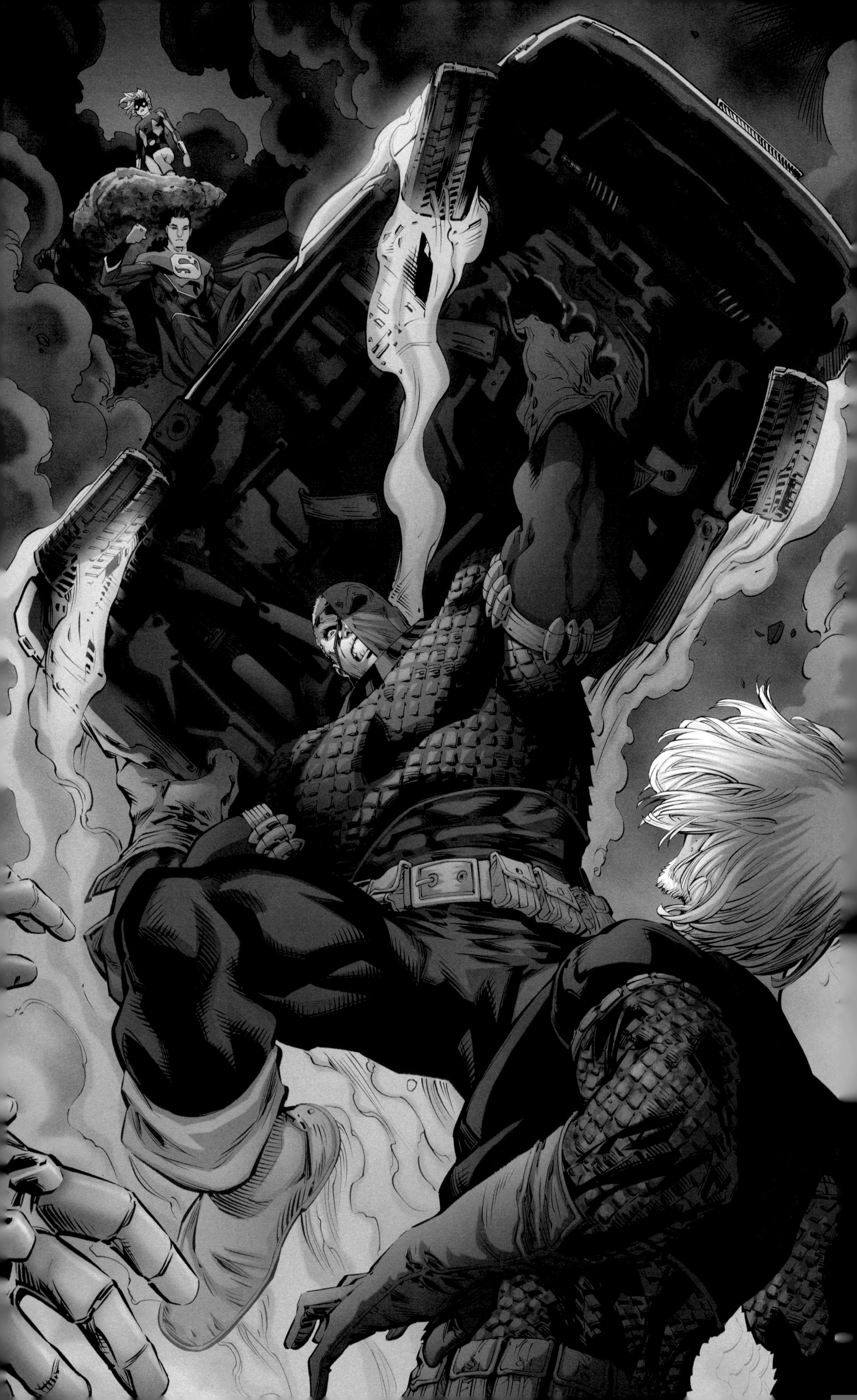

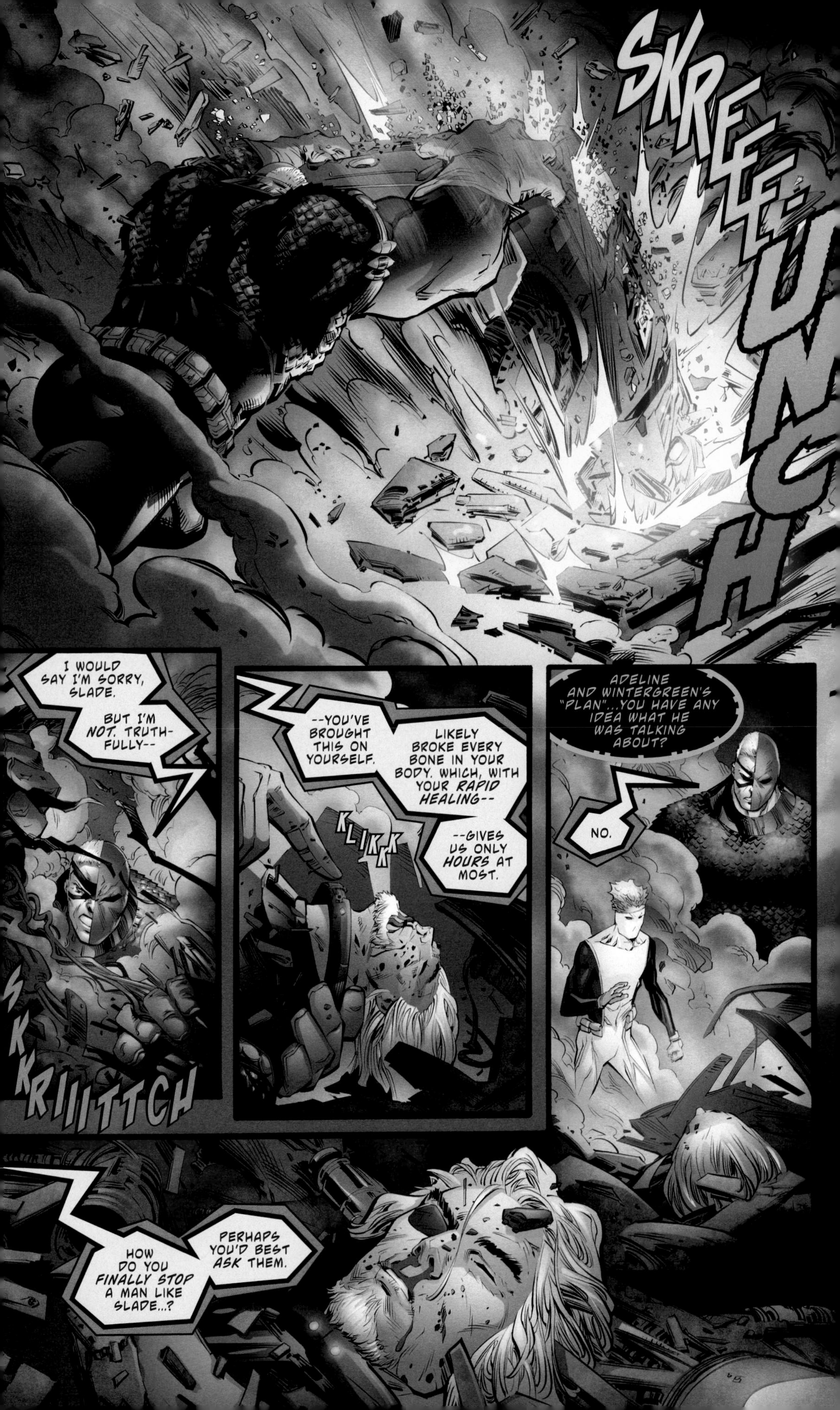

SKREEEUNGH
I WOULD SAY I'M SORRY, SLADE.
BUT I'M *NOT.* TRUTHFULLY--
SKKRIIITTCH
--YOU'VE BROUGHT THIS ON YOURSELF.
LIKELY BROKE EVERY BONE IN YOUR BODY. WHICH, WITH YOUR *RAPID HEALING*--
KLIKKK
--GIVES US ONLY *HOURS* AT MOST.
ADELINE AND WINTERGREEN'S "PLAN"...YOU HAVE ANY IDEA WHAT HE WAS TALKING ABOUT?
NO.
HOW DO YOU *FINALLY STOP* A MAN LIKE SLADE...?
PERHAPS YOU'D BEST *ASK* THEM.

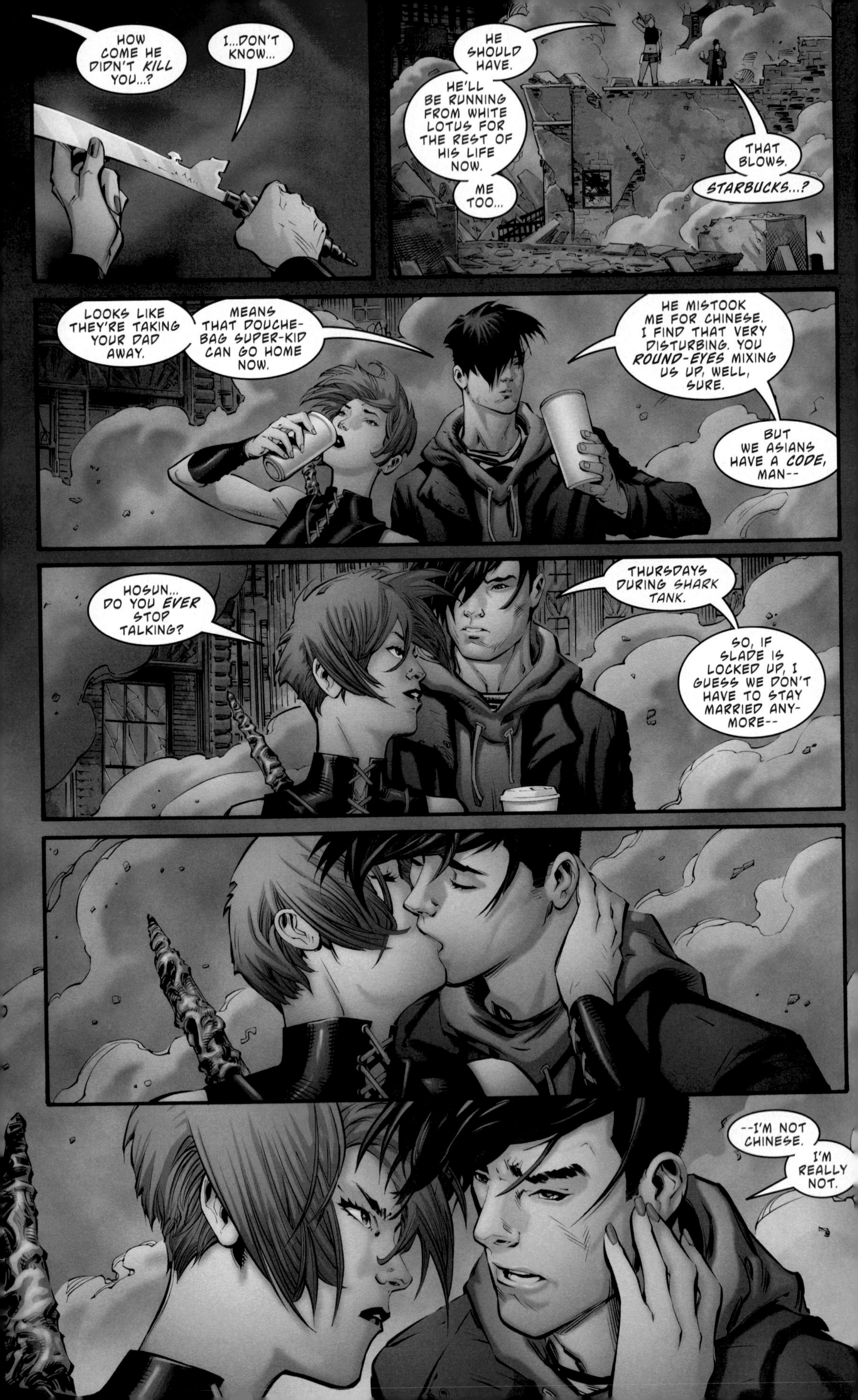
HOW COME HE DIDN'T KILL YOU...?
I...DON'T KNOW...
HE SHOULD HAVE.
HE'LL BE RUNNING FROM WHITE LOTUS FOR THE REST OF HIS LIFE NOW.
ME TOO...
THAT BLOWS.
STARBUCKS...?
LOOKS LIKE THEY'RE TAKING YOUR DAD AWAY.
MEANS THAT DOUCHE-BAG SUPER-KID CAN GO HOME NOW.
HE MISTOOK ME FOR CHINESE. I FIND THAT VERY DISTURBING. YOU ROUND-EYES MIXING US UP, WELL, SURE.
BUT WE ASIANS HAVE A CODE, MAN--
HOSUN... DO YOU EVER STOP TALKING?
THURSDAYS DURING SHARK TANK.
SO, IF SLADE IS LOCKED UP, I GUESS WE DON'T HAVE TO STAY MARRIED ANY-MORE--
--I'M NOT CHINESE.
I'M REALLY NOT.

Well, now, Slade...

...alone at LAST.

--
--IT FIGURES...

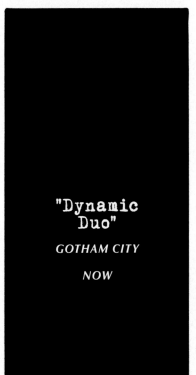

"Dynamic Duo"

GOTHAM CITY

NOW

Just you and me, Slade.

The way it SHOULD be.

So, then--

--shall we BEGIN again...?

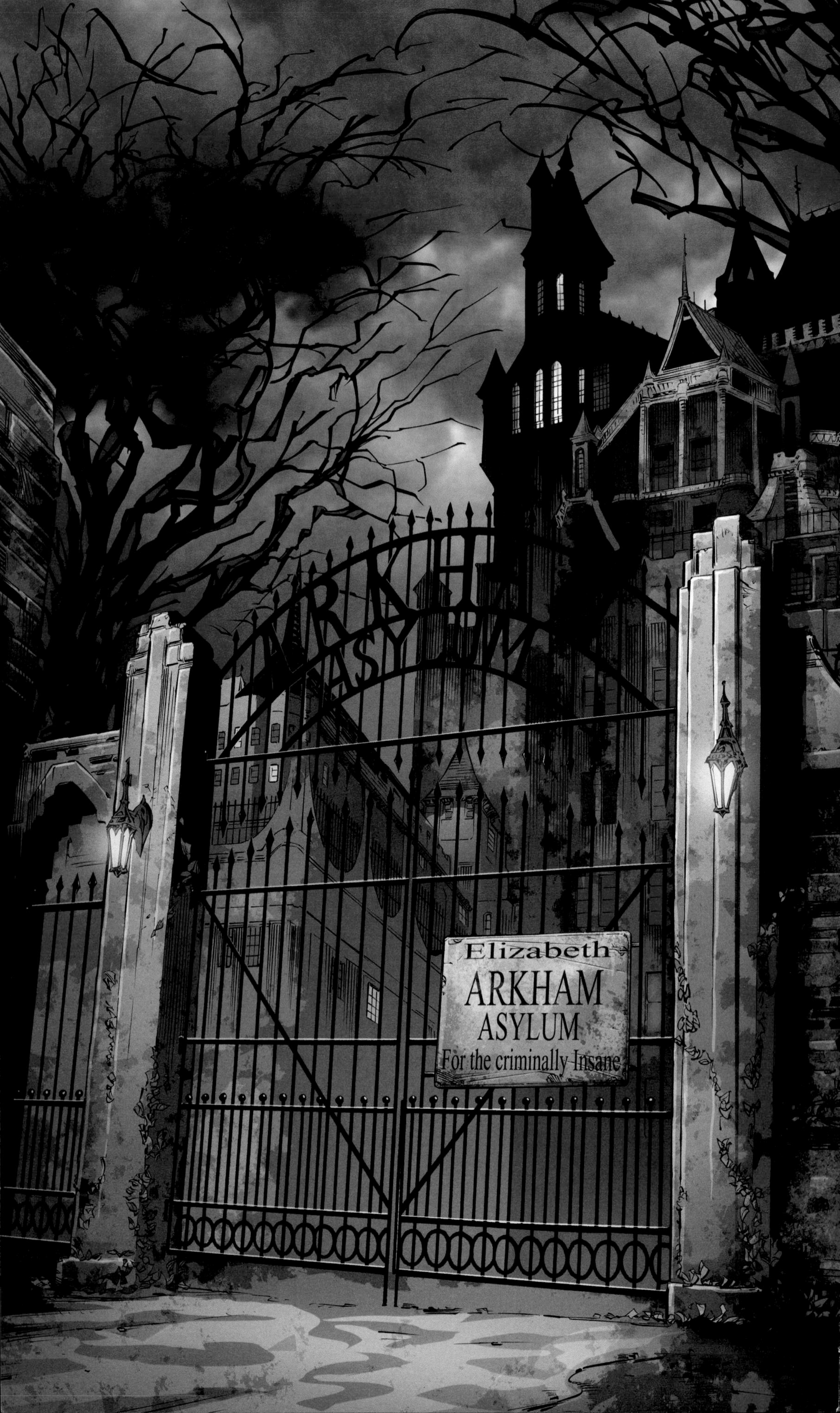
Elizabeth
ARKHAM
ASYLUM
For the criminally Insane

DEATHSTROKE

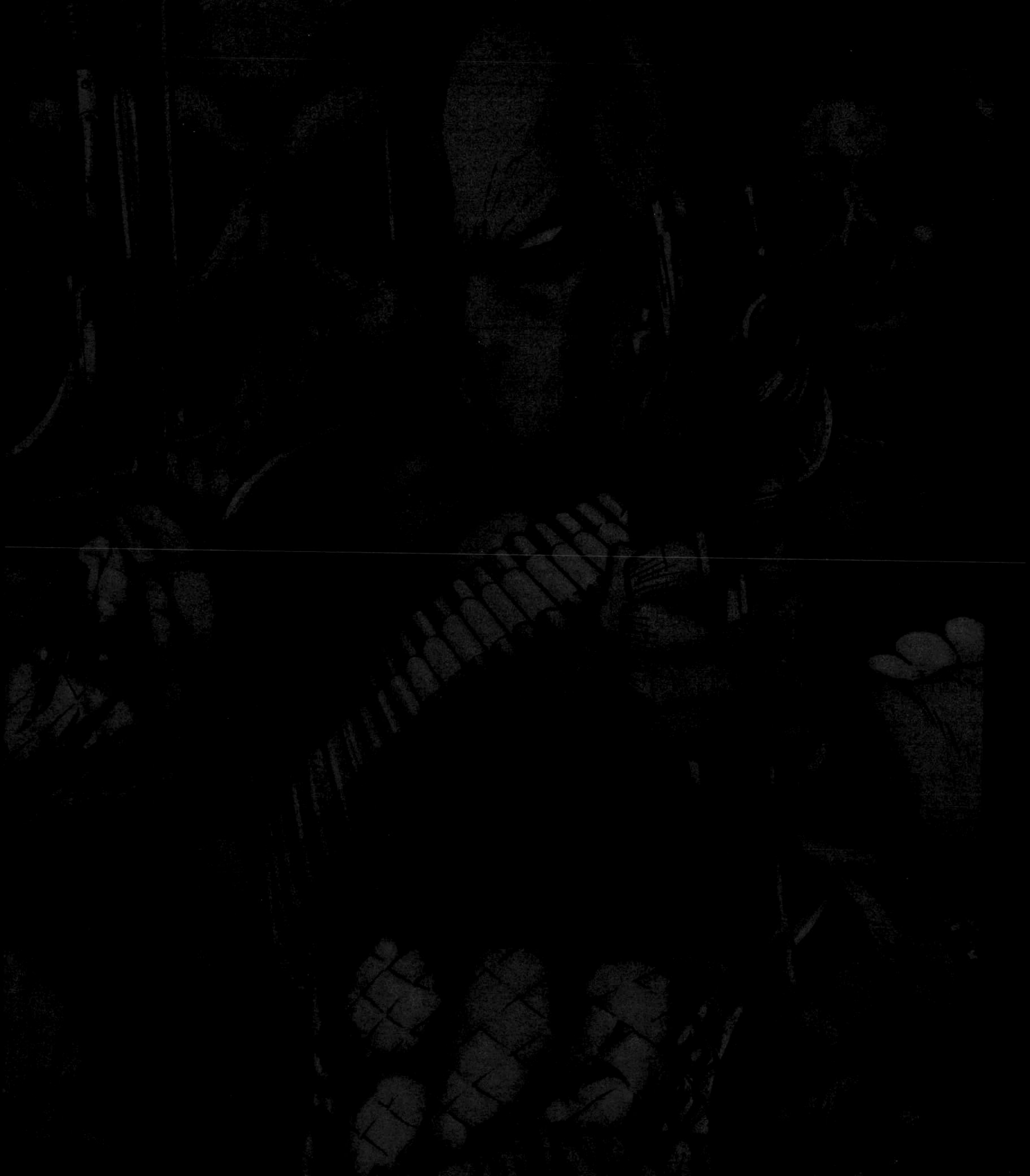

VARIANT COVER GALLERY

DEATHSTROKE #26 variant cover by
SHANE DAVIS, MICHELLE DELECKI and ALEX SINCLAIR

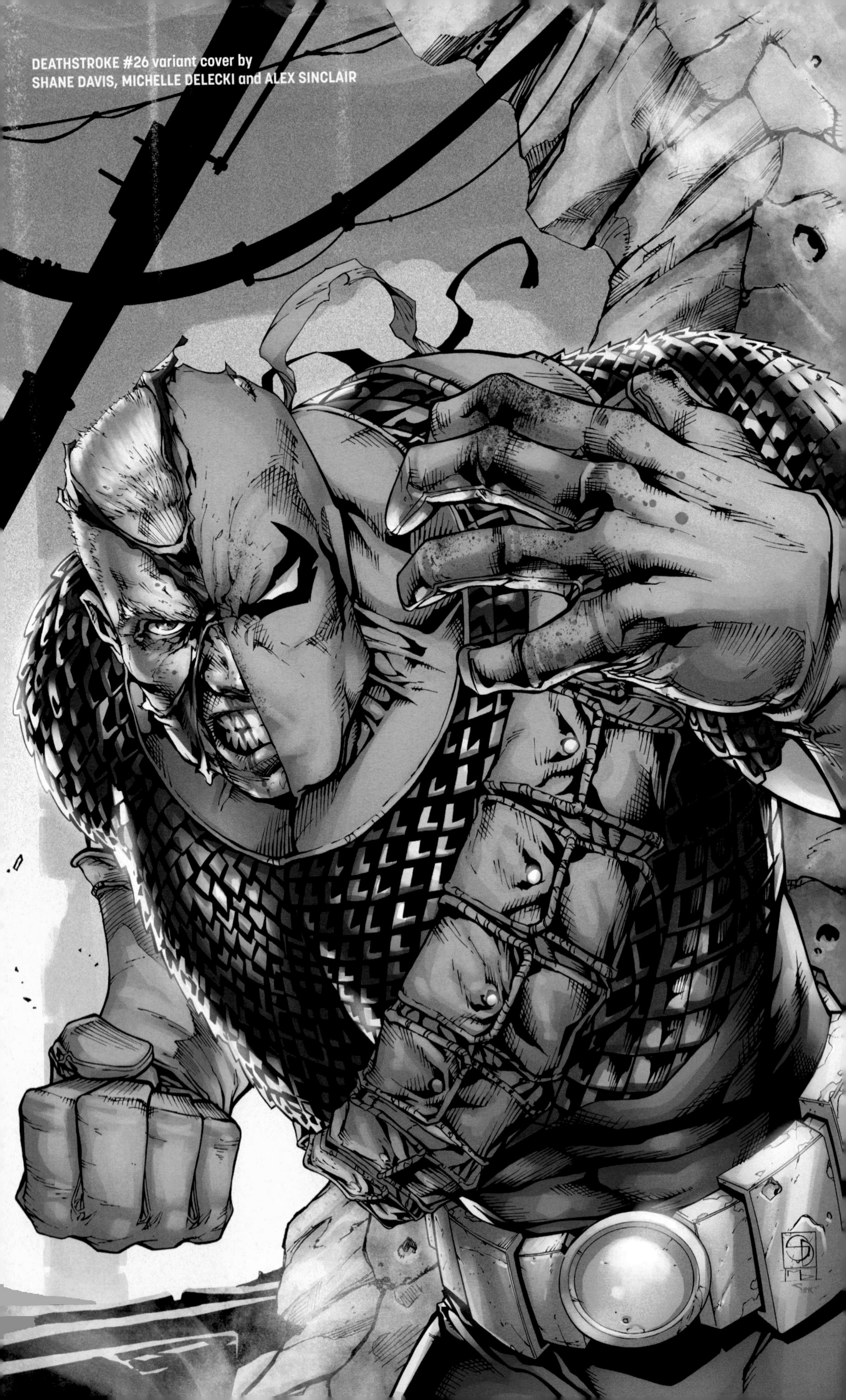

DEATHSTROKE #27 variant cover by
SHANE DAVIS, MICHELLE DELECKI and ALEX SINCLAIR

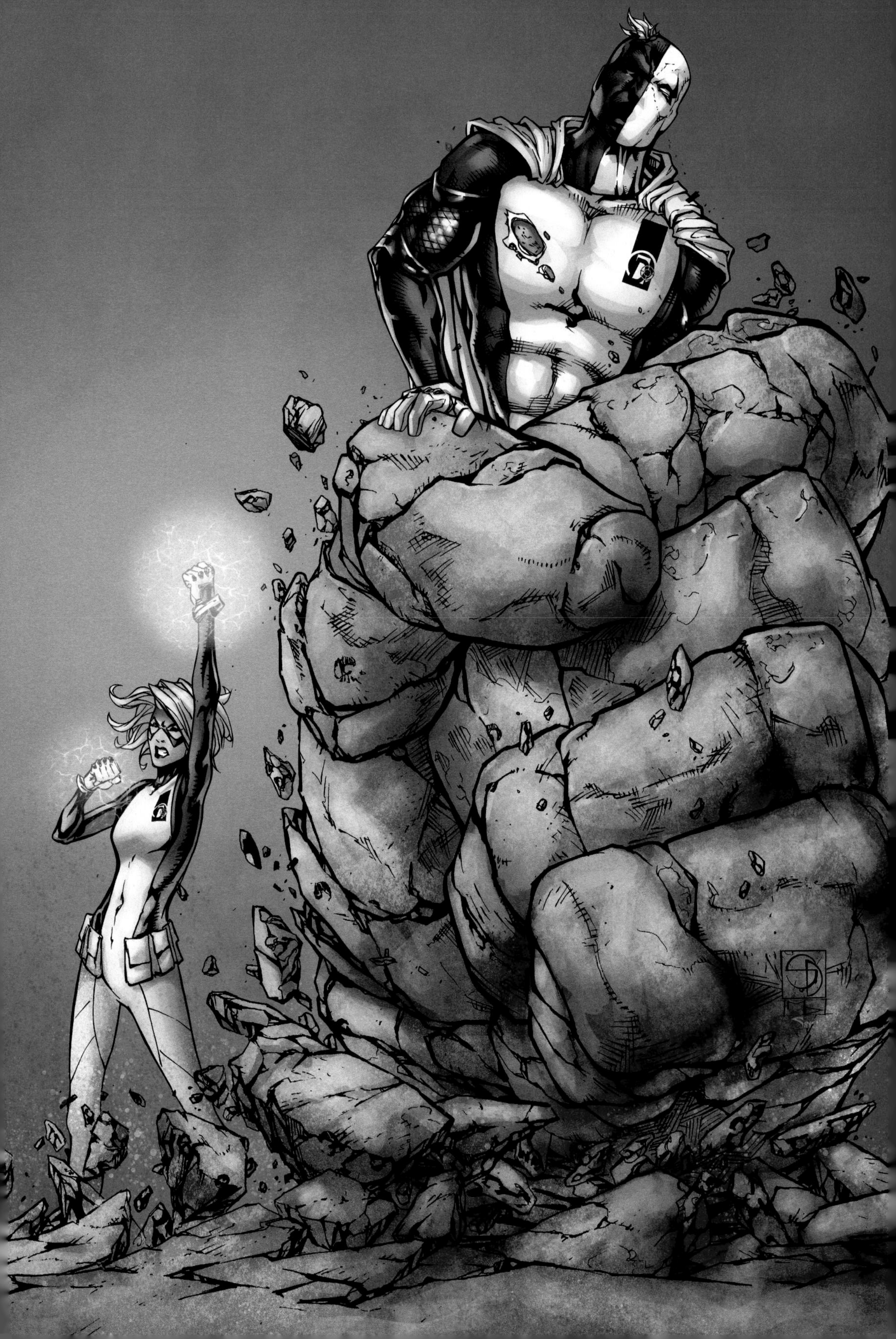

DEATHSTROKE #28 variant cover by
SHANE DAVIS, MICHELLE DELECKI and ALEX SINCLAIR

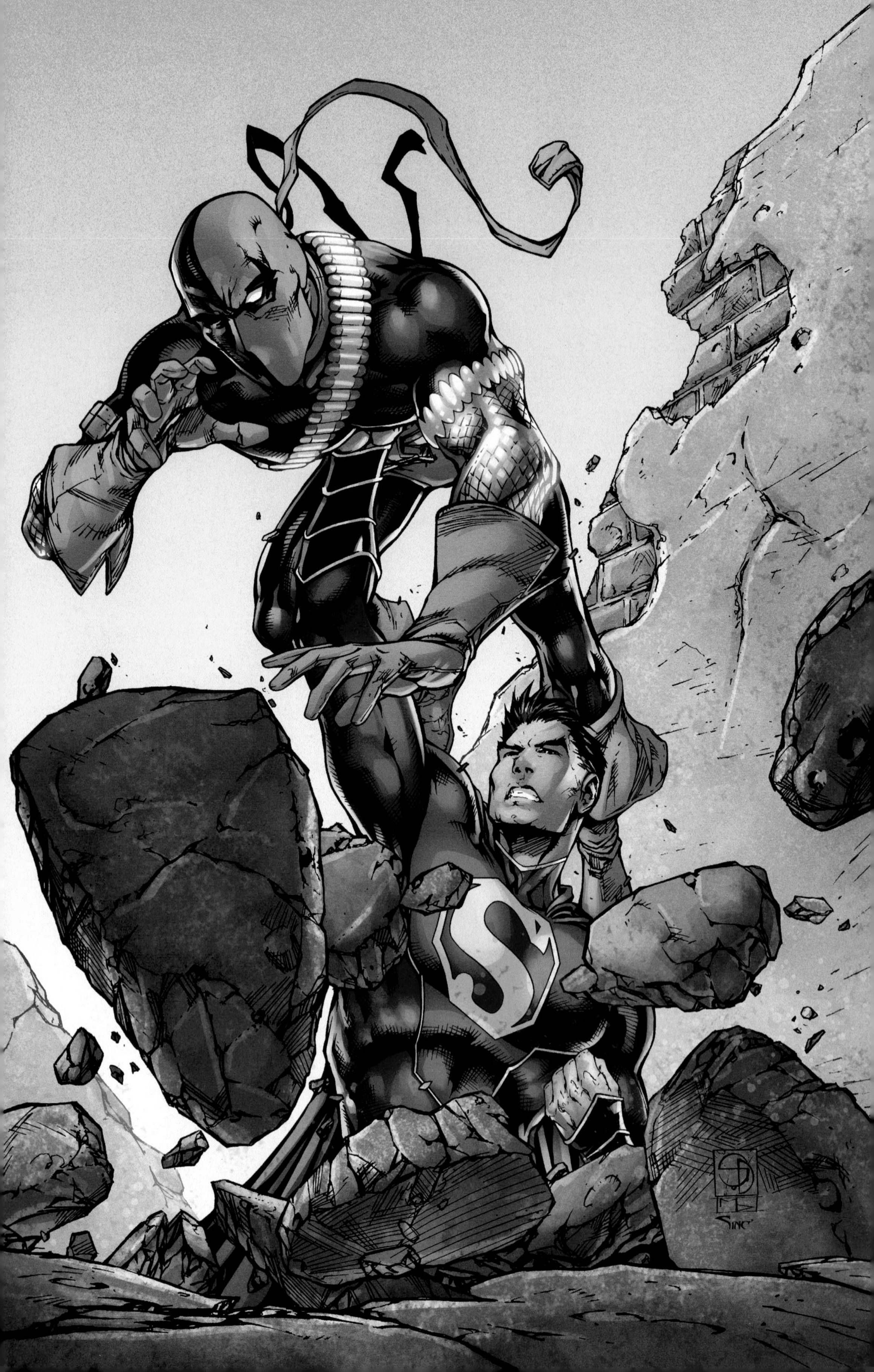

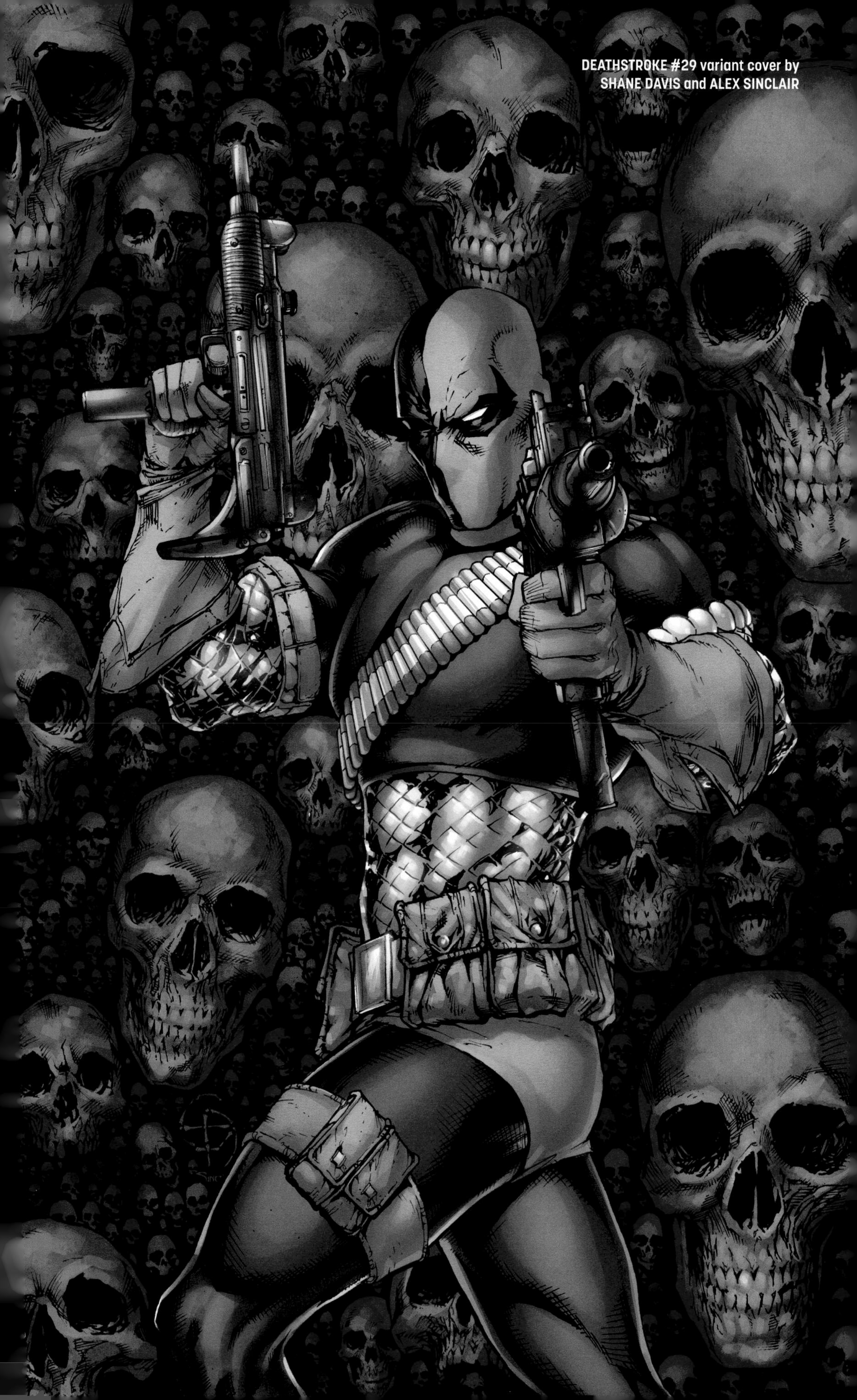

DEATHSTROKE #29 variant cover by
SHANE DAVIS and ALEX SINCLAIR

DEATHSTROKE CHARACTER SKETCH
by DIOGENES NEVES

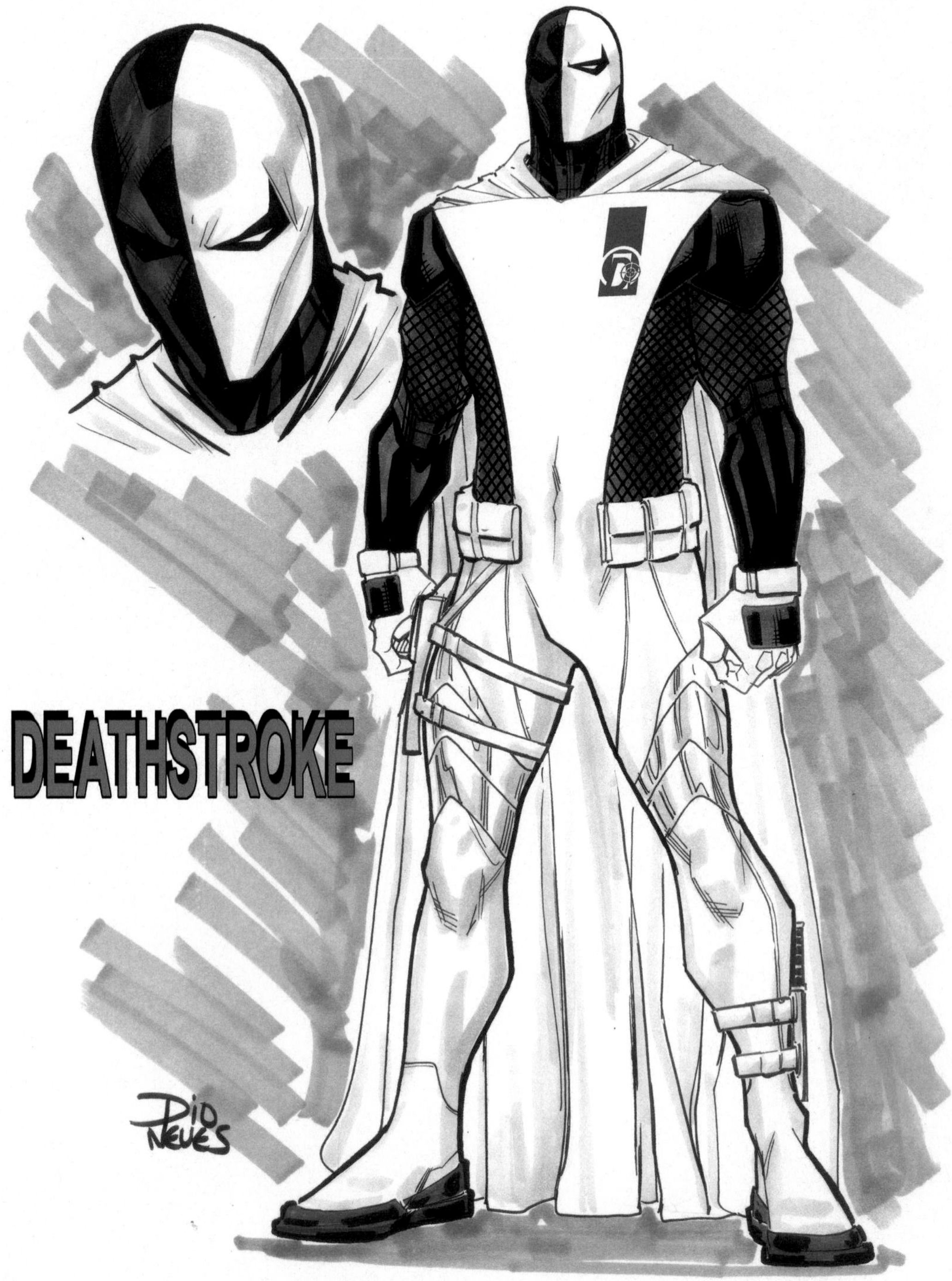
DEATHSTROKE
DIO NEVES

RAVAGER (ROSE) AND WILLOW CHARACTER SKETCHES
by DIOGENES NEVES

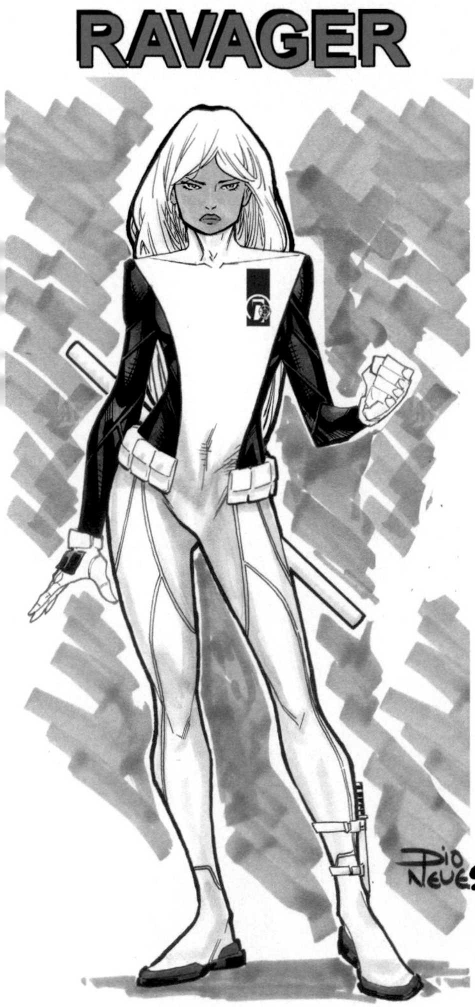
RAVAGER
DIO NEVES

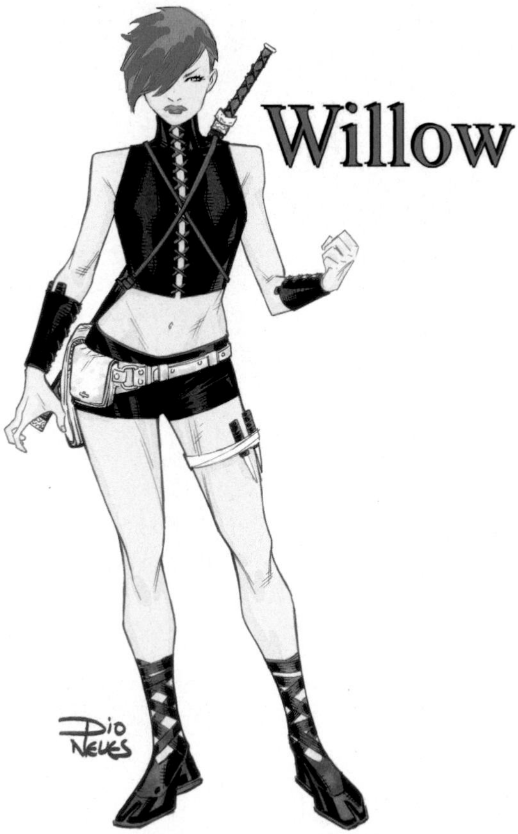
Willow
DIO NEVES

POWER GIRL AND KID FLASH CHARACTER SKETCHES
by DIOGENES NEVES

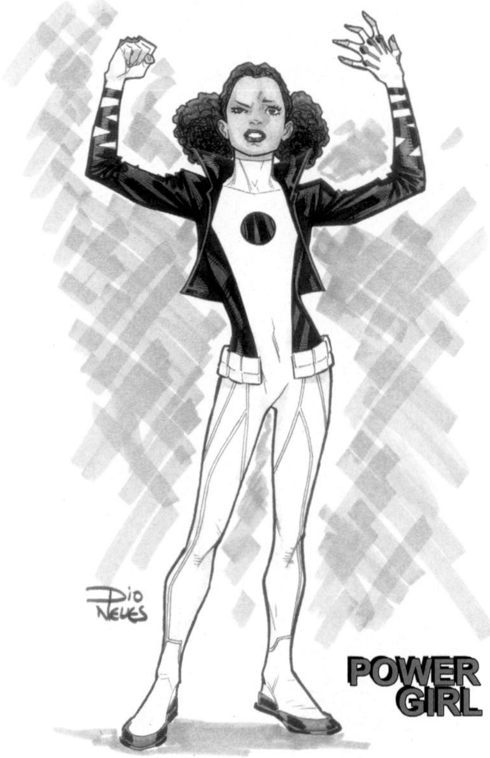
POWER GIRL

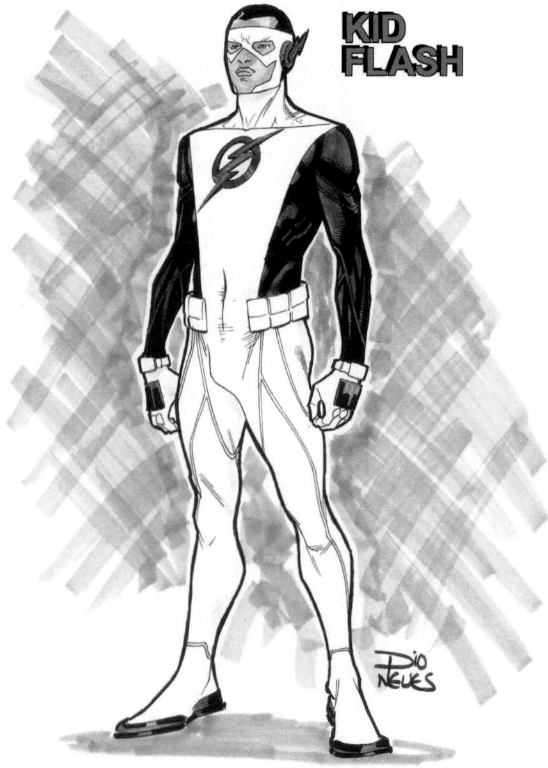
KID FLASH

TERRA AND JERICHO CHARACTER SKETCHES
by DIOGENES NEVES

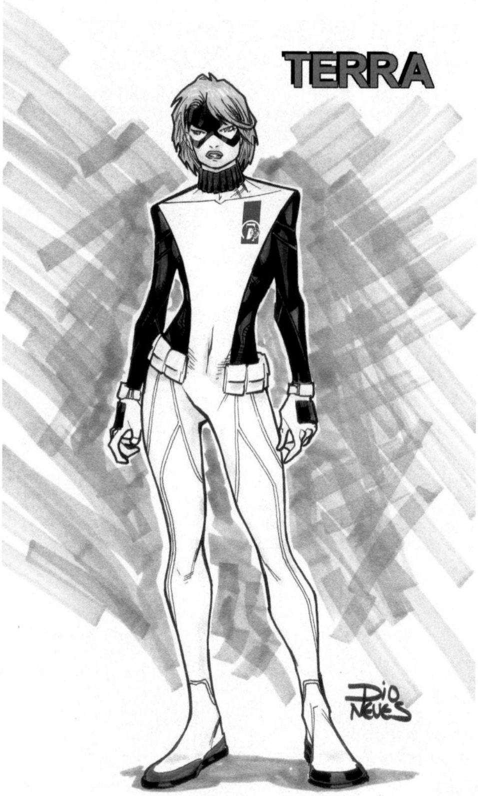
TERRA
DIO NEVES

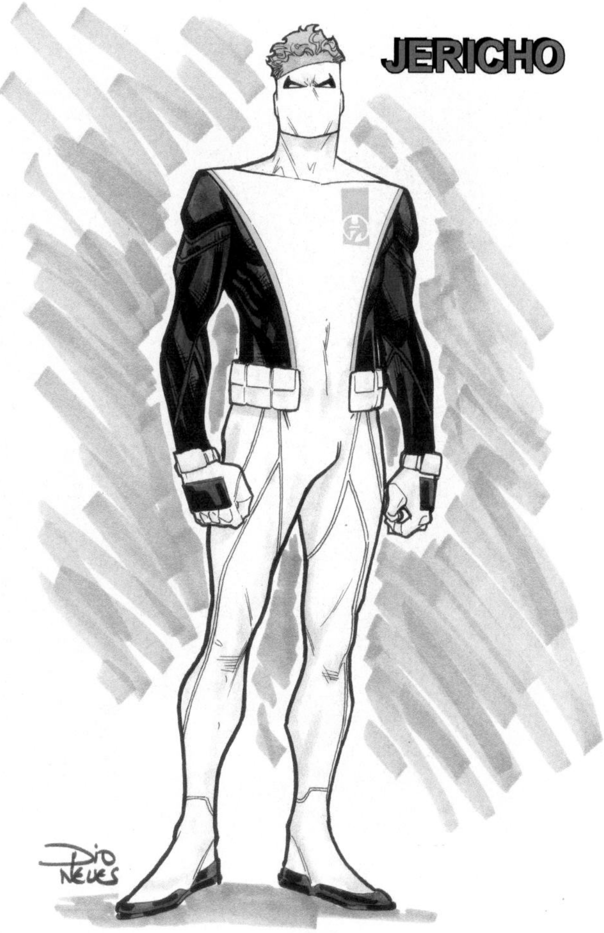
JERICHO
DIO NEVES

DEATHSTROKE ANNUAL

by RYAN SOOK

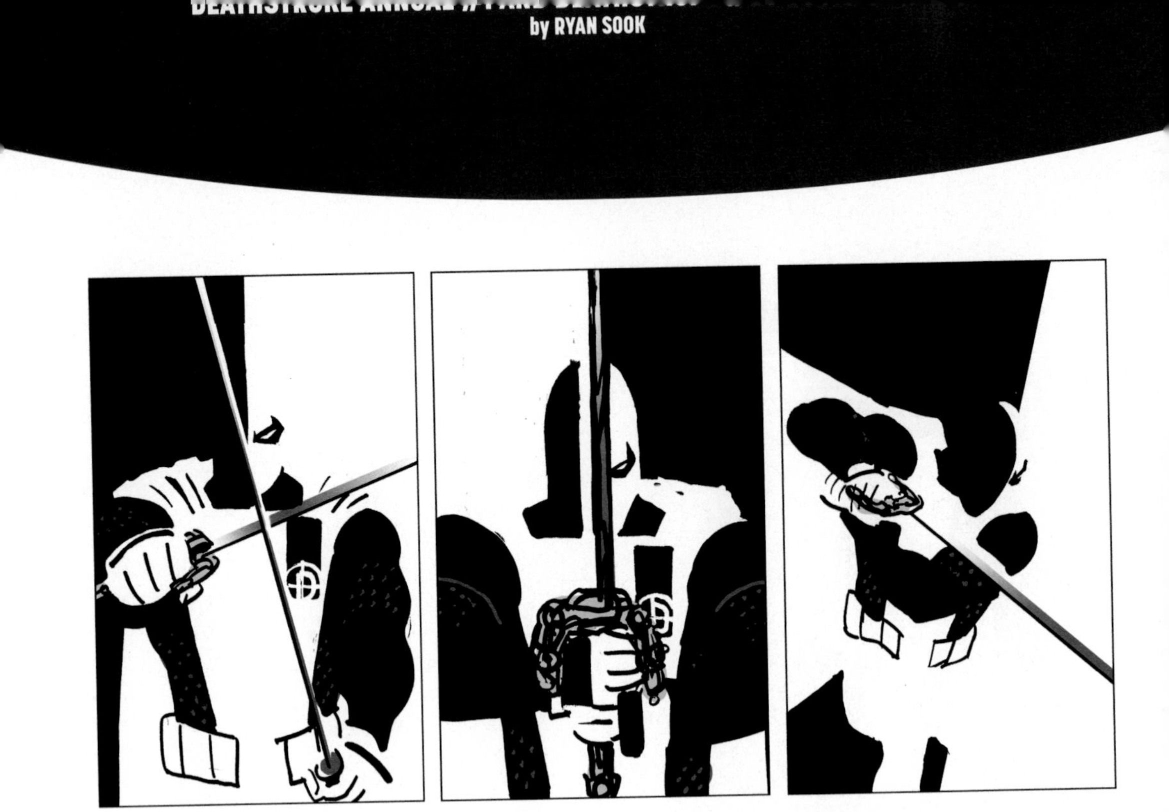

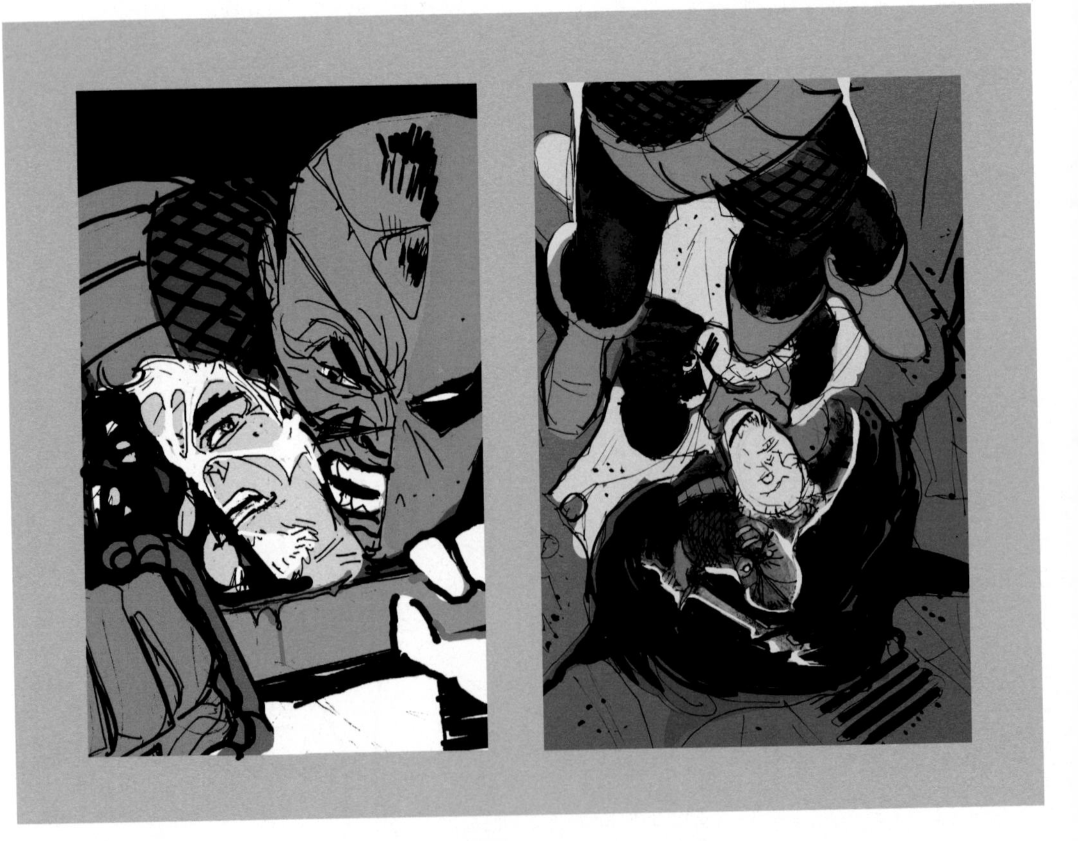

DEATHSTROKE #27 COVER SKETCHES

by RYAN SOOK

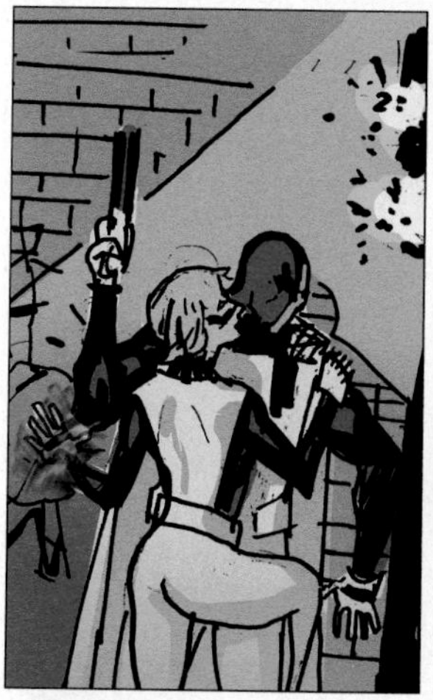

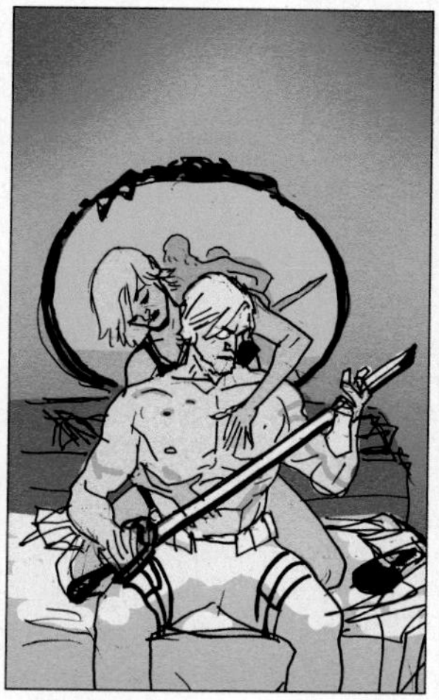

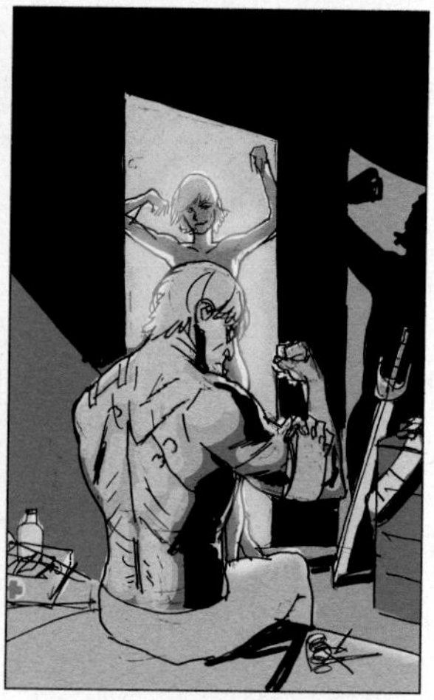

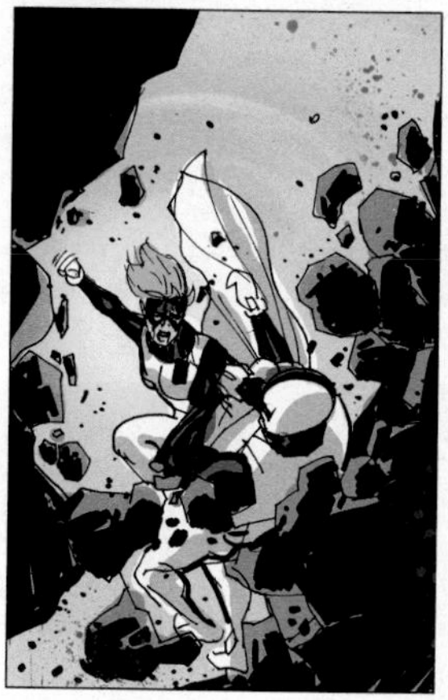

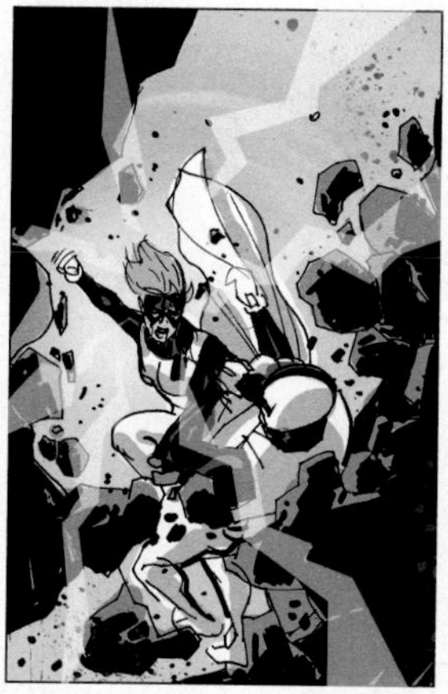

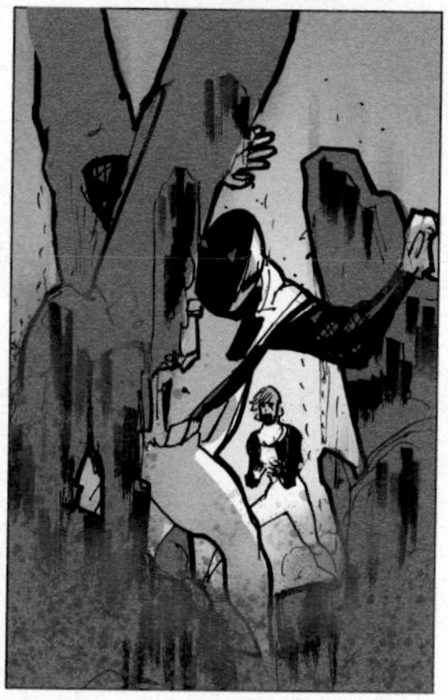

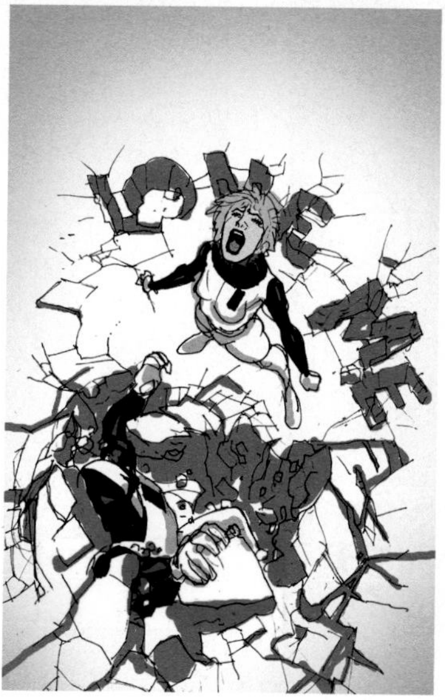

DEATHSTROKE #[illegible] AND #[illegible] COVER SKETCHES
by RYAN SOOK

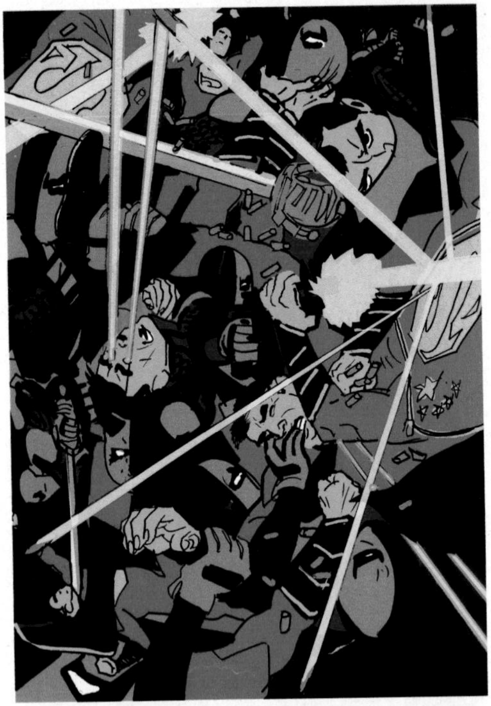

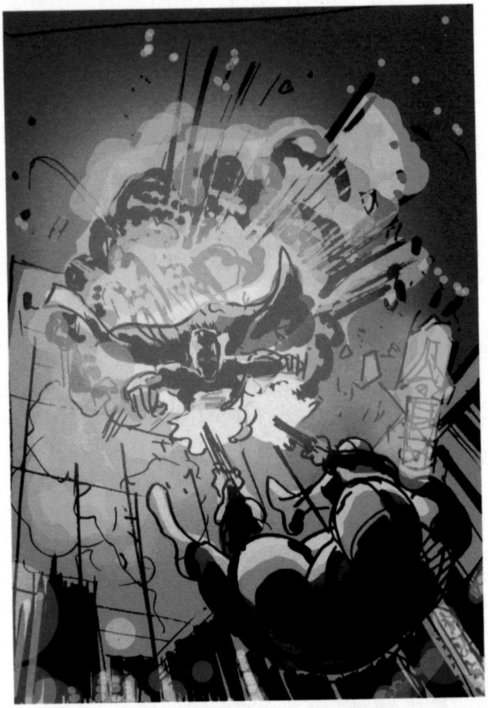

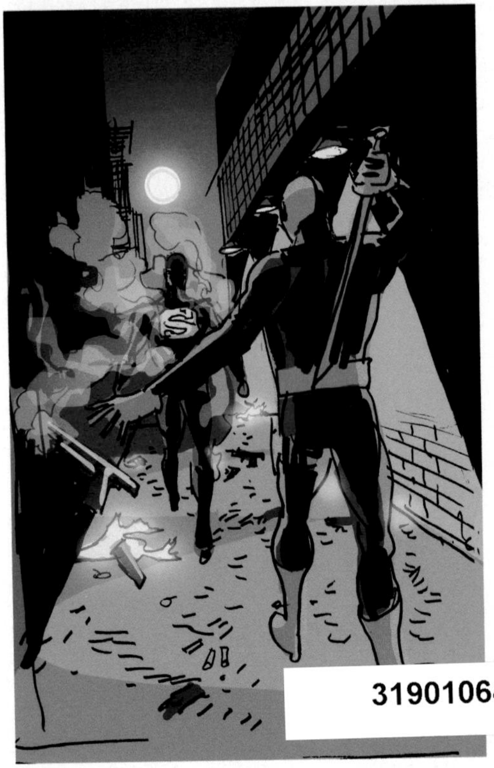

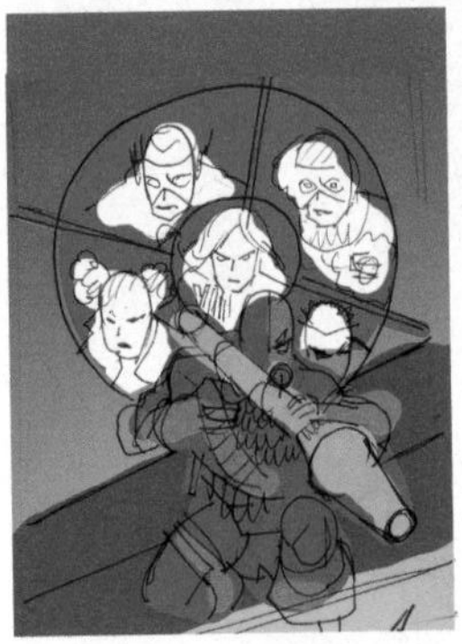

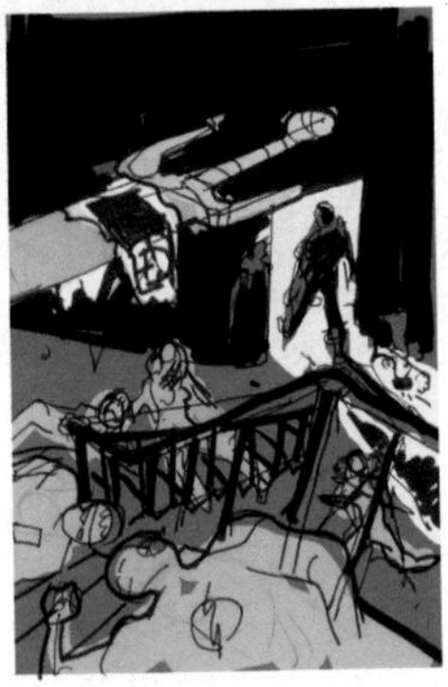

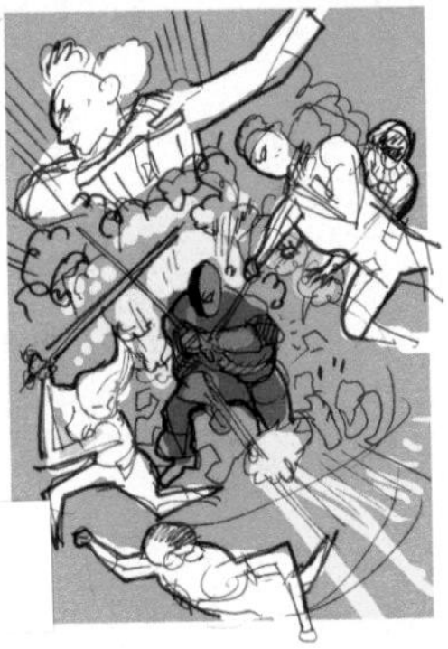